Foucault's Politics of Philosophy

Oriented around the theme of a 'politics of philosophy', this book tracks the phases in which Foucault's genealogy of power, law, and subjectivity was reorganized during the 14 years of his teaching at the Collège de France, as his focus shifted from sovereignty to governance. This theme, Sandro Chignola argues here, is the key to understanding four features of Foucault's work over this period. First, it foregrounds its immediate political character. Second, it demonstrates that Foucault's "Greek trip" also aims at a politics of the subject that is able to face the processes of the governmentalization of power. Third, it makes clear that the idea of the "government of the self" is – drawing on an ethics of intellectual responsibility that is Weberian in origin – an answer to the processes that, within neoliberal governance, produce the subject as an individual (as a consumer, a market agent, an entrepreneur, and so on). Fourth, the theme of a 'politics of philosophy' implies that Foucault's research was never simply scholarly or neutral; but rather was characterized by a specific political position. Against recent interpretations that risk turning Foucault into a scholar, here then Foucault is re-presented as a key figure for jurisprudential and political-philosophical research.

Sandro Chignola, Ph.D, is Full Professor of Political Philosophy at the University of Padua (Italy), where he teaches History of Political Philosophy and Political Philosophy, and Visiting Professor at the UNSAM (Buenos Aires).

Part of the
LAW AND POLITICS:
CONTINENTAL PERSPECTIVES
series

series editors
Mariano Croce
Sapienza University of Rome, Italy
Marco Goldoni
University of Glasgow, United Kingdom

for information about the series and details of previous and forthcoming titles, see www.routledge.com/Law-and-Politics/book-series/LPCP

a GlassHouse book

Foucault's Politics of Philosophy

Power, Law and Subjectivity

Sandro Chignola

Translated by Valeria Venditti

Routledge
Taylor & Francis Group
LONDON AND NEW YORK

First published 2019
by Routledge

2 Park Square, Milton Park, Abingdon, Oxfordshire OX14 4RN
52 Vanderbilt Avenue, New York, NY 10017

a GlassHouse book

Routledge is an imprint of the Taylor & Francis Group, an informa business

First issued in paperback 2019

British Library Cataloguing-in-Publication Data
A catalogue record for this book is available from the British Library

Library of Congress Cataloging-in-Publication Data
A catalog record for this book has been requested

ISBN: 978-1-138-74270-3 (hbk)
ISBN: 978-0-367-89533-4 (pbk)

Typeset in Galliard
by Apex CoVantage, LLC

Sueño el Sur, inmensa luna, cielo al revés.
Busco el Sur, el tiempo abierto, y su después . . .
Vuelvo al Sur

For Romina and Elisa

Contents

To the English reader viii
Preface xii

1 The impossible of the sovereign: governmentality and liberalism 1

2 Body factories: Foucault, Marx 26

3 The politics of the governed: governmentality, forms of life, subjectivation 43

4 *Koinōnikon zôon*: Stoics and the other modernity 68

5 'Phantasiebildern'/'histoire fiction': Weber, Foucault 86

6 The courage of truth: *Parrhēsia* and critique 108

Bibliography 127
Index 141

To the English reader

It is not easy to introduce this book to the reader. It is not easy because this is not a book on Michel Foucault, as it intends to be – and actually is – something less and something more. Something less, because its underlying intention is not (mainly) reconstructive. It is not a book that wants to extend the series of many volumes, most of the time excellent, produced in English. Here it is sufficient to mention two recent contributions by Stuart Elden. This book is not a comprehensive reconstruction of, or an introduction to, Foucault's overall thinking. Rather, or maybe, it wants to do something more.

I began to deal with Foucault as I was working on the history of the concept of society and on the legal and political thought of the nineteenth century in France and Germany. At that time, the studies gathered in *The Foucault Effect* prompted my research. I found particularly helpful the concept of governmentality advanced by Foucault in the second half of the 1970s and the use that Jacques Donzelot, Pasquale Pasquino, Giovanna Procacci, François Ewald, but above all, in that case, Colin Gordon and Graham Burchell made of it. They helped me to develop my hypothesis on the legal and administrative construction of the concept of civil society within German social sciences of the century (in particular in Lorenz von Stein) and to interpret Tocqueville in the light of his writings on pauperism, the prison and the social question. From that point on, my research interests moved along the line of the Foucauldian ontology of the present, the post-sovereign and post-representative settings of contemporary politics, the proliferation of biopowers, the deconstitutionalization of command and decision, and the governmentalization of power dispositifs, within the ambit of that which I believe is a decisive crisis of contemporary democracy vis-à-vis the neoliberal regulation of the regimes of capitalistic accumulation. To trace the genealogy of the modern political form and the transformations it underwent, I believe Foucault's philosophy of politics is crucial.

Foucault's is a politics of philosophy, not simply a (political) philosophy. The years in which neoliberalism rose as a political and organizational formula are the years in which, not only in Italy, structural adjustments were imposed on the system of knowledges as well as the university. Accreditation systems, the evaluation of teaching and research activities, customer satisfaction: these models, on the one hand, foster types of intellectual work and transmission of knowledge based on the market as a means of reproducing the academic system; on the other, they rigidify and standardize the canons of knowledge. As far as my field of study is concerned, political philosophy, this all ended up impoverishing the research, or at least emphasizing repetition, hampering the problematization of its contents and its traditional archives. It is a profound deresponsibilization with respect to the meaning of the intellectual work. Foucault and Weber, the Weber of 1919 lectures, helped me to bring this question back to the fore.

There are two senses to the expression "politics of philosophy" in keeping with the objective and the subjective value of the genitive. Philosophy endures politics. It is an important part of its institutionalization as a type of knowledge within academia. But philosophy can also assume a subjective responsibility. Foucault's intellectual style, his producing his own research in the historical archives, his collaboration on the problem of the continuous transformation of the present, his ethical choice to partake in the ongoing confrontation between power and what resists it – for Foucault there is no "outside" of power, just as there is no "outside" of language – his practicing philosophy as a position taking in a battle, that which a radical problematization of the status of academia, its role and its knowledges entail: all this was decisive to my everyday practice, the unspoken and implicit aspects of my teaching activity.

This is therefore a book on Foucault, but also a book on the current transformations of politics. Recently, Wendy Brown pointed out, also with reference to Foucault, that neoliberalism is 'unthinkable' without governance. When Foucault introduced the term "governmentality", I believe he did so exactly in relation to the transformations of politics introduced, even prior to Thatcher and Reagan, by the discussion on the crisis of democracy and the problem of its governance, especially in the way it was framed, for example, by Michel J. Crozier, Samuel P. Huntington and Joji Watanuki in the Report on the Governability of Democracies to the Trilateral Commission (1975). Between the end of the 1960s and the first half of the 1970s, social movements witnessed and reproduced the disaffection for the mechanisms of representation and an excess of claims, which in fact made democracy ungovernable. Then the problem that arises is that of undoing the *demos* and disseminating in the social body a series of legal, normative and institutional dispositifs designed to 'dedemocratize' politics (as Wendy Brown puts it), undoing ties (Mariano Croce and Andrea Salvatore) and constructing in another way the relationship between subjects by adapting it to what Toni Negri named, with reference to Marx, the real subsumption of society under the capital. When Foucault conjured biopowers as irreducible to the classical legal form of sovereignty, this is the transformation he hints at. A transformation that, in my view, to recall the terms of the discussion inaugurated by Alan Hunt and Gary Wickham, does not imply Foucault's dismissing law, as on the contrary it implies the fundamental role that the law plays in the construction of relationships whereby it gets disseminated.

Thatcher once said that 'there is no such thing as society'. Wendy Brown is right when she emphasizes the deconstructive structures of neoliberalism. But the neoliberal governance is mainly composed of constructive legal processes that pass through the individuals, tie up to the heart of individuation, to the freedom of subjects, and, exactly because of this, actually make it impossible to recentre democracy on the classical forms of expression of popular will. This is a question that I think is at the core of Ben Golder's and Peter Fitzpatrick's writings, as well as Etienne Balibar's, Saskia Sassen's, Sandro Mezzadra's and Brett Neilson's, as they all contributed to renovating the discussion on the neoliberal governance and its role with respect to the state (a role that, although transformed, it continues to maintain). The law still has a disciplinary and sovereign aspect, but at the same time takes a different role, since it emerges as the principal dispositif for the functioning of biopowers. And, after all, *pace* what many protagonists of the debate on biopolitics claim (Roberto Esposito, Giorgio Agamben), hardly ever has Foucault claimed that sovereignty, discipline and biopowers marked different epochs of the history of power.

When Foucault, in the 1978–1979 *Cours*, spoke of the state as a 'péripétie de la gouvernementalité' (Foucault 2004a: 253), I think he meant two things. First, he intended to *de-termine* – that is, to attribute to a precise mechanism of formalization – a phase of the modern legal experience. *Terminus* is the Latin name for the God of borders and the experience of sovereignty and the state is to be insulated. This experience is to be genealogically reconstructed within its conceptual and categorical limits. Second, Foucault did that because this is what defines the problem of the present, to reopen the terms of the confrontation between the governors and the governed as a primary effect of the resisting *excess* of life that he spoke of only a couple of years before in *La volonté de savoir*, at the moment when he introduced the concept of biopower.

The relation of government is a constitutively dual relation – this was the case with the Ancients, as well as with the phase that antedates the constitution of the modern state, and is destined to become like this again in the phase that has been initiated with the end of the modern state. This relation cannot be reduced to unity, as happens in Hobbes' dispositif of authorization. Ch. XVI of *Leviathan* – and I know this might sound paradoxical – represents the heart of the modern concept of democracy. The representative sovereign is irresistible as he manifests his will, because the will that he expresses is authorized by the individuals who make the covenant. Only through the representation that the sovereign exerts do these individuals become a people. Subject and sovereign identify with each other to such an extent that nothing remains before the one(s) who – a person or an assembly, says Hobbes – wield(s) sovereignty. The governed and the governor, on the contrary, always face one another, in that the relation that encompasses them draws an ellipse.

With explicit reference to Foucault, Partha Chatterjee talked about a politics of the governed. In fact, I think Foucault had in mind the elliptic relationship between the governed and the governors as he spoke of the *parrhēsia* of the governed. The relation of government remains irreducible, as I noted above, because there is no space that is external to the exercise of power, given that power is not a form, but is a pure structure of circulation, or, as Foucault himself recognized with a nod to Wittgenstein, something that cannot be transcended just as language cannot. However, within the relation of government, the governed can subjectivize his own position. He can do that not necessarily by claiming rights or by deciding to upturn the relation that encompasses him – in either of these cases, the King's head would not be cut off. Rather, he can ask those who govern to account for what they do, he can revoke their (allegedly unquestionable) legitimacy, their power on the various level at which it is exercised. This does not mean restoring democracy but redefining the conditions of thinkability beyond the state and the legal-constitutional forms whereby the state somehow domesticated, disciplined and formalized democracy.

If, as I believe, one of the fundamental movements from "representative democracy" to "democratic efficiency" – it is a movement marked by unequivocal processes of deconstitutionalization and the administrativization of decision – is characterized by a radical temporal upturning of the definition of the criteria of legitimacy. The decision is no longer deemed to be legitimate on the grounds of the legal and constitutional steps that *formed* it, but on account of the effects that it is technically expected to produce once it has been made. Therefore it is measured against a bet, or a promise, on the future. The non-transitability of the governed can be re-determined as an instance of subjectivation capable of inventing and standardizing powerful dispositifs of resistance. This is just as true as, with the subsumption of life under the capital, life itself – all that one is and all that one can be, as Foucault writes in *La volonté de savoir* – is what is at stake in political struggles.

With the above, I think I have clarified my intentions in this book. It is not an introduction to Foucault, as it rather wants to be an attempt at expanding the effects of his thinking style.

Foucault with Marx and Marx *after* Foucault, as Toni Negri has recently suggested. Foucault with Weber and Weber *with* Foucault, I meekly suggest myself. The Stoics and philosophy as a form of life subtracted from the Platonic-Aristotelian series that dominates the history of political philosophy. The courage of truth as a form of individual and collective subjectivation on the part of the governed within the dual dispositif of governmentality, among other things. A book on Foucault that seeks to take Foucault *beyond* Foucault: this is the intention that I declare: I hope that the reader will bear with me.

***

In arranging the English version of this book, I ran up many debts of recognition on top of those mentioned at the end of the premise to the Italian version. I want to thank the anonymous reviewers for their comments, again Sandro Mezzadra, and then: Michael Hardt, Colin Perrin, Valeria Venditti and, above all, Mariano Croce.

Preface

Writing on Foucault makes me vulnerable to a double risk. On the one hand, the risk of making him an Author. On the other, the risk of dispersing him by severing his work too easily from formulas, categories and concepts to reuse them in other contexts and for other purposes. It is well known that Foucault was far away from the first option – one that would have sharpened his profile, reconstructed his coherence, ignored the stumbling-blocks or neglected his second thoughts to elevate him to a chapter of the history of philosophy. He rather wished his texts the second option. Writing as excavating mine tunnels. Producing texts that could enlighten the scene, determine position-takings and then dissolve into their own effects as a flare or a Molotov cocktail that leave no trace. This latter is the option that has mostly sedimented with regard to various Foucauldian reappraisals, dislocations and the interplays with other types of knowledge (not only philosophical ones) as well as radical interrogations of the status of academic disciplines. However, this is not the road I will go down in this book; nor is it the most relevant as far as I am concerned. Studying Foucault does not mean reassigning him to philosophy. Rather, it means rethinking philosophy itself, the consistency and the alleged autonomy of its archives, the limits within which it marked itself off as a scholarly knowledge. This activity challenges these limits and tries to exceed them. Yet, this does not entail jettisoning philosophy. On the contrary, this starts a back-and-forth movement between its interior – its authorial series, canon, styles – and its exterior, one that comprises processes, practices, conflicts. Philosophy has to be able to take up the challenge of this exterior and measure its own tenability against its background. On this account, Foucault can be studied as a philosopher and at the same time as someone who radically defies the status of philosophy as a knowledge. He offers an example, one of the most radical ones, of an authentic *politics of philosophy*. A politics of philosophy that is able to break the inertia of an overall tradition, in particular that of political philosophy along with the separation between practice and theory on which its specificity as a discipline is premised.

The courses that Foucault gives at the Collège de France represent a particularly felicitous opportunity to take this operation forward. An operation that Foucault carries out personally. He uses these courses as a workshop in which he can test his own arguments and thus modify, get back to and abandon them. We can also carry out this operation by following in his footsteps as we use these courses as an entry point to his oeuvre that is characterized by a constant disquietude.

The same goes for the interviews, reviews, comments and roundtables featuring in *Dits et Écrits*, which along with his courses at the Collège de France provide most of the material on which I worked to produce this book. The conclusion that these texts are but scarcely relevant moments of a contingent and occasional production vis-à-vis other books he authored evidently hinges on the tendency to assign Foucault an authorial stigma. On the contrary, these writings condense the general sense of an intellectual engagement that integrally unfolds in the name of the present. They are positions that most of the time indicate the direction to which his work heads and lend themselves as entry points or breaches that are particularly useful to the Foucauldian laboratory.

"Entry points", "breaches" or "accesses": it is no coincidence that I am using these terms. This book does not intend to provide a comprehensive or ultimate interpretation of Foucault. It refuses to do that for the reasons I clarified at the outset. These are not trajectories, paths or crossroads in Foucault's production that move from specific and unilateral viewpoints – though of course they are hardly casual. At least in my reading, my book aims to interrogate not, or not only, an oeuvre, but the status and discursivity of the types of knowledge to which it is tied by extending the effects of Foucault's oeuvre.

The title of the present book exactly intends to thematize this movement. Its chapters are not to be taken as parts that move according to a progression running from the first to the last. Rather, they are paths with an autonomy of their own. Repetitions and insistences might frustrate those who decide to read these chapters in sequence. But they will not do this to those who decide to read them separately, as is certainly possible to do. The texts that I put together are talks and papers that I gave in Italy and abroad. Among them, I would like to mention those that engendered the most vivacious discussion. Those at the École Normale Supérieure de Lyon; the Universidad Nacional de San Martin (Buenos Aires) and the Universidad de Córdoba in Argentina; the Université de Toulouse-Le Mirail; the Universities of Palermo, Rome La Sapienza, Bologna and Trento; the Scuola di dottorato in Filosofia; and the Scuola Galileiana of the University of Padua. I want to thank again those who partook in these discussions. Except for the unpublished text on Foucault and Marx that here features as Chapter 2, the others have appeared in some form with different titles and in different forms. Chapter 1, 'The impossible of the sovereign: governmentality and liberalism', which has been entirely rewritten, was included in Chignola 2006. Chapter 3, 'The politics of the governed: governmentality, forms of life, subjectivation', though extensively re-elaborated, originally appeared in Spanish in the Argentinian journal *Deus Mortalis* in 2010. Chapter 4, 'Koinōnikon zôon: Stoics and the other modernity', the only text that does not directly address Foucault, was written to tackle a few open questions relating to the interpretation of *Herméneutique du sujet*. It features in Gruppo di Ricerca sui Concetti Politici 2012. Chapter 5, '"Phantasiebildern"/"histoire fiction": Weber, Foucault', was published as a chapter in Cesaroni and Chignola 2013. Chapter 6, 'The courage of truth: *parrhēsia* and critique', appeared in the journal *Politica e Religione: Annuario di teologia politica*.

Many people have contributed to forming, revising and amending these texts, and to clarifying the interpretation that I advance here. Among them, my special thanks go to Emmanuel Biset, Claudio Cavallari, Pierpaolo Cesaroni, Edgardo Castro, Mariano Croce, Girolamo De Michele, Jorge Dotti, Bruno Karsenti, Sandro Mezzadra, Valentina Moro, Toni Negri, Michele Nicoletti, Judith Revel, Michel Senellart, Paolo Slongo, Lorenzo Rustighi, Giulia Valpione, Valeria Venditti, Adelino Zanini.

Padova – Buenos Aires,
Primavera – Otoño 2014

1 The impossible of the sovereign

Governmentality and liberalism

1. Let me start from the beginning. There is a text that I believe plays a crucial role in the last phase of Foucault's research trajectory. It is the text that, along with others from the same period, Foucault in 1984 devotes to Kant. It is called 'Qu'est-ce que les Lumières?' (Foucault 1984a/2001). Here Foucault places at the heart of his discourse – and he does so with an intention that goes beyond any reference to the letter of Kant's thinking – a question that is both disquieting and decisive for philosophy. A question that, Foucault avers, philosophy could answer neither back then nor afterwards, one that resonates throughout the grand twentieth century: 'The question of the present'. From Kant to Nietzsche through to Foucault, this question saturates philosophical thinking.

According to Foucault, Kant poses this question in strictly negative terms. The question of what Enlightenment is can hardly be answered if we place it in a historical horizon that can be grasped as a whole from an external point of view (Enlightenment is neither an "age", nor the "event" that comes, let alone the "dawn" of the progressive fulfilment of history). In Kant, this implies the need to delimit in a *differential way* the present to which thinking itself belongs by isolating it at the level of the mobile forces that characterize history. It is the acme of a path in which *Kritik*, as the general form and 'livre de bord' of the process of emancipation of reason, winds back to itself, bestowing the historical time in which one lives and thinks with a specific title ("Aufklärung": specific name, signature that identifies a moment, streak that critique traces in the smooth time of memory). For the first time with Kant, philosophy comes to interrogate its own meaning in relation to knowledge, to history in general and to the singularity of time in which and for which one writes (Foucault 1984a/2001: 1386–1387).

With Kant, modernity becomes an 'attitude' (*attitude*). For thinking falls back on its own contemporary reality as that which is called upon to establish the limits and the conditions of possibility of modernity, to assert what and who we are today as well as what "today" actually means – the mean time in which we begin "to dig under our feet" to come up with a *diagnosis* that is capable of crystallizing the lines of force that cut across the present and keep it in a tension between past and future by returning it to its own nature of event (Foucault 1967b/2001: 634). Modernity is an attitude in the sense that, within it, a special and irreducible modality of relation with one's contemporary reality is produced; an *ethos*, says Foucault. Modernity coincides with the decision that *tasks* thinking with its own present (Foucault 1984a/2001: 1387). This is the first point to stress.

In Kant's work an interrogation takes roots – the only one that can be said to be truly philosophical, according to Foucault. This interrogation brings up the relation between thinking and present, the comprehensive mode of historicity, the constitution of the subject in the fold of a belonging that makes no room for preliminary forms of exteriority. A belonging that destabilizes once and for all the position taken by the subject himself as the foundation for historical representation. For Foucault, being faithful to the Enlightenment does not imply being faithful to a system of doctrines or a form of thinking. Rather, it implies the constant reviviscence of an ethics of research and critique that can be expressed in terms of a 'critique of our own time' (Foucault 1984a/2001: 1390).

Here is the second step, then. The philosophical ethos that Foucault identifies in Kant as the distinguishing feature of the modernity of thinking gives another meaning to the term "critique" – insofar as thinking is an "attitude", Kant tells us, a style or an ethics; and this is worth emphasizing so as to take a position towards that interpretive trend that deems the later Foucault to be a weak thinker, one who progressively heads towards an unpolitical direction. On the contrary, the decision that is implied here parallels Weber's or Rimbaud's. Critique here does not express any refusal or denial. Rather, the term designates a 'limit-attitude', as Foucault dubs it. The subject is constituted in the *intern-exteriority* that the interrogation of the present of thinking sets forth as an inflection or a folding. The ethos of modernity is defined through the decision that keeps thinking on the boundary that separates and unifies the within and the without: in the perimeter that is marked off by the limits of the historical *a priori* which gives life to a particular intercourse between knowledge and power and in the re-opening that one can perform *beyond it* once one acknowledges the integral contingence of the present – specific configuration, simple segment of time in which a relationship of forces, pure "become", crystallizes. Nothing of the present is necessary. This means that freedom and movement are possible as long as one has the courage to take responsibility for the framework where the thinking subject gets constituted – the thinking subject from within the web of references and meanings that locates him in the system of knowledges and powers which assigns him to a particular present.

Therefore, *Aufklärung* for Foucault means choosing to fully belong to one's own time and yet regarding one's own time as a becoming – where time is the present in which one thinks and in which the subjectivity of thought is constituted. In the definition that Kant lends to the Foucauldian interpretation, *Aufklärung* is the history of reason and the site in which this very reason raises the question of what reason is, what its limits are, what its strength, what the task that it has to carry out "now" (that is to say, in the very moment at which one writes and, while writing, one takes a position towards this all). The thinking subject practices this limit-experience, according to Foucault. And the subject is modern insofar as he proves to be able to *persist* on this threshold: 'Il faut être aux frontières' is the imperative that conveys in Foucauldian terms the ethos of modernity as an 'attitude' (Foucault 1984a/2001: 1393).

Hence the third question that, in my view, we need to pinpoint before we go farther. The philosophical ethos of modernity coincides with the decision to take upon oneself this "limit-attitude" towards the present. This is the distinguishing feature of the modern, irreducible, mutual belonging of present and thinking. Such a *Kritik* does not merely entail rejecting the present, let alone a pure analytic of the boundaries that delimit it. Foucault places emphasis on this point because it is crucial to the overall significance of his work. Critique does not mean pure depletion of what exists from an image of thought that explains to us how the world should be. Nor, with Kant, is it a simple analysis of the general conditions for the exercise of judgement within the limits of pure reason. Rather, critique means – and this is a category that Foucault employs exactly in this sense – "practical critique" and "possible overcoming" of the universals whose unilaterality and contingency can be traced and identified (whether these universals are the teleologies that orient the representation of history, or the signs against whose background we can judge the latter, or the system of references that impose it on us). Therefore, *Kritik* can be re-transcribed in productive terms by building on a position that, in the Foucault of the second half of the 1970s, amplifies the archaeological inquiry by dint of genealogy. The present as the effect of selective procedures, as the product of a peculiar configuration of power relations, as the unilateral actualization of possibilities that remain virtually available to other combinations and beyond the mere negative that turns critique into a simple instance of dissolution: acceptance of one's own singularity, of one's own difference, of one's own liberty, instead of the general, the necessary, the obligatory.

Hence, in Foucault's reading, the process of constitution of the thinking subject, of the present in which he thinks as well as the form of thinking that enables him to think, comes to be assigned to a dimension that is fully temporal, thoroughly historical. Within modernity, the act of thinking comes about only through an excavation that the thinking subject carries out responsibly, commencing from himself and his own problem.[1] *Kritik* becomes an 'inquiry'; a procedure of 'événementialisation' (Foucault 1980b/2001: 842). It does not draw the limits of one's possible experience, nor does it canvass the formal structures of reason. Instead, it lends itself to a re-determination vis-à-vis the time in which one thinks and acts. Yet it can do that only once it has reconstructed the junctures, the breaks, the inevitably partial solution of power relations that comprise the history of truth – those that led us to be what we are and placed us in the present where we act and think. In this way, such a redetermination forces thinking to face what cannot be constitutively solved within it and remains irreducibly external to thinking itself: the materiality of the processes that produce it as a knowledge, the conflicts that involve it, the singular matrices of universality.

The "enquête historique" is necessary to thinking. It is the assumption of this pre-condition that makes Kant's text inhospitable to Foucault – and this is the fourth point that needs to be highlighted. "Événementialisation": mobilization and temporalization of what instead appears to be homogenous, necessary, universal. 'En ce sens', Foucault writes, 'cette critique n'est pas transcendentale, et n'a pas pour fin de rendre possible une métaphysique: elle est généalogique dans sa finalité et archéologique dans sa méthode', as I have just noted.

> Archéologique – et non pas transcendentale – en ce sens qu'elle ne cherchera pas a dégager les structures universelles de toute connaissance ou de toute action morale possible; mais à traiter les discours qui articulent ce que nous pensons, disons et faisons comme autant d'événements historiques. Et cette critique sera généalogique en ce sens qu'elle ne déduira pas de la forme de ce que nous sommes ce qu'ils nous est impossible de faire ou de connaître; mais elle dégagera de la contingence qui nous a fait être ce que nous sommes la possibilité de ne plus être, faire ou penser ce que nous sommes, faisons ou pensons.
> (Foucault 1984a/2001: 1393)

All that exists, in the eyes of the genealogist (Nietzsche: the radical thinker of the Enlightenment), proves to be the actualization of one among many combinations of the possibles that antedate it, that cross it, that exceed it; the unilateral outcome of a selection that accommodates multiplicity to a "form" which could have been otherwise.

For Foucault, Kant's work inaugurates this enterprise carried out at the edge of what we are. In particular, it positions philosophy within history. On the one hand, it forces philosophy to retrieve the materials on which to work outside itself – that is, in the philosophically spurious territories of politics and of the archives in which its "story", its process, sedimented. On the other hand, it makes reason permeable to curiosity and vigilance. Philosophy puts itself to the test of reality (an expression that recurs many times in Foucault's works of the 1980s and that we will come across again) to identify the fissures in which what challenges repetition irrupts. It does so to assess the instances that prompt change and transformation. What Foucault acquires from the Kantian philosophical ethos is an *experimental* style of thought and action. On the one hand, it rejects any projects of a global transformation of reality. For they sever the tie between thinking and actual practice, which serves as a precondition for philosophy. On the other hand, it rejects the temporal sclerosis that, in the dimension of anticipation, produces a crystallized or "protected" vision of the present and the future. Experimenting means being exposed to risk, practicing philosophy as a "critical ontology": genealogy of the present and mobilization of its truth effect. It means taking charge of the freedom that we are assigned and thinking of it as a pivot for the elaboration of the relationship between the thinking subject and the experience of subjectivity – 'comme travail de nous-mêmes sur nous-mêmes en tant qu'êtres libres', Foucault writes (1984a/2001: 1394).

For this reason, and this is the fifth and last point I want to make, *Kritik* cannot be seen as propaedeutic, as a mere preliminary work. For it represents the general form of thinking. On Foucault's account, *Kritik* does not represent a premise destined to culminate in a "this is what you have to do" – as in the scheme that determines the relation between theory and practice within modernity and that portrays the intellectual as a supervisor of the universal. What has to be done cannot be announced from outside the present that encompasses and constitutes the subject and robs him of any claim to sovereignty. History does not have spectators, Foucault points out elsewhere (Foucault 1976b/2001: 80).

The philosopher's sayings and doings do not correspond to the sayings or the doings of the prophet or the legislator – two further classical icons of veridiction. Theory neither anticipates practice nor comes up with prescriptive formulas. More akin to the clinics or to the navigation of the present (figures that reappear many a time in the late Foucault), the philosopher's work is the *diagnosis* of the present. Opening historical sites in which one can verify what one is, what influences the philosopher's position in the general movement of reality; the field of possibilities that belong to the philosopher, just as much as he belongs to them. Critiquing the present means making oneself available to those who keep the narrow door of the future open, and means nothing other than this, in that reality comes to be fluidified, and thought of, as the immanence of becoming. Critique is 'a challenge to all that is' (Foucault 1980b/2001: 851). Thus, it has to be interpreted as a work of 'unblocking' (*déblocage*). A work that frees thinking from its obsession with reality as a totality to restore (Foucault 1980a/2001: 834). Such a work draws connections among the present in which we live and think, the past that produced it, the future that remains accessible if the present is set in motion and hence can be performed as a cluster of possibilities and lines of force. Foucault writes: 'J'essaie de provoquer une interférence entre notre réalité et ce que nous savons de notre histoire passée' (1980c/2001: 859). The philosophical work of modernity is the production of an interference between the present and its history – a history that is understood as the critical ontology of the present, potential 'franchissement' of its truth effect, liberation of possibles that remain available if the history of the present coincides with the diagnostic tracking of the selective mechanism that moulded it. It is in the wake of Kant's research ethos that Foucault proceeds.[2]

2. Now we can move on. Restarting the modern attitude of philosophy means temporalizing history and giving it back to the event, as we have just seen. 'Diagonalizing the present through history', to evoke Foucault's expression; which is to say, foregrounding that the alleged necessity of what exists is not a genuine necessity and how its truth stems from a specific – and thus always revertible – selection of the possibles. Foucault does not advance a critique of ideology, but a politics of truth – and he restates it explicitly in many occasions when he is forced to confront the Frankfurt School (see e.g. Foucault 1977a/2001). He does not denounce the false consciousness of knowledges, nor does he look for the bare materiality of reality beneath them. The alignment of these two levels would produce the mere effect – "reactionary" in the end, according to Foucault (1978c/2001: 632) – of showing what the "true" reality is. This would ultimately confirm the inhospitality of reality. Truth cannot be enfranchised from power, because truth itself is power. This is how Foucault confirms the specificity of philosophy, his stance for it, his refusal to substitute it for another kind

of critical-theoretical work, often far more naïve. As is the case with those who think of power as "removed" from smooth communication practices or as a truth rehabilitated by means of a denunciation of ideological mechanisms of duplication based on which power works. Truth produces institutions, makes knowledge hinge on power and brings about effects. This is why what we are supposed to do is to liberate – Foucault writes 'détacher' – truth from the regimes of 'veridiction' in which it works or has so far worked, 'pour l'instant', and thus in an always revocable way (Foucault 1977a/2001: 160). This is the way in which Foucault reaffirms the bond between philosophy and history, between "inquiry" and the present, between philosophy and the critique advanced in Kant's text. The reference to history makes the phantom of reality disappear. The level of discursivity becomes the form through which traditionally the link between words and things is produced as well as the hierarchization between the former and the latter. In other words, the idea that a truer reality is available in the more rarefied and neutral vision of pure theory. To the 'vérité-ciel' Foucault's genealogy opposes the 'vérité-foudre' (Foucault 2003: 238). To Plato, Foucault opposes Nietzsche. The Kantian ethos of philosophy as Enlightenment thrusts truth into history, because truth does not lie in an elsewhere, as it belongs in this world (Foucault 1977a/2001: 158).

We can summarize the general sense that Foucault assigns to his work. He opts for a philosophy that is entirely embedded in history. This means that he works is such a way as to produce an inquiry of regimes of veridiction that can be placed at the intersection of an archaeology of knowledges (treating what is done or said as an event of discourse) and a genealogy of knowledge (in which any residues of that 'in which we are pleased to look at ourselves when we wish to exorcize the discontinuities of history' [Foucault 2002b: 147] is dissipated). Entirely internal to the materiality of processes, philosophy can take on itself a political task: analyzing truth from within the connection between knowledge and power that constitutes philosophy itself.

Is this still philosophy? A philosophy that comes to be practiced outside its own tradition, intertwined with archive work, attuned to the present as if it were a battlefield whose dynamics are to be assessed. What happens to philosophy when the universals to which it refers and with which it works are effaced, so much so that it is treated as a knowledge among others? And again: what kind of philosophy are we referring to when the truth it addresses has to be extracted from regimes of veridiction in which it operates as a supplement to power? Or as a code for discriminating between what can be, or cannot be, said and done? According to Foucault, philosophy has to be thought of in a tension that irretrievably links it to its own becoming, one that constitutes its turning point and the constant renewal of the possibility of experience. Philosophy is to be practiced as a decoding of – and a positioning into – the power strategies that organize veridiction "on a daily basis" (needless to say, this Wittgensteinian term is not selected randomly), as it determines the rules and roles of enunciation. A philosophy understood in a Nietzschean sense as "journalism", then. A philosophy centred on "today" as something that needs to be thought of and that acquires a liquid, restless, mobile

(Foucault 1979/2001: 783) form in order to adhere to the specific temporality of the "games of truth and power". These "games" are to be mapped out with perfect detachment so as to grasp them as a language, as something that purely exists and works and can never be eradicated, as a chart of resistance and multilateral strategies of domination. The relation between philosophy and history, between inquiry and the present, emphasized by Kant, cannot be concertinaed back: philosophy can no longer exist as an "autonomous" activity – and Foucault overtly reclaims this view and seizes on it (Foucault 1970/2001: 973).

Accordingly, we need to take a further step. As a legacy of his ongoing controversy with phenomenology, Foucault coherently calls back the theory that takes the subject to be the prerequisite for enunciation, as well as the apophantical form of true judgement (Foucault 1975/2001: 1562).[3] Truth is an event. If this is the case, truth cannot be gauged, demonstrated or retrieved. Not even as a substratum on which ideology exerts its effect of distortion. Truth is to be ***produced*** by the power relation that imposes it (Foucault 1997: 22). Hence, an analytic of power in the everyday relationships that power itself establishes.

It is worth noting once again that the type of *Kritik* Foucault advances, even when he muses on power, does not have anything in common with critical theory. Power is neither a substance nor a thing; it does not only work in terms of interdiction or repression. Power is not stabilized, secured or fixed in its form or in the modes of its exercise by the resistance it meets with and that, paradoxically, it feeds. Working on an analytic of power means clearing a research path in which power is seen as a system of rules and is assessed against the background of the specific character of the "games" it enables, time after time. Foucault refers directly to the late Wittgenstein and to Austin. The question is to assess power outside its moral frame of reference (power in itself is not good nor bad, it simply circulates; on a daily basis it allots the relations to which it is applied) and to resist the temptation of substantialization. (Power is not kept captive by anybody who owns it as such, nor does it deploy a total and unquestionable domination. Depending on the relation at stake, power can either head towards a direction or be capsized: the power a scholar exercises during a lecture can be immediately upturned when he goes back home and finds himself at the mercy of a nagging wife, or falls prey to a symptom that gives him anxiety and thus lends himself to the inscrutable judgement of a doctor.) According to the immanent field in which power operates, it has to be analysed in terms of mere assessment – it exists, and there is nothing more we can say – and in the regularity of strategic games that it shapes, reproduces and keeps in tension (Foucault 1978b/2001: 540–542).

The work of philosophy is not the work of transcendental critique, let alone the one of the history of philosophy. Either of them is quite ineffective. The relation between philosophy and history (distinguishing feature of the ontology of the present) is the constitutive relation that modernity establishes as a covenant with itself – an ethos, an attitude, a decision, as I wrote above. It builds on the bare fact that there is no referent for thinking outside the flow of becoming. Foucault takes history in terms of Nietzsche's "wirkliche Historie". A fickle, centrifugal, diffracted history composed of everyday moments which is up to us to foreground as we cast light on the powers that inhabit it. There are powers that wage battles and impose conventions; insubordinations and disobediences that re-emerge as something that have to be put under control, harnessed; governmental technologies capable of stabilizing organized relationships; codes of normalization of individual and collective behaviours; apparatuses and strategies of "veridiction" that determines truth effects. The modern attitude of philosophy comes to be constituted in the "sagittal" relation that it establishes with its own present (Foucault 1984c/2001: 1500). As the ethos of a vertical interrogation that subjectivizes the position of the interrogator, the space of the belonging to a present that evolves and keeps moving and that, for this reason, captures philosophy always *outside* it, 'entièrement politique et entièrement historienne', as Foucault puts it (Foucault 1977a/2001: 266).

A few lines above I raised the question: is this philosophy still? I can now ask: what *can* philosophy do? Philosophy does not merely criticize power by assessing the conditions under which it is exercised from a moral or "political" point of view. It is aware that power as such cannot be abolished. Neither does the truth claim of philosophy allow us to take reality as a bare fact, on the basis of which the falsity of "ideology" can be denounced. If philosophy can still do anything, Foucault tells us, it is capable of getting truth out of things at the level of pure observation: it is a pointer to reality being controversial (Foucault 1978c/2001: 633). It exhibits the "jeux de pouvoir" as the threads that embroider everyday life (and in doing so, it brings to light its many layers, its differentiation, its "enjeux", its contradictory and contrasted dynamics [Foucault 1978b/2001: 542]). It shows that these "power games" (which are the "historical-concrete" analogous of the late Wittgenstein's language games) can be analysed only in tactic-strategic terms, as a cluster of moves gesturing towards the resolution of conflicts and the imposition of perspectives.

Needless to say, the philosopher is an interested party, a non-detached spectator, of such a contradictory reality – of this struggle, which is also a struggle for truth, if at the end of the day truth itself is a struggle. The truth that he is able to draw from "power games" (drawing them out and unearthing them from the anonymous circulation of discourses) is temporary and contestable, just like every other truth. It dissolves the illusion that power is a "thing". And also gets rid of the idea that the speaking subject can get back a universality that does not exist – being the sovereign who imposes the law or the philosopher herself who plays the role of the sovereign institutor of meaning. Truth, likewise the subject, is a product. In such an everyday struggle, every saying corresponds to a specific stance and an irreducible partiality, not the irenic neutrality that should characterize any impossible skirting stance.

'Pour dire les choses clairement' – Foucault (1980b/2001: 846) writes – 'mon problème c'est de savoir comment les hommes se gouvernent (eux-mêmes et les autres) à travers la production de vérité'. Once again, here truth should not be understood as the production of (allegedly) "true" enunciations, but as the regulation (Foucault writes the 'aménagement') of domains in which the partition between true and false can be "governed" and continue to pertinently work. Power as such does not exist (Foucault 1977c/2001: 302). It circulates, distributes, organizes the social space.[4] Power is a bundle of relations more or less hierarchically ordered, more or less coordinated, constantly threatened by the very liberty that power itself tries to dominate and by the forms of resistance that intersect it. It is impossible to build an ideal-type of the power – Foucault observes, using an expression that invites us to problematize – as we will do in another of these seminars – his relationship with Weber (Foucault 1980b/2001: 846–847). Nor can power be univocally ascribed to institutions or things. Power should be "spatialized"; treated as a juncture where truths articulate and intersect – and it is exactly there that its *effect* lies. Through these truths, the relations between subjects can be organized and deciphered.

Based on the above, we can draw a few more consequences. First, in the heterogeneous forms that characterize it, power (as an anonymous, silent, elusive structure that multilaterally traverses reality) can be analysed only where it exposes itself. Namely, *through the emergence of what resists to power.* Resistance to power (the body to discipline, the subject to educate, the insane to confine) should be considered as the "chemical catalyser" that allows tracing the features and trajectories of power itself (Foucault 1982a/2001: 1044) – here the experimental attitude that Foucault ascribes to thinking is confirmed. Resistance is what delineates the space where power relations are inscribed, as well as the scope and the methods of power. The second consequence is even more important. Not only freedom, resistance and the surplus that exceed the code of power *anticipate* and *precede* power itself. More than that, power should not be analysed by accounting for an alleged internal temporality (a teleology, an intention, a linearity). What characterizes power, according to its different fields of application, is its capacity to resolve (or not) strategic confrontations. The "truth games" on which Foucault's analytical-political philosophy lay emphasis should be attributed to a reality that appears to be agonistic and divided. At the basis of power relations lies the bellicose clash of forces (Foucault 1997: 17–18). The third and last consequence that results from my analysis so far is that, according to Foucault, understanding how human beings govern themselves through the production of truth means analysing power outside and beyond the legal scheme in which it has been framed within the Hobbesian frame of modern political theory. Once the teleological-political problem of the foundation and legitimation of power as sovereignty collapses, it becomes decisive to try to understand the way in which the production of truth (in accordance with the features that turn it into a historical effect) regulates and discriminates the circulation of our discourses; determines our individuation; permeates the social spaces we dwell in.

Drawing from Kant, the most compelling task for philosophy, as I pointed out, is to answer the question: "Where are we now?". This is not meant to relegate the question to what can be discovered by isolating the present from the universal development of history but rather to *reject* what we find out we are (Foucault 1982a/2001: 1051).

3. Finally, then, we can get to the point. What is it that characterizes the present? How do power devices work as they act at the moment in which philosophy throws light on the present? On which kind of transformation of political

structures should the historical inquiry and genealogy intersect in order to shed light on this transformation and clarify its character of event? This a question that arises when Foucault takes the floor at the Collège de France, between 1977 and 1979, and with Deleuzian creativity forges the concepts of "biopower" and "biopolitics". What is it that operates as a further space of dispersion for Foucault's analysis once it reaches the point at which the role of power appears as not merely restrictive, but productive, reticular, microphysical? "Dispersion" here indicates a problematization that is constantly revived, rather than the product of a univocal and coherent analytic doomed to settle into a work, as we know. This question is also linked to that which Foucault calls the 'inversion of Clausewitz's principle' (issue that he tackled in the 1976–77 lecture series, according to which war cannot be seen as the continuation of politics 'by other means'; in that politics itself, as well as the reality it encompasses, turns out to be a war). It offers an analysis of the mechanisms that keep something that can never be assimilated or neutralized, as it is completely *external* to the power and procedures of juridification through which power itself tries to exorcize the structural crisis that characterize its process.

In this chapter I am not concerned with further reinforcing – though I am perfectly aware of this risk – the effects of continuity and coherence that these pages might project on Foucault's research. For it is pointless to adopt as an interpretive scheme the question of whether, and to what extent, as some claim, the courses held at the Collège de France between 1977–78 and 1978–79 (*Naissance de la biopolitique* and *Sécurité, territoire, population*) suggest a drastic defection from his previous analyses and, in particular, from the model of "war" presented in the 1976–77 lectures (*Il faut défendre la société*). However, I find it reasonable to see the whole Foucauldian production – at least from the second half of the 1970s onward – as intended to challenge the traditional paradigm of modern political philosophy and its reduction of the question of power to the juridical scheme of sovereignty. It makes sense to say (regardless of the glaring simplification this might entail) that Foucault's work consistently takes a twofold path. On the one hand, he questions the outcomes of the passage that sets the critique of ideology in motion and turns it into a normative philosophy. This entails abandoning the idea that regards philosophy as a true discourse capable of amending and limiting the exercise of power and requires moving on to a study of power that looks at the devices and rules which produce and secure effects of truth (Foucault 1997: 22). On the other hand, thanks to the valorization of genealogy (the re-discovery of the battle within peace, of the clash occurring within that which appears as neutralized; the understanding of politics as the continuation of war, as I have pointed out), Foucault takes a step beyond the analysis carried out in *Surveiller et punir* and the isolation of the disciplinary peak in which the triangulation of power, rights and law in penal devices of the classic age is abridged. Based on an accurate diagnosis of the status of politics in the current era, of the processes of subjectivation that intersect it, of the governmental devices that mark it, Foucault steps away from a political philosophy centred on the modern problem of the genesis and legitimation of the sovereign. The decisive transformation that concerns power relations, from the nineteenth century to the second half of the twentieth, moves the site of "veridiction" from the state to the market. It is the market (and not the legal scheme of the composition of rights) that defines the system of relations whereby subjects represent themselves as individuals. By taking a leap beyond the foundational scheme of modern political theory (it is the sovereign who makes the people, and not the other way around, as Hobbes would have it), it becomes clear that what has to be governed are interests, needs, valorization processes, linked to the singularities that embody them and allocated along curves of generalization that the sovereign can neither foresee nor institute – once the sovereign has been eventually deposed from the panoptic position of the frontispiece of *Leviathan*. Such a double *déplacement* – a *déplacement* that produces new institutional dimensions, assigns relevance to other knowledges, downplays the political sphere and the notion of subject with which the law works – is considered by Foucault as key to starting to think of the present in which we belong.

In Foucault's theory, this passage is marked by the introduction of the terms "biopower" and "biopolitics". On the one hand, these become indications for the deconstruction of the concept of individual. In the view that portrays the individual as an agent involved in trade and the marketplace, this individual is radically different from the "natural" rights-bearer – rights that are claimed vis-à-vis the state and can be used as a natural shelter against the expansion of the state action. On the other hand, the concepts of biopower and biopolitics overstep the burdensome sequence of events that led to the state and paves the way for an inquiry into the devices of governmentality. This research marginalizes the state – the alleged cornerstone of Western constitutional history – and demonstrates that the series of events that led to it is but a mere "peripeteia" (literally: 'péripétie', as Foucault writes) of more general processes – ones that antedated the state, crossed its legal profiles and its institutional dimensions, and exceeded and overflowed it continuously (Foucault 2004a: 253).

Foucault now works on the margin of the law and opens it outward. He is concerned with how, in the present, the government and the production of truth come to be installed in another centre of 'veridiction'. Particularly he homes in on the production of the truth in which obedience is rooted, once obedience ceases to be understood as what the law brings about straightway and is viewed as an indirect effect of individual, free and yet regulated conducts.

Let us follow Foucault's argument. First step: law is not opposed to power, nor can it be thought of as a separate instance. Rather, the legal discourse has historically represented the code on which the state apparatuses have settled down. There is no doubt that Western monarchies embodied a pure will (*arbitrio*) of domination, particularly in the phase of absolute sovereignty, whose devices have been inherited by the modern constitutional state. Despite this, they have been established as systems of law, they thought of themselves through legal theories, while their power mechanisms have been set in motion through the legal form. Here, Foucault takes up the well-established outcomes of legal history: through the jurists' expertise, monarchy gained the monopoly on the Political, emptied out the constitution based on guilds and corporations, subjected the nobility by absorbing their prerogatives and powers. It is true that various critiques (formerly from the nobles, then from the revolutionists) tried hard to detach politics from law and to isolate the legal form as a separate instance able to defend society from the prominence of the sovereign and from the violence that might be exercised by the unquestionable power of the sovereign (for example, the idea of fundamental rights, the idea that law can be represented as a pure form of obligation – one has only to think of Kelsen). Nonetheless, Foucault notes, the legitimation of power has long depended on the legal scheme (Foucault 1998a: 78–79).

Second step: we need to realize that, until sovereignty is deemed to be the core of political theory, the King's head has not been cut off yet. Hobbes' ghost is the obsession that not even critical thinking – let alone the revolutionary one – has so far managed to get rid of. For Foucault, thinking of liberation means giving up once and for all the question of the takeover of power or its democratization. For power is a residue of the juridical formulation of the question itself of the foundation and authorization of the sovereign which has percolated into the bourgeois theory of law from Hobbes to the French Revolution. This deflects our attention from the state and its apparatuses to its margins, to subjectivation and domination, to local strategies that are not marked by the universality of law. The strategies through which power affects bodies and moulds individuals. Foucault (1997: 25) writes that we need to grasp power where it is exercised in a less and less legal way. Once again, what is key is the inside of power (an alleged intentionality that can be unveiled), but the *line of extroversion* whereby it relates to what remains outside it: individuals, bodies and the system of dense and opaque relations that the interests have turned into what will be called (from the seventeenth century on) "civil society".

Third step. Power is no longer "a thing" that can be in the hands of someone. It is no longer the sovereignty that can be overthrown and changed and legitimized once it is appropriated "from below". It is no longer the stake of a clash that can be regarded as a clash between opposite "rights": the right of the subject and the right of the sovereign. At the same time, the place of the sovereign is no longer the lynchpin of theory's space of gravitation. If this is the case, it is necessary to decentre the analysis and refocus it on the circulation of power. We need to verify the trajectories that power draws within the social body, within the interactions between subjects, the relationships between them. Foucault is not particularly, or at least not only, interested in the fabrication of the sovereign (a topic that has largely concerned modern political theory from Hobbes to Rousseau). Rather, he deals with the concrete fabrication of individuals and the way power devices work. These devices are linked to, and intersect, the complex game of individual and collective interests. Getting rid of the obsession with Leviathan, to use a Foucauldian expression, means analyzing power inside the thick texture of relationships that dislocates it from the legal form and reinvests it in the overall "vitality" of social processes (Foucault 1997: 39).

It is a transformation that concerns the law and political thinking between the eighteenth and the twentieth centuries, although it had important antecedents in previous centuries. Foucault embarks on what is, literally, *another* genealogy of politics. Here "biopolitics", whose technologies are not those of the law (in a truly formalistic legal sense), is coupled with "thanatopolitics" to which sovereign devices attach (attachments that correspond to sovereignty as far as the history of criminality reconstructed in *Surveiller et punir* is concerned). From the beginning, the logic of sovereignty is linked to life and death. In Hobbes, this juncture acquires decisive importance, since it enables the interplay between the monopoly of violence and the juridical representation of power. The sovereign incorporates the multitude as it bounds its tidy distribution to the existence of laws, secured by the sword. For the individuals transfer their power through the covenant whereby they step out of the state of nature, one that removes the *metus* that individualizes them around the concrete threat of violent death – 'continuall feare, and danger of violent death' are for Thomas Hobbes (1998: Part I, Ch. XIII) what makes life in the state of nature 'solitary, poore, nasty, brutish' and, above all, 'short'. The liberty that 'individualizes' the individuals by taming their predacious drives, their wild soul, is adjusted and privatized by the system of sanctions that the sovereign power is required to administer in everybody's interest: 'the Liberty of a Subject lyeth therefore only in those things which in regulating their actions, the Sovereign hath prætermitted: such as is the Liberty to buy and sell, and otherwise contract with an other' (Hobbes 1998: Part II, Ch. XXI). This 'frees' the relations between individuals as it removes the obstacle that every individual represents for each other when there are no common rules.[5] Hobbes writes (with reference to the bonds that he previously defines as 'Artificial Chaines' of civil laws) that '[i]n relation to those Bonds only' is it possible to speak of a 'Liberty of Subjects' (Hobbes 1998: Part I, Ch. XIII). In what Thomas Hobbes labels state of nature – a scenario that for the first time in the history of political thought assumes that living beings are equal – there is no liberty.

Power makes free. This is Hobbes' extraordinary finding and what of his work largely radiates on modern legal-political theory.[6] Laws enchain the wolf of the state of nature and tame its instincts. The sovereign's sword produces subjects by *subjecting* the beast that the human being is and by subduing him to a *reasonable* and *appropriate* use of freedom. The sovereign and his right guarantee life. Still, only in the *unbalance* whereby life appears to frame itself as a stretch of time crossed by death and suspended over its abyss. It is to this constitutive *asymmetry* between life and death that Foucault draws attention (Foucault 1997: 214). Death hangs over the processes administered by the sovereign, just as his sword does. The law of the sovereign is deployed as a right to give life or death. It *decides* between life and death. The monopoly on legitimate violence, conferred to the sovereign in order to pacify relations among subjects and to end the war between them, becomes entirely visible in the right he claims (and that the laws confer on him) to sentence to death those who continue to act as a wolf among humans. "Re-bel" is the one who reintegrates the *bellum* within the space of peace. The sword of justice has no sheath because it has to threaten and hit continuously, as De Maistre (1821: I), disenchanted reactionary, observes. The black heart of modern sovereignty is a "thanatopolitics" whose paroxysmal icon is the divine function of the executioner.

4. The passage from 'thanatopolitics' to 'biopolitics' does not trigger a linear succession of devices. It does not initiate a different "epoch" at the level of history. Between the seventeenth and the eighteenth century, the right to put to death or let live epitomizing the typical trait of sovereignty was infiltrated, penetrated, shifted by a different political rationality. After all, for Foucault, a device never produces a totalizing effect on reality. Nor can it be thought of as a discourse that saturates an entire field of relations by stitching it as a "system" to its repertoire of categories and concepts.

While the history of the juridification of power – between the Middle Ages and Absolutism – adopts death as its own referent and "taking possession" as its own constitutive trait (to rescue people from death, dispose of the culprit, segregate the insane, eat up the resources of the territory), the perspective that replaces it overturns the sense of the strategies and the techniques of power. From a certain moment, Foucault claims, a device, which is completely *heterogeneous* to the one of the law and sanction, progressively gains centre stage. It is a device that considers human beings not as forms, as legal "persons" or abstract subjects, but rather as bodies and living "animalities" (Foucault 1998a: 80). The right of sovereignty as power to *put to death and let live* is replaced by the one to *make live and let die* (Foucault 1997: 214).

In Foucault's account, this passage has two phases. Or better, it grafts two different technologies into one another. On the one hand, the one that Foucault calls 'discipline'. The system of practices that invest the body of the distinct living being, in the process that Marx in the first book of *The Capital* calls 'primary accumulation', to make the body socially compatible and economically productive. 'Discipline' shapes the human being in accordance with the criteria of socialization of the field in which one is placed (the field of valorization, of the army, of the correction-schooling, for instance). It denotes both the cluster of tools through which the body is trained to a specific function, the modalities and the contents of the training itself, as well as the results of the process as a whole, that is, a subject's commitment to it. This tends to naturalize 'discipline' in the form of an everyday behaviour.[7] Discipline produces individuals from the bodies it controls. It aligns the work of militaries, pedagogues and officials to the jurists' and the social contract theorists' (Foucault 1995: 185). Both in the case of the former (the "experts" of the training knowledge) and in the case of philosophers, Foucault deems the problem to be the same: how to set the stage for a general action on the basis of a scheme of individuation that produces subjects as junctures in which individual and collective behaviour are integrated.[8] In both cases, the norm is conceived as a scheme of *normalization*. The individual is observed, watched, kept in check. His behaviour assessed, analysed, examined. The movement of his body in the disjointed, rationalized, better organized space. Education and training to a constant self-examination objectify the subject so as to 'pin' him (as Foucault writes with an outstanding expression) to his singularity. An individual singularity (since it is ascribable to the subject) and yet anonymous (because it is produced as the effect of a general scheme).

Discipline inverts the process of "classical" individuation, as Foucault observes. While the latter only knows memorable individualities – the human's *bíos* which is able to make himself immortal on account of his deeds (see Arendt 1958); the "name" in which dynasty and nobility tie up (Rancière 2014) – normalization works downward. Which is to say, it evaluates the wastes. What in the conjunction of social sciences and psychology Foucault calls the generalization of 'function-Psy' (Foucault 2003: 86) is the complex of technologies that work on the measure of the differential between the single and the norm.

On the other hand, there is the governmental scheme. This is the second passage on which Foucault insists. In addition to clutch of power on the body, aimed at crafting individuals (the discipline of the barracks, the boarding school, the factory, as devices designed to deal with the unruly multitude of loafers, proletarianized farmers, vagrants), there is the one that proceeds in the opposite direction, to wit, in the sense of a massification. This is how economics, administrative sciences and the police understand the population as a set of processes, needs and vital interests. Between the eighteenth and nineteenth century, "biopolitics" as a technique of management of metabolic exchanges among society and the state[9] replaces that which Foucault names the 'anatomopolitics' of the eighteenth century (the production of the individual on the back of juridico-political social contract thinking based on the disassembling and reassembling of its own movements and its singular and collective gestures [Foucault 1997: 216]).

The panoptic principle of centralized surveillance, which is the heart of discipline, is not alien to the biopolitical process. The disciplinary device of power is able to represent itself and to deal with the general, and not only to bound itself to individuality. Foucault detects it, for example, in the guidelines on epidemics drawn up by the police.[10] The segregation-city of leprosy (the lazaretto wherein sick people are kept captive as the model of a binary code inclusion/exclusion) is not the plagued-city, integrally covered and reproduced by the disciplinary gaze. The plague is not leprosy, and the contagion it threatens is an inescapable risk because the agent of contagion cannot be isolated. Furthermore, despite the ongoing epidemic crisis, the city has to keep functioning. This means taking care of the living, constantly providing the population with food and water, mapping out the development of contagion, disposing of corpses and looking after sick people, as far as possible. The plagued-city, the inquired-city, the regulated-city, produced as the scene of total visibility of bodies and exchanges-city, represents for disciplinary theory the equivalent of what the state of nature is for political theory, Foucault (1995: 198–199) writes. In the health and administrative regulations that refer to it and inform it, it represents the precondition for conceiving the 'utopia of the perfectly governed city' (Foucault 1995: 198).

From there the ultimate step to the delineation of the functioning codes of biopower devices. The disciplinary city, the well-governed city, brings to light what might otherwise risk lingering in the shadows. Power disassembles, corrects, perfects the corporeal attitude and the individual performativity. Still, it does so not only to restrain the potential insubordination of the subjects or to exorcise the definite threat of their freedom (goals that bring discipline to make itself up in accordance with the schemes of modern penalty), but also – in more general terms – to make the overall social exchange safer, more affordable and efficient. Discipline *amplifies* and *intensifies*, more than it produces control.

It adopts as its own task the growth and the multiplication of forces to which it applies. On the one hand, the enclosed institution: the factory, the prison, the military camp. On the other hand, the disciplinary society, the extension of the administrative-statutory rationality to cover the entire web of relations between subjects. Physics of a relational power that finds its highest intensity not in terms of authority, in the person of the King or the sovereign, but rather on the front of the bodies that it allows individualizing and empowering by enhancing individuals and collective performances (Foucault 1995: 207–209).

The establishment of biopolitical technologies can be observed in the shift produced here. It is an acknowledgement of the vital processes of a social body that increasingly emerges as mass or population (exchange volume, cluster of statistic curves, knot of relations weighted on agents' freedom of movement and trade) and that can be hardly confined to the distinct individual bodies that compose it. Objects of biopowers are the problems of birth rate, mortality, longevity, dealt with on the basis of an inclination that values, as political knowledges, demography, economy and statistics far more than private or public law (Foucault 1997: 216–217). The new subject that hits the scene is the "population": no longer "society", still anchored to sciences of the state; nor the "individual", who corresponds to disciplinary technologies. "Population": a framework of relationships defined by a specific state of interactions of humans and things (employment and unemployment rates, evolutionary composition of demand and supply, the degree of healthiness and morbidity rate of a territory, mark of the power or degeneration of a civilization). It is vital to secure the regulation of this framework, whose reproductive circuits factually remain *unavailable* to the sovereign.

The genealogy of the governmental reason can be traced back to the point of derivation of biopolitical technologies – 'Entstehung', 'Herkunft', rather than 'Ursprung', as Foucault remarks in a very important text devoted to Nietzsche (Foucault 1971) – in the particular torsion imposed by the anti-Machiavellian literature on the issue of the conservation and enhancement of the state forces. Torsion, and not a simple overturning of the *Prince*; 'représentation ancrée' of the device rather than its replacement, as Foucault (1978d: 640) comments. What the new "art of governing" imputes to Machiavelli is the relation of singularity, exteriority and transcendence of the Prince with respect to his dominion. The unidirectionality of a relation that appears to reproduce the discontinuity of power which is implicit in a legal theory of the sovereign, as if in a sort of reversed anticipation. In Machiavelli, Foucault believes, the Prince conquers and maintains his power by handling the political matter as something that can always slip one's control and therefore has to be, and can be, brought back under his power and subjected to it.

Instead, the "correction" that is produced in the anti-Machiavellian literature of the reason of state (that pulls the general logic of power in the direction of an art of governing which is irreducible to pure sovereignty) valorizes the web of social power and the ascending/descending continuity of a governing circuit that intercepts, and does not abolish, all that lies outside and to which it is related only in terms of an exchange. The might of the Prince depends on the might and magnificence of his princedom, on the modalities through which he governs the population, increases its wealth and floridity, which functions as the constant validation of the goodness of his action. His glory is neither military nor a predatory glory, a glory of conquest. Rather it is an *indirect* glory. His good government is demonstrated by the citizens' prosperity, the volume of exchanges, the increment of accumulated wealth in his territories. For this reason, what is at stake here is, literally, a new *economy* of power.

From this derives the history that Foucault deploys as a genealogy of "governmentality". On the one hand, the body of texts of the *specula principis*. The ascending continuity of a governmental function that the Prince must be able to administrate first and foremost in terms of self-government and then as the wise exercise of the *patria potestas* over his wife and sons; as the broadened management of the "gentleman's residence"; as general political functions with regard to the territory. Good government is primarily constituted by the Prince's self-government. On the other hand, the descending continuity of an overall *police* of "social" relations that, in the well-governed city, allows the order to be kept even in the most minute private spaces as well as the general finalization of the collective action towards good to be adopted as a norm of the individual behaviour (Foucault 1978d/2001: 641). It is an economic model of power in which, in a completely classical form, the management of humans and things operates in various domains of action that only the modern juridical representation of power tends to isolate from each other[11] – from Aristotle to the German *Hausväterliteratur*, that is to say, according to a second order of discourse that does not oppose economy and politics but rather takes on governmental functions starting with the *oikonomia* of the household as a system of regulated political relations. Within the household, a social ontology of the human living being comes to be developed and generalized on the basis of the cluster of political relations.[12] 'L'introduction de l'économie à l'intérieur de l'exercice politique, c'est cela, je crois, qui sera l'enjeu essentiel du gouvernement' (Foucault 1978d/2001: 642).

However, a further step is needed. The governmental reason at its beginnings still appears to cling to the political cycle described by Machiavelli. It unearths an extended dimension which is nonetheless still marked by a tinge of unilaterality. What is at stake here is only the relationship between the Prince and the maintenance, the ordering and the preservation of his Princedom. A blocked relation between too stiff and abstract a conception of domination and a notion of trade and economy which is still too narrow and indefinite, says Foucault (1978d/2001: 650). In order for the new political governmental rationality to unfold completely, a radical *regression* of the legal principle has to be accomplished. Put otherwise, what must fade away is the notion that the governmental function has to be carried out in a decretal form and coincides with the extension range of the sovereign's will. A referent of the administrative action must emerge which is able to melt with the system of processes that intersect and characterize it as an intermediate site of the articulation of far more general and impracticable regularities. It is the very "family" to which the Ancient governmental art referred at its beginnings to thematize the specificity of *oikonomia*. According to Foucault 1978d/2001: 652), the ultimate inversion of the juridical scheme is brought about by the appearance of "population": a subject that has interests and needs of its own, which are irreducible to, and independent from, the Prince; and an object of governmental technologies which do not aim to increase the Prince's power, as they have to maintain and optimize relationships and forces to which they are applied.

The population is not merely the arithmetic sum of individuals. Instead, what defines the population – a political concept whose history is marked by its introduction in economic and cameralistic sources, rather than in strictly philosophical writings – is the opaque mass that resists the sovereign's gaze and manifests itself only obliquely, through demographic and statistical data, the curves of the birth and death rates they trace, the graphic representations of exchange and trade, and the assessment of epidemiologic risks. However, the population is at the same time the collective singular that emerges as interwoven with individual dispositions and limits (job skills to train, social costs to keep down, risks to avoid: as is the case with what nineteenth-century rising social sciences labelled the "social question", urging for a reformation of knowledge with a view to disciplining the moral restlessness of the working class – drunkenness, promiscuity, irresponsible exposure to harmful productions, scant propensity to savings[13]). These dispositions and limits call for the adoption of a managerial mindset that might prove capable of firmly connecting normative production, disciplinary devices and the governmental technology.

Foucault emphasizes that governing and administering a population does not simply entail the management of the mass of phenomena it involves at the level of general processes. It also entails taking care of a population more in depth, namely, by adopting a logic of the detail in which government and discipline are coordinated and not opposed to one another. In other words, the relation between governmentality and discipline – like the one between the legal society and sovereignty, the disciplinary society and the "governed" society – is not a linear 'remplacement', a sequence. This is particularly the case if we refer it to different time lines that allegedly allow us to identify a disciplinary and a governmental phase of modern politics. Instead, the process has to be framed in the triangulation of sovereignty, discipline and "governmental management". It also has to be considered as an effect of the shift whereby sovereignty (regarded as the fundamental descriptor of politics and as the privileged referent for the legal discourse) slowly and inexorably withdraws from its central position as it is absorbed by problems of governmental decision and the controlling mindset that it embraces. The "population" appears to be the converging point of the internal renewal of police sciences and the isolation of political economy as a discourse that progressively becomes autonomous within the domain of knowledge. The population imposes itself in the oscillation between disciplinary and biopolitical technologies. It is an objective fact (the population as a configuration of relations that can be captured by statistics), a specific area of intervention (intermediate point between the individual and society), and the general object of the governmental action (that finds the efficacy of its own action in the desirable prosperity of the population). Thus, population contributes to congeal that 'série solide' of economy and politics, as Foucault (1978d/2001: 654–655) calls it – one that can scarcely be disaggregated and that, because of this, turns out to be the key feature of the system of relations on which the present to which we belong develops.

5. It might be worth recalling that genealogy always proceeds from the end. It is materially steeped in history, as we know. It breaks up the linearity and the effects of continuity typical of a facile representation of history. Genealogy does not trace origins but unearths the grafts among heterogeneous logics that determine deviations, breakdowns, new beginnings, in the link of knowledges and powers. The genealogist needs history, Foucault reminds us, precisely to eschew the chimera of the origins (Foucault 1981c/2001: 1008) – he needs archives in which dossiers sediment as the memory of struggles and conflicts between freedom and power; he needs the battlefield that the everyday analytic reveals.

Again, then, the starting point of Foucault's analytic of biopowers is the urgency of the present. The enlightened philosopher, the one who works with the keen awareness that there is nothing outside history, has to take a position on the present, the time to which his work and his word belongs. Setting forth a genealogy of governmentality means taking the transformation of the political as a problem; it means questioning the transformation that is triggered by the imposition of a new principle of reality on politics, by its own settlement in the inaccessible "Umwelt" of social interests. Governmentality is the cluster of the instances that adapt the exercise of power to the centrality of economy rather than law. But it is also the 'lines of force', in Foucault's words, that gets a particular function, i.e. the government, to acquire pre-eminence over the mechanisms of sovereignty and discipline. Finally, it is the point of view that exorcises the spectre of the state, and the effect of 'survalorization' assigned to it, both in its lyric form (the 'cold monster' whose presence haunts our relationships) and in the (paradoxical because seemingly reductive) form that makes it a superstructure of the processes of reproduction – processes that cut across the state and accentuate the importance of attacking and conquering the state as the authority that guarantees the general system of domination (Foucault 1978d/2001: 655–656; 2004a: III). For Foucault, the state never had the unity that has been ascribed to it: neither as the "subject" of constitutional history nor as the sovereign sum of its functions. The state has always been a cluster of procedures and legal and extra-legal technologies that only the philosophical-political enchantment of modernity could portray as unified, as the sovereign monopoly on decision. If something characterizes the "liberal" present to which we are assigned, the indicator that permits grasping the tendency that drags the present is not the process of "statization" of the social to which critical theory refers, the intrusiveness of an exorbitant and totalitarian power able to permeate all the remaining interstices of cooperation and to one-dimensionally limit individual freedom. Rather, the characteristic of the "liberal" present – and Foucault (2004a: 112) grasps it very clearly, to the extent that he completely modifies his analytic of power – is the drastic limitation of the rationality of the state that imposes on the latter the 'governmentalization' of its own devices, starting with the centrality that market acquires.

Once again, we need to take notice of a separation, a rift. Not only the one determined by the operational environment of biopowers – with respect to which political economy (genuine *Kritik* in a Kantian sense) investigates the conditions of possibility and the limits of exercise (Foucault 2004b: 286) – vis-à-vis the authoritative code of the law. Even more radically, the separation determined by market agents, whose utility calculation (the only and free mover of the exchange) is somewhat impenetrable to power devices as it is the object of practices of government that are not in the position to train it. For the conditions and the possibilities of the market cannot be laid down from a sovereign point of view. An interest, to put it another way, is radically different from a right.

The shift from biopower to biopolitics is the specific trait of this passage in Foucault. On the one hand, in the eighteenth century biopower (the cluster of mechanisms through which humanity as far as its biological and vital functions are concerned) enters the space of intervention of power. Power objectivizes it as "population" – the police science, the cameralistic, statistical science; their referral to the jurisdiction of the sovereign not only in spatial terms, which are marked by law's operations, but indeed in economic, demographic, actuarial terms; the re-semantization of political science on the part of the knowledges that are instrumental in the development of the subjects' prosperity and wealth.[14] On the other hand, biopolitics, that is, the appearance in the political anthropology on which economy is premised of a subject whose cooperation interlaces webs of valorization that are addressed to the state only indirectly. It is a strictly egoistic cooperation as it calls upon the state to safeguard the conditions of freedom that feed various dynamics of appropriation and ownership and that express instances and needs that can never be fully formalized, foreseen or totalized from the point of view of the state.[15]

The site of "veridiction" moves from the state to the market: from the sovereign's law as what severs the legal from the illegal and lays down the possibility for action to a free and "spontaneous" exchange between individuals that mostly calls for regulation in order to find the same premises and the same conditions time and again. This does not only mean, in the transition between classic liberalism and Austrian ordoliberalism analysed by Foucault in his 1978–1979 lecture series, that the general logic of the relation between society and the state is capsized and that unequal mechanisms of competition come to set the rhythm of the institutional adjustment to the system of economic variables taken as fundamental (Foucault 2004b: 120–121). For it also means that the subject, more than ever, tends to constitute himself *outside the boundaries* of the traditional disciplinary mechanics and to rely on a kind of autonomy that sizes on the reasons of interest by promoting a liberty that must be continuously given back to him.

While the space of disciplines is a space of full visibility, a closed "territory" on which the panoptic gaze of surveillance devices unidirectionally radiates, the biopolitical "environment" is instead a non-transparent circuit of interests and exchanges that makes the point of view of the sovereign literally *impossible*; a fact that consolidates the system of unavailable references based on which one can verify the social utility of the governmental functions (Foucault 2004b: 47–48 and 285–286).

However, Foucault takes a further step. Inside this transition dispels other "universals" with which history and political theory (even the "critical" one) work. Once it has been transposed into market, the "society" of individuals cannot be thought of as an insurmountable limit to the state, as is the case with classical liberal theories; nor can it be evoked to integrate its institutional dimensions, as is the case with the rhetoric of citizenship. At least with German ordoliberalism, society reveals itself as a concept proper of the governmental technology that allows linking the law to the dynamics of exchange (Foucault 2004b: 299–300). "Society" only exists as a petition and demand of a "government" whose functions are at one and the same time necessary and minimized.

What the subject of interest asks the state is to be kept in the un-tie imposed on him by the calculus of utility. And, far beyond what meets the eye, *it is exactly for this reason* that this operation is possible insofar as the government exists. The cluster of relations that the governmental technology fosters and keeps in tension defines an extremely frail system. On the one hand, the intangible element (in relation to the exercise of power) of the interest of which the individual is the only depositary; on the other hand, a "soziale Umwelt" constitutively intertwined with the individual interest (the game of the free market, the offspring of a 'contrat social à l'envers', as Foucault (2004b: 207) calls it, that encompasses all the subjects without them asking for it; one that can function only provided that nobody pulls out in advance and hampers its mechanism). Such a "soziale Umwelt" has to be maintained in optimal conditions in order for the web of the exchanges to go on without it being instrumental in a collective good, which can by no means be the goal of the market.[16]

It is here that the connection of biopower and biopolitics becomes visible. The relation of government is a relation that, unlike sovereignty, is contingent on an environment and not on a territory. The social environment of market relations is determined by variables (the game of supply and demand, the dynamics of exchange, the valorization or devaluation of available human resources, the competition of interests) which are entirely independent from any political agenda. The *homo oeconomicus* who dwells in it is an 'élément intangible' to power; literally, it has to *let him do* (Foucault 2004b: 274). His action is a free action, one that *consumes* freedom and that thus requires the "government" to offer and guarantee freedom continually. A "government" capable of performing at one and the same time an effective and indirect action. This freedom is the specific object of governmental care.

The action of government is, then, a critical action. It is produced as the optimization of the conditions in which the subject's freedom of action can be exercised. A subject that is unavailable, as he is not produced as subjected to the sovereign law, is not confined to a legal territory, mostly irreducible to the formal scheme of the *persona*. Yet he is "malleable", as he, along with his freedom, is sensitive to the variations of the environmental constants in which his freedom is implemented. Governmental reason: not the design of a process, but "strategic design" of the comprehensive coordinates for organizing the free competition of individual interests. In this context, the very wage labour is neo-liberally re-transcribed in terms of a corporate activity, or the mobility of migrants in terms of subjective investment in one's own self-promotion skills (Foucault 2004b: 232–233; 236). It is possible to say that the governmental reason always teeters between a *lack* and an *excess*.[17] The government *ought to* take action in order for the free rider to freely pursue his own interests in the game of competition that is open to everybody, at the same conditions, whether or not this – in the neoliberal politics whose specificity Foucault grasps immediately – leads to the demolition of the Fordist compromise with labour unions and to the opening of the markets of healthcare, education, energy.[18] At the same time, though, the government should not take *too much* action, as it runs the risk of invading a space that does not belong to it – one that is completely heterogeneous to the state and that, according to the characteristic inversion that Foucault investigates in the writings of American and Austrian economists of the 1930s, cannot be "liberated" from a self-limitation of the state as was the case with the doctrines of continental public law theory at the beginning of the twentieth century. A space that should be immediately recognizable as the place of an immanent legal-political self-regulation.

Producing freedom – instead of making up subjects or disciplining bodies, as was the case with the devices previously analysed by Foucault – does not mean laying out the overall existence conditions of freedom. For it means making sure that the possibilities for the individual exercise of freedom remain constantly open. It means indicating the economic space in all subjects and at the same time governing the risks that freedom implies with no recourse to universal legal schemes, but by singularizing the responsibility attached to its exercise. In this regard, it is definitely worth noting that not even the notion of interest allows anchoring the action of government to an objective reference. The interest, which neoliberalism adopts as its fundamental notion, is thought of in terms of "will" ('une forme de volonté à la fois immédiate et absolument subjective', Foucault [2004b: 277] writes). It eludes the representative scheme of equivalence. Inequality (which from time to time might concern the interests at play, individual performances, particular goals) is the engine of competition. This entails that, once the law has got rid of its equalizing universality, it only operates as the guardian of a differential space, re-transcribed along the lines of subjectivity.

This means that the very "society" to which governmental technologies are addressed cannot be delineated through the recognition and rearrangement of the interests at play, sticking to traditional mechanics of balance enabled by trade and the uniformity of goods. Rather, it has to be produced as a multiple system of individual "enterprises" linked to the differentiation of the options and subjective choices (Foucault 2004b: 154–155). After all, 'there is no such thing as society', as Margaret Thatcher is claimed to have said. The normative surface on which the individual and governmentality meet each other is comprised of managerial and administrative processes. These concern the optimization of performances with a view to attaining growth and the reduction of complexity of a "soziale Umwelt" which is hazardous insofar as it is crossed by entropic tendencies (both on the side of the subject, whose entrepreneurial capacity might fall short, and on the side of the collective, when exchanges go down, monopolies rise, losses are socialized). Such a normative surface requires to be governed and exactly for this reason defines the system of relations that continually fathoms the efficiency of its own action and procedures. Governmental rationality is an ***insuring*** rationality (see in particular Ewald 1986). It dumps the costs on the subject and holds him responsible for how he uses his own freedom and for the self-valorization of the human capital he has been endowed with – through diffusive processes that upturn the traditional centripetal trajectory of disciplines and that however have to do with consumption habits and psychological-affective attitudes of individuals with a capillarity never experienced before (Foucault 2004a: 46). Neoliberal governmentality directly passes through the subject. The idea of the welfare state is deconstructed on account of the idea of a risk that can be socialized only in the guise of costs. For this reason, by virtue of governmental interventions that are much subtler but far more pervasive than traditional ones, these costs are reassigned to the single subject who is called upon to take it on himself.

The addressee of governmental technologies is the individual as a self-entrepreneur and a social environment that is able to regulate its own connections as far as it is not subjected to interference. This freedom – like the individual who bears it – is not a fact, but the product of "governed" relations. They are enabled by a power that does not own them, but grows ***within*** them, and reproduces their conditions of possibility.

The subject – this is one of the major results of Foucault's inquiry – ***is*** not free but is ***produced*** as free. Then, he comes to be thought of, moulded, disciplined as circumscribed by securitarian devices that govern the system where he operates. Securitarian devices adjust the individual and the market to what they are expected to be to one another. The self-entrepreneurial subject is not the free subject of the liberal rhetoric closely linked to the doctrine of natural law, but the subject who is made free by technologies that give him back the possibility of being free within a potentially unsafe environment. Such a complex environment is the one of competitive interests and the webs of optimization that cannot be entirely domesticated, subdued by the law – certainly not in the way Hobbes' wolf was turned into a citizen. For the self-entrepreneurial subject is delineated by the uncompressible trajectories of an action with respect to which he must always be capable of acting freely.

Governing – this is the decisive characteristic of this concept – does not mean controlling the subject, imposing constraints on him. Not even the typically democratic one in which the entire history of sovereignty is summarized,[19] that is, a general will formalized in procedural terms as the effect of a contract of all with all. Governing means ***conducing***, orienting. In particular, it means adjusting free behaviours, habits, conducts to suitable purposes by regulating their distinct aspects and general coordinates.

Foucault (2004a: 129; 1978e/2001: 719) comes up with a specific genealogy of this governmental function, one that *is not rooted* – if not in part – in Greece. Government is the management of a system of relations that are at the same time general (as the population considered is the specific object of a genealogy of government) and individualized in each person (as the "government of self" is influenced by the governmental discipline in terms of an impalpable direction of the self-reflective consciousness). This government is, says Foucault, an Oriental and biblical idea. It is an idea that belongs to the pastoral power that is imparted through the Church, cameralistic sciences, police devices, the economic paradigms of Physiocracy, and then percolates into Keynesianism and the institutions of the welfare state. German ordoliberalism and American anarcho-capitalism put to the test its general logic.[20] And yet the return to the 'libéralisme frugal' they recommended – minimal state, maximum openness to individual freedom, responsibility for the latter according to its exercise – developed schemes of regulation that were just as invasive.

The entire life of the subject is subsumed under the market, so much so that everybody's conducts must be formed, and then initiated, in keeping with a praxis of exchange and valorization. The liberal society, just like each individual who dwells in it, requires government. It has to be supported by an intervention that creates the conditions for attaining the aims that inherently pertain to such a society – through each individual knot. It is exactly for this reason that governmentality always plays a specific rhythm that strictly pertains to the *oikonomia, omnes et singulatim*.

If "liberalism" – another false historical universal, Foucault maintains[21] – can be identified with anything, this is the hard recognition of the necessity of harmonization, one that, in order to be determined, does not require a point of view external to the social, for no such point of view is possible once the social is finally assumed as non-transparent and is deemed to be determined by the unfathomable game of individual interests. Rather, harmonization requires going through all the points of the relation, on condition that each of them satisfies as much as possibile the general criteria of rationality that maintain the tension between the market and the exchange.

This inclination is precisely the government: conduct of conducts, adjustment of individual freedom to collective freedom, re-instantiation of an exteriority, of a power which is pastoral in the end, at the heart of the relation that each individual establishes with himself. If Greeks do not have any clue about it, this is because they have another idea of the process that constitutes what we may call "subjectivity", however inappropriate this concept may be for Antiquity. It should then come as no surprise – no makeshift or withdrawal in the "ethical" research of the 1980s – that the last lectures given by Michel Foucault revolve around late Antiquity to understand the outdated, intransitive truth of that process of subjectivation, otherwise related to the "government" of the self, with an eye to imagining a liberation that keeps up with the present and is able to support it with a Weberian disenchantment.

Notes

1 'Mes livres ne sont pas des traités philosophiques ni des études historiques', Foucault (1980b/2001: 840) writes some years before, 'tout au plus, des fragments philosophiques dans des chantiers historiques'.
2 'L'ontologie critique de nous-mêmes, il faut la considérer non certes comme une théorie, une doctrine, ni même un corps permanent de savoir qui s'accumule; il faut la concevoir comme une attitude, un êthos, une vie philosophique où la critique de ce que nous sommes est à la fois analyse historique des limites qui nous sont posées et épreuve de leur franchissement possible' (Foucault 1984a/2001: 1396).
3 On the topic of the apophantical, see Foucault's lessons which now appear in Foucault 2011, in particular: 64–65.
4 As Deleuze (1989: 186) observes, it is simply a 'third dimension of the space'.
5 'A Free-Man is he, that in those things which by his strength and wit he is able to do, is not hindred to doe what he has a will to' (Hobbes 1998: Part II-Ch. XXI).
6 On this topic, see the collective researches collected in Duso 2003a; 2003b.
7 On this topic, see Schiera 1999: 29–105.
8 Gerhard Oestreich (1969) too draws attention to the scheme of individual disciplining in the construction of the modern experience of politics.
9 If a "break" between the 1976–77 course (Foucault 1997) and later courses (2004a, 2004b) comes to be produced, it has to be understood as deriving from the way in which Foucault's analysis shifts from the topic of "state racism" to the analysis of liberalism.
10 For an outline on the administrative "Police", see *Filosofia Politica* 1988; Piasenza 1990; Cavalletti 2005.
11 G. Duso (1999, in particular: 55–85) views this gap as the primary feature of the transition that concerns politics in the passage between premodernity and modernity.
12 On this topic see Brunner 1970.
13 On this see Ewald 1986; Procacci 1993.
14 See among others Schiera 1968; Maier 1969; Scattola 1994.
15 On the Foucauldian analytic of the economic discourse, see Zanini 2005; 2010.
16 See Lemke, Krasmann, and Bröckling 2000: 7–40, in particular 14-ff.
17 On this topic see Burchell 1991: 119–150; 1996: 19–36.
18 For an overall analysis of these processes see Dardot and Laval 2009.
19 On this topic see Duso 2004.
20 To which Foucault devotes the lesson held the 31st of January 1979, see Foucault 2004b: 77ff.
21 For a general account see Bonnafous-Boucher 2004.

2 Body factories

Foucault, Marx

1. Let me make a detour. Both the term *corpus* and the Greek word *sôma* have an obscure origin. It is said that *corpus* might be an extension of the Indo-Iranian root **krp*. Here it means "shape" or "beauty". Evidently there is a symmetry underlying the use of this term both in Latin and in Greek. Homer always refers *sôma* to the inanimate body, to the corpse. When he speaks of a living body he uses *démas*. *Démas* is an interesting term. According to Benveniste, it develops an Ancient verbal root, **dem* – meaning construction. This root produced the "political" terms of the household (the Iranian *dam*, the Latin *domus*), such as *despótēs* (lord), *dmōs* (servant) and *dmōē* (handmaid), as well as the term *démas*, which actually indicates a form or a visible and corporeal appearance of an animated living being: its "construction". Latin takes notice of this terminological opposition – that between *sôma* and *démas* – as it opposes *corpus* to *anima*, the principle that gives form to inert matter. Here article missing: a further consideration is needed. *Corpus* is not only, by analogy with *sôma*, the corpse, the dead cadaver of a man or an animal. For it is the term that Latin utilizes to indicate, in a much broader sense, any material object – *omnes quod potest uideri corpus dicitur* (Servio, *Commentarii in Vergilii Aeneidos*, 6, 303) – as well as, by extension, any aggregate of parts once it has taken form (See Chantraine 1968; Ernout and Meillet 2001; Benveniste 1969). *Corporo* first and foremost means: I kill, I make, or provide, a corpse. But, in its passive form, the verb *corporare* – that is, to take on the appearance, the shape, of a *corpus* – means to incarnate, to embody, to materialize. Whence the political terms *corporatus, corporatio* and the verbal forms *concorporo, incorporo* that relate not only to the aggregate in which the parties get assembled but also to the vital principle that animates them. *Anima, animal*: yet another semantic field. I can't expand on that. I can just say that the lexicon of the organic that has to do with the metaphoric and conceptual field of "political life" (suffice it to refer to Aristotle, *Politics* 1253a; 1281b) is predicated upon an opposition between animated and inanimate matter – animated: activated through breathing (*psychē*: in Greek "soul", "breathe", "air") by the *animator* who gives it life – where there is a directive element, a principle of movement that somehow exceeds its being inertial, for its body to acquire an 'organicness' (see Cavarero 1993). Soul: *archē* of the living being, according to Aristotle (*De Anima*, 402 a7).

I am coming closer. In the Elizabethan era, in England, royal jurists find the best formulation to solve the problem of the continuity of the body politic. It is the theory of the King's two bodies. In a declaration to the Serjeant's Inn, they agree that 'the King has in himself two bodies'. It was meant to justify the fullness of the King's power even if he was not of age, 'a Body natural and a Body politic'. The natural body of the King is a mortal body 'subject to all Infirmities that come by Nature or Accident', while the political body – 'consisting of Policy and Government, and constituted for the Direction of the People and the Management of the public Weal' – is incorruptible and not subject to imperfections, nor can it be affected by age and illness. This body is entirely separate from the natural body (see Plowden 1816: 2123).

It is known that this juridical construction has been elaborated on in its ultimate form in specific conditions, that is, to legitimize the full exercise of royal power on the part of the successors of Henry VIII. Edward, still under age, Mary and Elisabeth, women. On the basis of the Christological paradigm, that is, of the twofold nature of Christ, royal jurists overcome the existing duality between the doctrine of the *corporatio* – the supratemporal *corpus mysticum* of the political community – and the doctrine of the *maiestas* of the King, time by time embodied in a mortal body and a physical person. For my purposes, what is more important is the theory of "migration" on which jurists build the continuity of the body politic as the King dies. Within English common law, the death of the King is not called "Death", as they emphasize with reference to Plowden's *Reports*, but "Demise". For the body politic of monarchy does not die. With the decease of the physical person of the monarch, the two bodies of the King come to be separated again. The corpse that is buried is the natural King's, but his "Dignity", the institution's immortal *anima* (soul) transmigrates with no interaction to his successor, re-embodying the body politic in a human being of flesh and bones: *dignitas non moritur*. Thus, *anima* and *corpus* of the kingdom again.

Here I cannot trace the long history and the tacit aspects of the monarchic institution. Famously, Ernst Kantorowicz scrutinized its rites, iconography and textual sources (Kantorowicz 1957). However, what concerns me is the way in which Pierre Rosanvallon referred to this very theory by studying a different institution, that is, the universal franchise in France. We can then take a further step, the third, towards the topic which I want to deal with at present. A theological-political device is also at work in the democratic election. In Ch. XVI of *Leviathan*, Thomas Hobbes nicely articulates it as he introduces the modern concept of political representation, whereby he overcomes the dualism of corporatist representation – one that had hitherto allowed thinking of the relation between the Prince and the corporations as a relation of juxtaposition and resistance among separate instances (see von Gierke 1880; Näf 1951; Hofmann 1974). The sovereign represents the unity of the people and towards his *persona* (which is a theatrical term that in Latin means "mask", as Hobbes points out) confers an existence on it that it does not possess on its own. It is exactly in this sense that it is the sovereign who makes the people and not the other way around, as could appear on the surface, based on the authorizing *fictio* of the social covenant (see Duso 2003c). The unity of the "people" comes to be produced, within the scene of the political theatre, by the representative act that pieces together the dispersed multitude of individual wills into which the bodies and the corporations of the medieval *societas civilis sive politica* dissolve. A dissolution that Hobbes equates to a pre-political state of nature with a view to obtaining the equality of the subjects of law. The *Commonwealth* is a mystical body organized through law as a unified expression of the sovereign's representative will.

Such a complicated juncture does not exclusively relate to the political theory of sovereignty. On the contrary, as far as it contrasts two Hobbesian terms – "multitude" and "people" – in order to disentangle the two stages of the covenant for legitimation purposes, this juncture is reproduced and maintained even in the constitutional history of democratic institutions. Rosanvallon takes universal franchise to be the operator that accomplishes the progressive political integration of the social. He employs the metaphor of the King's two bodies to account for the modes whereby the inequality of the harsh materiality of social processes can be minimized by the immaterial temporality of legal equivalence. As there are two bodies of the people that go across the constitutional history of the nineteenth century, the history of suffrage coincides with their transmutation. Suffrage is a genuine technology designed to turn the body of the people (a dirty, irreducible, undisciplined body, to which the liberal and conservative political rhetoric between the eighteenth and the nineteenth centuries referred with depreciative terms like "populace", "plebe", "mob", "swinish multitude") into the glorious body of the nation that is at the origin of constitutional preambles ("people", "popolo", "peuple" [von Treitschke 1871: 226]).

The fact that Rosanvallon's book seems to represent a sort of mirroring upturning of the young Marx's position in *Zur Judenfrage* (1844) (see Rosanvallon 1992) is of little importance. It makes indeed an apologia of the process of depoliticization that, throughout the long French Revolution, urges the proletariat to give up weapons and to get integrated into the democratic game of elections, where the equivalence of the right to vote is supposed to even, although formally, the unevenness of social processes. Rather, I am concerned with how the metaphor of the people's two bodies – the collective body where the "citoyen" is inscribed and the natural, savage body of the "prolétaire" – is re-actualized to gesture to the opposition between the *form* and the *matter* of subjectivity, one that is seemingly overcome and redeemed within the inclusivity of universal citizenship.

2. I can now get to the core of the issue. I am interested in analyzing another mode of this opposition between the two bodies of the people. The opposition that most of the nineteenth century identifies with that between the barbarian and the worker, between the "dangerous class" and the "working class".[1] Put otherwise, I am not so much concerned with the political-constitutional register whereby it is elaborated as with, and maybe preliminarily, how the working body is actually "thought of" – that is, designed, fabricated beyond any mystique or legal *fictio* – as a docile body or as a useful body. In doing so, I will make two contentions.

The first has to do with Michel Foucault's relationship to Marx. A problematic and evolving relationship that, according to some interpreters, is marked by deep reconsideration. In *Les mots et le choses* (Foucault 2002a: 272ff) Marx is wholly steeped in the modern *epistemē* and integrally reabsorbed in the framework of the Ricardian categories. Non-transitable 'instaurateur de discursivité' (Foucault 1969/2001: 833) just a few years later (see Cuccorese 2001 and Leonelli 2010). According to other interpreters, the relationship simply does not exist and this is a sign not only of Foucault being utterly uninterested in economics as well as the history of economic thinking – whose categories are claimed to be "made invisible", if not completely cut out from his analysis of power devices.[2] It also signifies a sort of aversion to Marxism and Marx that is believed to unveil the liberal outcome of Foucault's philosophy. The second contention I want to make – and it evidently feeds back into the first – concerns the way in which Foucault thinks not only of the body but, *with* Marx, of the productivity of power – one that exceeds the conceptual grid with which political theory has tried to exorcise it by keeping the ways of exercising it within the legal framework. It is at this level that the reference to Marx, I believe, assumes its true importance. 'Comment pourrions-nous essayer d'analyser le pouvoir dans ses mécanismes positifs?'. This is the question tackled by Foucault. He does so in the years when, by clarifying in depth the objective of his research, the processes of subjectivation come forcefully to the fore. 'Le pouvoir' – eventually and beyond any mediation – 'c'est la lutte des classes', he averred a few years before in an unpublished interview.

Power is an ensemble of asymmetrical relations of force, characterized by inequality, and yet continually mutable and amenable to being subverted. These relations can arise in a particular social body (Foucault et al. 1977). For Foucault, thinking positively of power implies not only desubstantializing it, taking it out of the system of references that conceptualizes it as a "thing". It also implies thinking of it in the difference of relationships that it imbricates as it produces them, crosses them and, at least as long as it manages to do so, reproduces them as ordered. In Marx, and particularly in *The Capital*, Foucault finds some of the fundamental elements to achieve that goal.[3] First, the Marxian analytic of the relations of production casts light on the multi-laterality of power mechanisms and their coordination. By insisting on the specificity and localization of the factory domination, Marx underlines the difference between this particular form of exercising power and those legal forms that cross the social space. The relative autonomy of command that is exercised within them – it is worth noting: not as a reality to which the legal ideology is to be reduced and confronted in order to unmask it, but as a system of relations *thoroughly heterogeneous to the latter* – makes it impossible to think of that very command as a specific repetition of an original central power or as a direct derivation of it. This is the second Marxian element that Foucault values. It is the theoretical-political scheme of legal modernity that gets upturned. According to modern contractualism, society is enabled by the power that organizes it and locates it in a system of secondary powers, hierarchically subordinated, put in motion and authorized by the unity of the sovereign. On the contrary, according to Marx, it is the existence of local and diffused forms of exercising power within the whole social space – private property, slavery, the factory, the army – that paves the way for, and determines the construction of, the grand state apparatus. This Marxian move imposes an extra-legal analytic of power and an evidently strategic view relating to the specific modes of its exercise. Finally, there is a third element that Foucault finds in *The Capital*. If a univocal rationality is to be detected in these local and heterogeneous mechanisms of power, such a rationality cannot be mere prohibition. The 'archipelago of different powers' which Foucault identifies with the social space is crossed by an imperative of production rather than instances of repressive power. Production of effectiveness, production of attitude, production of producers (Foucault 1981c/2001: 1006).

It is here that Foucault quells its own misgivings about Marx. He does that in a perfectly coherent manner, I believe. The straightforward integration of Marxism into the epistemological disposition that makes room for it derives from the Hegelian residue that marks the dialectics and the "naturalisim" of the economic categories it employs – 'Marxism exists in Nineteenth century thought like a fish in the water', Foucault (2002a: 285) wrote in 1966 with a famous expression. Evidently, he denies Althusser's 'coupure' depicting *The Capital* as 'a real epistemological mutation of its object, theory and method' (Althusser and Balibar 1970: 15).

In a text written a few years before, Foucault explicitly drew attention to this tension inherent in Marx's thought. A tension between a systematic attitude and a political attitude, we can possibly say if we pay heed to Foucault's ongoing attraction to the Marxian historiographic practice. It is a practice where the systematic attitude gets constantly exceeded and challenged, while premises and outcomes get unbalanced and shown to be untenable by the analysis of the mutual position where processes of subjectivation and tactical-strategic power dispositions are detected. What determines Marx's belonging to the nineteenth century and the order of economic discourse is the idea that labour can be thought of, as Hegel did, as the 'concrete essence' of the human being ('das sich bewährende Wesen des Menschen', Marx wrote).[4] Quite on the contrary, according to Foucault, labour is an effect. Or better, it is the product of a set of technologies of domination designed to conquer the body and bridle it in its logic of production. 'Le travail n'est pas l'essence concrète de l'homme. Si l'homme travaille, *si le corps humain est une force productive*, c'est parce que l'homme est obligé de travailler. Et il y est obligé, parce qu'il est investi par des forces politiques, parce qu'il est pris dans des mécanismes de pouvoir' (Foucault 1978a/2001: 470; emphasis added).

The duty to work is conquered with a series of interventions that mobilize extra-economic factors and operate disciplinarily on the production of subjectivity. It is Marx who primes such an analytical reorientation. Marx's account of circulation and currency emphasizes the surface where the whole phenomenology of power relations and their effects are inscribed – a "platitude" where any references to an outside disappears and the negative, never rescued by any dialectics, persists as openness, indeterminacy, possibility, in such a way that the latter might be truly upturned (Foucault 1967a/2001: 597). Marx goes beyond the discourse of political economy because he exhausts it and takes it out of its own paradigm. He lends the processes and categories of economy as knowledge to the bare materiality of history.[5]

Shortly thereafter it will be *this* Marx – a Marx beyond Marx – to orient the 'inversion of Clausewitz's principle' which Foucault raises as an interpretive grid of the historical discourse and the social process. 'Qu'est-ce que cela met donc au principe de l'histoire? D'abord, une série de faits bruts, faits qu'on pourrait dire déjà physico-biologiques', he will say then:

> vigueur physique, force, énergie, prolifération d'une race, faiblesse de l'autre, etc.; une série de hasards, de contingences en tout cas: défaites, victoires, échecs ou réussites des révoltes, succès ou insuccès des conjurations ou des alliances; enfin, un faisceau d'éléments psychologiques et moraux (courage, peur, mépris, haine, oubli . . .). Un entrecroisement de corps, de passions et de hasards: c'est cela, qui, dans ce discours, va constituer la trame permanente de l'histoire et des sociétés.
>
> (Foucault 1997: 47)

The fact that politics is the continuation of war and not the other way around is the lesson that Marx learns from the French historians of the Restoration. Foucault places this principle at the heart of his analytic of power. And he comes to a key conclusion: power relations are neither univocal nor disposable. Again, he acknowledges that Marx broke the spell that portrays the relation of domination as unilateral and its inversion as a simple de-activation of its code. Marx

> sait parfaitement que ce qui fait la solidité des relations de pouvoir c'est qu'elles ne finissent jamais: il n'y a pas d'un côté quelques-uns, de l'autre beaucoup; elles passent partout: la classe ouvrière retransmet des relations de pouvoir, elle exerce des relations de pouvoir.
>
> (Foucault 1981c/2001: 1020)

From the *subjective* vantage point of its social and political composition, the working class is not subjected to subalternity and domination but has and exerts power. This is the lesson we can learn from Marx.

The human body is a productive force. However, a productive force is not a biological fact or bare matter at our disposal. In the framework that ascribes a productive force to it, the human body is a historical invention. It is the effect of the specific procedures that concern it. To put it differently, if we consider the concept of history endorsed by Foucault, the body is a historical product. It is the outcome of a selection taking place in the irreducible confrontation between conquest tactics and tactics of subtraction or counter-power. Not only from the mid-1970s, but even before, Foucault works within the Marxian framework established in the first book of *The Capital*. He does that with a twofold end. First in relation to Marx, he wants to 'liberate' Marx from Marxist dogmatics. A scandalous assertion at the time, 'Marx is dead', has to do with the fact that the Marxian context and categories have been embalmed in the theoretical and political practices of communist parties. In an important interview of 1983, a year before his death, Foucault admitted to having cited Marx too little on account of a sort of 'obligation' to do so established in the intellectual *bon ton* of the time. 'Mais je pourrais retrouver', he could say 'bien des passages que j'ai écrits', without quoting him, 'en me référant à Marx'. More than that. Hinting at Nietzche, who had been totally disqualified by 1945 but had subsequently reappered in the second half of the twentieth century as a vital philosopher, Foucault (1983b/2001: 1276) maintained in that same occasion: 'il est certain que Marx, même si l'on admet que Marx va disparaître maintenant, réapparaîtra un jour'. As Foucault radically rejected prophecy, I am inclined to believe that this reappearance denotes the emergence of the Marxian thread that intersects his analytic of power.

The second end, on the contrary, does not only concern Marx, but the structure itself of such an analytic of power. Foucault always tried to do so, but in the second half of the 1970s did so more convincingly: he intends to de-juridify power to get it out of the machine that confines it to the model of the law. In Marx, he does not only find a productive, positive notion of power. He also finds a conspicuous structural hitch that could be set against the social democratic compromise which was augmenting the social pervasiveness of biopowers. By overemphasizing the state apparatus and its conservative features, by identifying it with a legal superstructure (as the Marxist dogmatics and Althusser himself evidently tend to do) one ends up 'rousseauiser Marx' (Foucault 1981c/2001: 1008). This does not only mean turning Rousseau into a simple pivot for a strategy of legal democratization. Rousseaunizing Marx by including him into the legal apparatus – the social-democratic strategy of the end of the nineteenth century – ends up gluing together Marxism and the state in the planning, management and reformist maintenance of the Fordist social covenant. This has noticeable effects on the diffusion of powers in the circuits of social reproduction.

The emphasis on a non-juridical and non-strictly economic notion of power (one that Foucault ascribes to Marx) brings out the modes through which fluxes of valorization are minutely regulated by agencies that, in their individual gestures and rhythms, enable, fluidify and intensify the production of goods. By breaking the enchantment that only attributes power to the state, Foucault gains access to the whole set of – legal and disciplinary – strategies that concretely actualize market institutions and produce their agents. Those strategies achieve the aim of curbing illegality and at the same time entirely transform life-time into labour-time ('alle Lebenszeit in disponible Arbeiszeit für die Verwertung des Kapitals zu verwandeln', Marx [1962: 430] wrote). What Foucault calls, with an evident nod to Weber, the 'grande mutation technologique du pouvoir en Occident' is achieved through the multilateral and discontinuous assemblage of a 'mécanisme de pouvoir'. While this mechanism controls things and people down to the minutest detail, it proves to be neither costly nor predatory towards society. Thus, it reverses the subtractive and rapacious fiscal model of Absolutism as it exerts itself 'dans le sens du processus économique lui-même' (Foucault 1981c/2001: 1009).

3. So, let me go back to the body. This time, I would like to go back to it directly through Marx. In the first book of *The Capital* there is a set of expressions that are relevant to the trace I am following. The first expression has to do with the Marxian use of Hobbes' terms. The point of departure of Marx's *Darstellung* is commodity. It is for this reason that, in the marketplace, commodity-owners enter the scene as *persons*. They give shape to the web of contracts and legal relationships that comprise the sphere of circulation. Marx draws literally on Hobbes' expression. The *persona*, however, does not merely epitomize legal equivalence. Rather it is the direct personification, 'Charaktermaske', as Marx writes of capitalist economic dynamics (Marx 1962: I, 2, *Ware und Geld*). This means that not only the commodity-owner, but anybody, any private will that expresses itself through the contract, appears in the scene as a mirror of the relation of production that takes place within it (Basso 2012: 47-ff.; Mezzadra 2014). The second has to do with the form of commodity. It is not a natural fact, of course. Products take the form of commodity only on the basis of an utterly specific mode of production, that is, the capitalist mode of production. Commodity absorbs a significant portion of the history of capital. In order for the commodity-form to exist, the product must not be produced 'as an immediate means of subsistence for the one who produces it', and, at the same time, a strong division of labour must be already in place (Marx 1962: *Verwandlung von Geld in Kapital*). The third expression is that the condition of existence of capital cannot be reduced to the mere circulation of commodities and money. The capital comes about, and thus marks the epoch of the social process of production, only if the owner of means of production and subsistence finds on the markets the free worker who sells his labour-force. The latter is defined by Marx (1962: 183) as a 'natural attitude of a living individual', as something that 'nur in seiner lebendigen Leiblichkeit existiert'.

'Lebendige Leiblichkeit', Marx writes. "Leib" is one of the two German terms denoting the body. Obviously the other is "Körper". I already touched upon the Latin semantics of this latter word. On the contrary, "Leib" refers to the gothic root **leif*. Both the German "Leben" and the English "life" derive from this root (Kluge 1899). The labour-force is *innate* to human beings. It enables them not only to produce what they need to survive, but also to replenish 'muscles, nerves, brain' that production eats up. They have to be replenished for the labour-cycle to resume the moment after. Labour-force here evidently means something that antedates the organization of the working day and the fact that that very labour-force is "purchased" by the capitalist. Just because it is an attitude inscribed in the 'Lebendige Leiblichkeit' of the individual, one's labour-force does not amount to a specific class of labour actions (this or that job which is carried out), but the generic capacity to produce that pertains to the human nature. Therefore, Marx understands the labour-force as an Aristotelian *dynamis*: as a potential or a capacity (see Virno 2002: 82 and Vadée 1998). More precisely, it is the sum of all the physical and intellectual attitudes that exist in the corporeality of a man ('Inbegriff der physischen und geistigen Fähigkeiten, die in der Leiblichkeit, der lebendigen Persönlichkeit eines Menschen existieren' [Marx 1962: 181]).

This point looks decisive to me. What is at stake is the specific human nature as potential for relation and potential for production. Marx uses the term 'lebendige Leiblichkeit' exactly to refer to that plastic knot of forces which identifies the living being as a system of an anatomical structure ('muscles, nerves') and a bundle of cognitive-linguistic dispositions ('brain'). Putting the working body to work predates subsuming the labour-force under the capital. This is the attainment of imposed conditions whereby that potential is actualized. Thus, the capitalist does not purchase this or that service. Rather, he purchases the indeterminate productivity which is inscribed in the human nature as potential. The capacity to produce as such, not yet applied, is the centre of the exchange between the capitalist and the worker (Virno 2002: 83). Indeed, the object of the purchase is not an actually accomplished job (the act that exhausts a potential) but the generic productive *dynamis* that inheres in life (*Leben*) and that the capitalist can put to work in order to extract a surplus value exactly as long as its generic character is hampered. The material backdrop to which this potential pertains is the living nature of the human being: what his body – which is indeed understood as *Leib*, not as *Körper* – *can* do.

A series of remarkable consequences ensues. First, what the capitalist cherishes is not so much, or not only, the worker's "body": muscles or arms, the pure toil that a body can endure. The body becomes an object of domination not on account of its intrinsic value, but because it is the backdrop of an immaterial thing, the labour-force, that coincides with the typical trait of the human nature – here lies part of the difference that, according to Marx, separates the Ancient slave economy from the capitalist form of production. As a good deal of interpreters have recently recognized only in this way is the term biopolitcs likely to become meaningful and to assume a "categorial" value outside and beyond the Foucauldian textual canon (Virno 2002: 84-ff; Marazzi 1992; Lazzarato 2005; Vercellone 2007; Fumagalli 2007; Hardt and Negri 2009). The worker's potential, bought and sold like any other commodity, is not-yet-objectivized work. However – and this is the second consequence – it is inseparable from the worker's immediate corporeal existence. The third consequence is that it is on account of this connection that Marx takes a decisive step in his *Darstellung* – in his *exposition*, according to Hegel's systematics – of the process of capital. The energetic consumption that Marx links to the body is at the same time a 'process of production' ('muscles, nerves and brain', that 'consumption' of labour force that has to be continuously replenished in order for the economic cycle to be reproduced). More in particular, it is a production which is not exhausted by the commodity that is produced, as it is irretrievably valued as a supply of surplus labour and therefore as a source of surplus value ('Der Konsumtionsprozeß der Arbeitskraft ist zugleich der Produktionsprozeß vom Ware und von Mehrwert').[6]

This is a decisive step. Hobbes' circulation is a theatre where buyers and sellers, also when it comes to that particular commodity that labour force is, meet each other on the scene as 'Charaktermasken' of contract and exchange. Such a view is overcome by that which Marx calls the 'secret laboratory of production' ('die verborgene Stätte der Produktion'). Well beyond the rutilant sphere of simple circulation, where the perfect representative transparency works as a presupposition,[7] the 'physiognomy of the *dramatis* personae' that animated the first four chapters of *The Capital* changes radically. The owner of money walks in as the capitalist, while the bear possessor of his own labour-force follows him as *his* worker ('folgt ihm nach als sein Arbeiter'). While the former smiles, the latter is timid and reluctant 'as somebody who has put his own skin on the market and cannot but wait for it to be tanned'.[8]

His own skin. Therefore, his own body. But under what conditions? What concerns me now is this juncture – one that is not only logical or purely internal to the Marxian *Darstellung* of the process of accumulation, as it unfolds historically, that is, as the subsumption of society under the capital. This juncture renders the generic labour-force inherent in the human 'lebendige Leiblichkeit' into the factory worker's useful, docile and productive 'Körper'. And this does not happen once and for all, given the plastic character of the human nature. Every different technique of production entails a modification of subjectivity strictly linked to the clutch on the body – this is a further lesson that Foucault learns from Marx.[9]

4. To get there, however, a further step is needed. Going beyond the sphere of circulation (and beyond the contractual dynamic of the exchange of performances) opens up to the process of production. Which is to say, according to Marx, to the valorization that is produced within it. The capitalist transforms money into value by incorporating living labour-force (*lebendige Arbeitskraft*) into dead labour (*tote Arbeit*) that gets objectivated in the productive factors mobilized by the capitalist with a view to producing surplus value. In this way, what is inserted in the process of production is the potential for valorization that inheres in the labour-force. The latter allows a capitalist to make a profit out of the invested capital, just because it is established by the capacity to provide unpaid surplus labour. Revived dead labour: 'ein beseeltes Ungeheuer'. Capital is an 'animated monster' that starts working 'as if he had love in its body' (Marx 1962: 209).

Famously, Marx uses this kind of metaphor in many places of his work. Capital is portrayed as a vampire or a werewolf. *Necropolitical* figures, as we could say by drawing on an expression that Achille Mbembe (2003) coined for different purposes. There is something that Marx intends to bring to the surface as the reality that tears to pieces the mirror game introduced by commodity fetishism: it is the series that gets underway from the inversion that generates the specific features of the capitalist process of production and its historical dimension. The worker, that worker in flesh and bones who is forced to sell "his own skin" in the exchange of performances with the capitalist, is subjected to the capitalist's control. What the worker produces belongs to the capitalist, as well as the entire time of production that exceeds the working day established by the wage. It is not the worker who uses objective factors in the production, as an ingenuous definition of labour wants us to believe. Instead, it is the dead labour "crystallized" in the capital that utilizes and 'sucks up living labour-force' and seizes on its potential for valorization. Beyond the metaphors of monstrosity, this is a gesture to the semantics of corporeality that started my discussion. The cadaverous *corpus* of productive factors *gets animated*. In front of the worker – and in particular the socialized worker, whose life is subsumed under the great factory system – the 'wholly objective *organism* of production' ('einen ganz objektiven Produktionsorganismus' [Marx 1962: 404]) rises (see in general Meyer 1969). This organism reproduces class domination, with the same tension that within Aristotelian physics qualifies the living organism (matter, form, movement). The system of machines is an 'Automat', for Marx. Still, this mechanism is an animated mechanism; the body of production, which the worker finds in front of him ('vorfindet') as the bond that subsumes him, literally takes on a *life* of its own.

It is on this sequence that I'd like to muse, as it illustrates a problem that is key to my argumentation. I am concerned with how this passage is materially produced and what it emphasizes. Above we came across the figure of the two bodies of the people, the "low" – but not that low – counterpart of the political theology of the King's sovereignty and the mystic body of the kingdom. Within democracy, the electoral machinery effects an analogous junction insofar as it turns the street "populace" (the mobs that haunts the bourgeois literature of the nineteenth century) into the bright sovereign "peuple", in whose name laws are issued and judgments are pronounced. Nineteenth-century liberalism, particularly in France, conceives of this transformation as the *éschaton*: that which lies at the very edge, in Greek. Culmination and resolution of tragedy in Aristotle's *Poetics*. And yet, no tragedy ends here. For Tocqueville, for Guizot, for Lorenz von Stein – to mention some of the authors who in that period toy with the politicization of the social question – the revolution does not "end" with the constitutional advancements and is revitalized through the issues of property and labour. While it was political, it actually becomes *social* (see Chignola 2004a; Conze 1954; Pankoke 1990). By dint of that, governing amounts to developing technologies to have an impact *on* the body and *within* the body of society. Assistive technologies and social safety, hygiene-sanitation technologies, pedagogy and responsabilization (Ewald 1986; Procacci 1993). Among them, maybe the most important, is the discipline of labour. As long as it is able to transform the indolent and idle body of the proletarian into the productive body of the worker.

When Marx begins to deal with production and valorization – when the body of commodity production comes into life – he evokes the sphere of circulation (the contract as transaction of the labour-force). For this sphere represents the necessary mediation to get access to the "secret laboratory" of production. This is evidence that the seeming symmetry of the will of the buyer and the seller of the labour-force is not a real and genuine symmetry: what the capitalist purchases is not "labour", the accomplished labour that is objectivated in a product that ends the trajectory of production. Instead, it is a power, a "living yeast", that keeps augmenting the value of the capital as it is embedded in the process (Marx 1962: 200). The worker does not alienate his own individual attitude (his skills, his particular talent, the strength of his body), but a generic capacity that can be exteriorized and organized in keeping with subjecting norms and reparation conditions that turn its capacities into *social* labour, surveilled cooperation "incorporated" into the capital ('dem Kapital einverleibt') (Marx 1962: 352). Within a planned cooperation with the others, the worker disposes of his own individual limits and develops the capacities of his own species ('im planmäßigen Zusammenwirken mit andern streift der Arbeiter seine individuellen Schranken ab und entwickelt sein Gattungsvermögen') (Marx 1962: 349). And yet: how is this "incorporation" accomplished in terms that do not only pertain to the mere configuration of abstract labour?

It is known that in his seminal work devoted to the formation of the British working class Edward P. Thompson pinpointed a decisive fact. The working class did not make its appearance at a given historical moment. Instead, it is 'a fluency', a relationship whose composition evades any attempts to grasp it as if it were dead in order to anatomize it.[10] The first phase of this relationship is, as it were, the fabrication of the working body as a productive body. Both within the individual and within cooperation. This is a passage that comes about as a practice – doubtless neither pacified nor pacifying – for subjecting the habits, rhythm, vital acts of individuals to the labour discipline. Fixing the vagrant, training the minor, organizing a collective movement are strategic assets of a process of social disciplining occurring within the multiple institutions (penal, educational, military) that contribute to the modern production of subjectivity.[11]

As Marx analyses the so-called original accumulation, it is to this complex phenomenology of extra-economic coercion that he refers while writing on the *naturalization* of the capitalistic code of production. To establish it, it is neither sufficient to postulate the *persons* of the buyer and the seller of labour force as the two poles of simple circulation, nor, on a genetic level, to assume the bare act of domination – the act whereby the seller, forcedly deprived of livelihood (*commons*, land, forms of community solidarity) is compelled to sell himself voluntarily and 'whipped, branded, tortured by laws grotesquely terrible, into the discipline necessary for the wage system'. Rather, what is necessary is the process that is intertwined with – and *redoubles* – the development of the productive system bound to waged labour. Which is to say, the system of practices that reproduces an 'Arbeiterklasse' that by 'education, tradition, habit' acknowledges the requirements of capitalistic production as 'natural laws' (selbstverständliche Naturgesetze). The incorporation of the worker's cooperation comes about as a *naturalization* of exploitment and command, that is, as subjection of the social body to the discipline of mandatory labour. Insofar as this process pivots on the depth of life – muscles, nerves, brain, i.e. the nexus of repetition and habit – it determines a clash between disciplinary technologies and the withdrawal of the workers. The fabrication of the useful body meets with strong opposition.

5. This is proven by at least two elements that keep re-emerging in Marx's texts. The first is the way in which the "expropriation" of independent workers is achieved. The proletariat 'is brought to life' by means of a multilateral and converging process that, as I recalled, comprises the stealth of ecclesiastical goods, the fraudulent alienation of state goods, the stealth of commons, the transformation of feudal properties into private properties. The first step to the original

accumulation is the production of the poor, the vagrants and the miserable who are compelled to work. Their being condemned to poverty is immediately redoubled in legal terms: 'the legislation treated them as 'voluntary' criminals and under the assumption that whether or not they continued to work in conditions that no longer existed depended on their good will ('die Gesetzgebung behandelte sie als 'freiwillige' Verbrecher und unterstellte, daß es von ihrem guten Willen abhänge, in den nicht mehr existierenden alten Verhältnisse fortzuarbeiten') (Marx 1962: 762). With its logic of imputation, the law attaches the subject to a 'free will', but only to crush his resistance, put him to work, bind him to the wage-form. Marx describes not only the law's social impacts but its 'use' as a weapon in the disciplinary battle. The second step has to do with the regulation of the working day. Which is to say, the imposition, on the part of the working class, of a series of limitations to the boundless extension of the working time on the part of the employer. By getting hold of the whole 'Lebenszeit' of the proletarian, the employer has no difficulties extending indefinitely the time of production and therefore securing a neat extraction of absolute surplus value. And yet, he is faced with the body of the worker as a form of resistance that makes it impossible. The technical organization of cooperation – with the perverse effects that Marx keeps describing in terms of alienation, repetition of acts, impoverishment of the worker's cognitive capacities – is basically instrumental in implanting a device able to increase the balance of the relative surplus value. However, the working counterpower imposes a regulation of the working day that opposes such a device. This counterpower is a 'resistance' ('Widerstand') that enables the working class 'subdued by the uproar of production begins to come to its senses' (Marx 1962: 762). It is almost impossible not to think that, amongst the many passages that are not quoted but are directly tackled by Michel Foucault, there is one in particular. The one devoted to the 'minute dispositions that regulate with such a military uniformity, to the ring of the bell, working periods, limits and breaks' ('diese minutiösen Bestimmungen, welche die Periode, Grenzen, Pausen der Arbeit so militärisch uniform nach dem Glockenschlag regeln') which Marx speaks of as a workers' conquest. While the regulation of the working day certainly depends on state intervention, it does not represent the vertical movement of a disciplinary act. It unfolds in the circumstances – 'allmählich aus den Verhältnissen herau' – and as a result of enduring class struggles (Marx 1962: 299). At the outset of *Surveiller et punir*, Foucault juxtaposes two archive texts whereby he foregrounds the range of oscillation of modern criminality. Here it is difficult not to have the sensation that it is those pages of Marx's that point him to the problem.[12] A law which is not only law. A power that circulates and activates opposite and antagonistic positions. An economy, not only of the punishment, constantly interlaced with a technology of government.

6. The publication of the *Course* he gives at the Collège de France in the first semester of 1963 finally dispels, I believe, several interpretive ambiguities relating to Foucault's analytic of power (Foucault 2013). The domination of capital over the worker – one that, according to Marx, is sealed by a 'silent compulsion

of economic relations' ('der Stumme Zwang der ökonomischen Verhältnisse') (Marx 1962: 765) – is conquered in the course of a century-long battle that exhibits the *warlike* matrix of social relation. As I pointed out above, the fabrication of the docile body, which is the objective of the disciplining strategy, is neither one-way nor pacific. And yet, the worker's body has to be subjected to the discipline in order for the force-labour inhering in it as *dynamis*, as potential, to be transformed as productive force.[13]

In this latter case, it is a twofold passage that lies at the heart of Foucault's *Cours* devoted to the *Société punitive*. It casts a sharp light on the analytic of law and penalty which he is deploying in those years. The human nature is not labour, he remarks in the last lecture. What really articulates the unruly life of the human being, as a hub of savage connections able to develop autonomous and collective relationships regardless of the rhythms of production, is rather 'plaisirs, discontinuités, fête, repos, besoins, instants, hasards, violence' (Foucault 2013: 235). In practice, the uninterrupted flux of instances and attitudes that capital always tries to force under its command – that is, the smooth chronometric temporality of the productive process. By traversing subjectively this flux, the working class meets with the forms of its own composition and exploits them as occasions for resistance and organization.

Here Foucault foregrounds two things that make him come as close as possible to Marx and at the same time make him move away from Althusser. First, the key role of conflict as a tensor of the analytic of power. Second, the passage whereby disciplinary technologies (and among them penalty) do not simply guarantee the reproduction of the capitalistic relation of valorization – that is to say, the repression of proletarian illegality and, more broadly, the "restructuration" of the general economy of illegalities that get accomplished along with the development of the capitalistic society.[14] These disciplinary technologies guarantee the organization of the disposition to produce to which the worker's body is to be subjected (Legrand 2004). On the one hand, the criminal system has to achieve the conditions of its own effectiveness through techniques of seizure and enclosure, techniques that fix mobility, that impact with violence and infiltrate microphysically the mobile and elusive body of a 'populace' of vagrants and inert individuals. Here Foucault's first radical statement: the 'guerre civile' as the *general matrix* of the rationality of punishment, because it does not aim at the imposition of peace over naturally conflicting relations, as in Hobbes or Rousseau, but at the ceaseless continuation of a war of conquest.[15]

On the other hand, like in Marx, the definition of the strategic horizon, continuously contested, within which both social relations and subjectivation processes have to be thought of once one reckons with the fact that the decisive problem of the genesis of capitalism coincides with the transformation/constitution of life into labour-force (Dardot and Laval 2012: 202).

Foucault's research objective is the comprehensive process of fabrication of the labour-force as a subjective disposition objectively attuned to the conditions of production, to draw on Stephan Legrand's nice formulation. Which is to say, based on the Marxian analytic of the genesis of capital, the process of real subsumption whereby labour gets incorporated into the process of valorization. The fact that the latter can be objectivated into a system of "natural laws" of economy – and this objectivation is not a simple ideological concealment but a truth effect, as it were, of the fetishism of commodities – derives both from the design of the body and from the discipline of the soul. The unruly and useless body of the inert individual is rendered into the useful and docile body of the worker – the plasticity of tamed life, trained to the rhythms and the gestures of production – on account of a series of knowledges that do not have the disciplinary inclination of economy, but remarkably affect its process. Law, morals, pedagogy, military sciences, to mention just a few of those that are key to separating, within the opaque mass of the multitude, the dangerous classes and the working class, which will then be recomposed in the disciplinary process. These knowledges are productively invoked not only to segment, to subject to an efficiency formula and to recompose an anatomo-politics of the body (as Foucault calls it). Rather, they link to the soul the work of normalization (a legal and above all an extra-legal one) that objectivates and reproduces the relation of capital and the objectivation of the soul.

It is in this Marxian framework that Michel Foucault develops his analysis of penalty and his clear-cut inversion of the Platonic tradition. At the threshold of modernity, as a constitutive break that imposes new functions, it is not the body that is the prison of the soul, as the soul becomes the prison of the body (Foucault 1975: 34). The transformation of the multitude into labour-force is the product of a sort of transcendental schematism of discipline. It redesigns and conquers space, and reorders and records time. Discipline organizes functions and hierarchies by operating on space. It isolates individual segments in the social cooperation and establishes operational links among them. By controlling time, discipline constitutes it as useful in its entirety. As Foucault writes in *Surveiller et Punir*, accuracy, application and regularity are the fundamental virtues of disciplinary time. The so-called original accumulation is the effect of the production of docile bodies and of a stabilization of a periodicity entirely subsumed to the performance (Foucault 1995: 138-ff and 152) – 'the human body was entering a machinery of power that explores it, breaks it down and rearranges it' as it seizes it, it affixes it to the repetitiveness of a gesture, a functional location, a particular junction between gesture and object. Fourier's sentence recalled by Marx becomes real within this twofold constitutive process: the factory is a mitigated jail (Marx 1962: 450). According to Foucault, the shared nature, which can be genealogically inferred, of the prison-form and the salary-form (Foucault 2013: 72).

To sum up, transforming life time into labour time means disposing of the body. Which means grounding the operativeness of a power *device* on the body. Here, "power" does not mean a "thing" that someone owns or could own. Rather, it is the always unsteady trajectory that leads the battle between a resistance and that which managed to defeat and tame it. According to Marx, the incorporation of the labour-force into the capital (the subsumption of life under authority and valorization) is produced as the pure extraction of absolute surplus value in the institution of the working day. Yet, the indefinite extension of the working time stimulates the invincible resistance of the physical corporality of the worker – in its very anatomical composition. The matching of the working day and the technical organization of production means developing the intensification of productive processes and the valorization of relative surplus value. But, for Marx, it also means concentrating on and increasing the power, subjectivity and the counter-power of the working class, as well as its likely political composition. What is at stake in the constant reorganization of powers and knowledges is the working body, in both an individual and a collective sense, in its being faced as a mobile, literally *dynamic*, irreducible instance.

The functions of government of this irreducibility which ties up with a wage-form and a prison-form – understood here as the ordered bounds of the factory and as the disciplinary code of the working day – finally faces a crisis – at least in that part of the Western experience of the world that is related to Foucault's direct experience, between the end of the 1960s and the end of the 1970s. One of the reasons that bring his philosophy back to the fore is the radical force with which he questions his own categories in a direction that I dare to define not *post-*, but *ultra-Marxist* (Negri 1979).

What now is directly put to work and exploited by the incrementally *extractive* functions of capital is not so much, or not only, the body of the human being, its disciplined usefulness. Rather it is the human nature understood in keeping with the qualities typical of its species, those that are immanent to the human being as a linguistic and relational animal: his affectivity, his faculty to cooperate, his potential for socialization (Mezzadra and Neilson 2013). Labour is no longer directly organized, unified by a command, confined to the perimeter of the working day. It gets spread around, set 'free', made precarious. Its model: that of autonomous entrepreneurship.

What happens, then, to the body within the broad social factory of the post-industrial society? There is a discipline maybe even more invasive then the one that is intertwined with the body in the series of extra-economic devices that are coupled with the structure of capitalism of the eighteenth and the nineteenth century. It is the discipline that, in the design of the society of neoliberal individuals, is coupled with the rhetoric of the human capital and the individual as a self-entrepreneur (Dardot and Laval 2009). Here the body – a performing body, hyper-connected body, cyborg body – is kept captive not by a directive, governmental function instrumental in a commanded accumulation. Rather, it is the subject himself who meets with, and recognizes, the basis for its own valorization as an individual enterprise. More than that. The body – a branded body, a body marked by the infrared scanner of the inspection personnel, a digitalized and scanned body in every airport – is governed, filtered, slowed down, but never fixed in its mobility. This becomes a function of valorization of capital in its own right. What is moving is more and more *Leiber* and less and less *Körpern*, one might say.

In the history of the working class the resistance of the individual and the collective body has produced remarkable processes of subjectivation. Counter-conducts, as Foucault calls them, when he tries to think of them beyond the organizational forms and the claims of the mass-worker. Today we should envision new tactics of resistance and subtraction also at this level – the level of mobile, flexible, precarious, global and hybrid corporality, that is interlaced with governmental devices of control and valorization.

Notes

1 See Chevalier 1958; and for the metaphorical field of the "barbarian" or the "savage", Michel 1981.
2 See Tellman 2009. For a general account of the relation between Foucault and economics see Amariglio 1988; Zanini 2010.
3 See Foucault 1981c/2001: 1005. In this case, Foucault quotes the second volume of *The Capital*. Clearly, he is referring to the second volume of the edition of *The Capital* published in eight volumes by Éditions sociales. Foucault is actually indicating the second tome of the first book, that is to Sect. IV of the I book of *The Capital*. Leonelli (1999) expands on this.
4 Marx (1968: 574) explicitly acknowledges this.
5 This point is emphasized by the literature that re-evaluates Foucault's relation to Marx. While many scholars believe Foucault can be considered as utterly useless for historians (see as a paradigmatic example Megill 1979), other scholars think his analytic of power should be appreciated, in the wake of Marx exactly in historical terms. In addition, it is amenable to fruitful developments, see Poster 1982; 1984.
6 Marx 1962: 189.
7 This is a transparency that the law renders the symmetry of the will into a legitimate feature of the exchange and the "innate rights of men" are claimed to embrace the whole process of negotiation and to guarantee it.
8 Marx 1962: 191.
9 '[J]'ai voulu décrire à la fois la spécificité de ces techniques et de leur interaction constante. Par exemple, le rapport entre la manipulation des objets et la domination apparaît clairement dans le Capital de Karl Marx, où chaque technique de production exige une modification de la conduite individuelle, exige non seulement des aptitudes, mais aussi des attitudes' (Foucault 1988/2001: 1604).
10 'The notion of class entails the notion of historical relationship. Like any other relationship, it is a fluency which evades analysis if we attempt to stop it dead at any given moment and anatomise its structure' (Thompson 1966: 9).
11 As regards the category of social disciplining see at least Oestreich 1969.
12 It is the lasting of the slow, excruciating agony of Damiens, where the resistance of the body of the victim hampers the ritual of sovereignty on the scaffold and kindles the complicity of the "populace" with the culprit as they watch the scene. The second is the regulation issued by Léon Faucher for the House of young prisoners in Paris, where violence is passed over in silence, but drum roll, organized movements and the ringing of the bell mark a day thoroughly saturated by discipline.
13 On this see the important Macherey 2013a.
14 This "restructuration" concerns not only the suppression of illegalities, but a government of them made up of thresholds of tolerance, differentiation of crimes, gradation of punishments. See Foucault 1975: 89.
15 In the 1976 Lecture at the Collège de France, 'Il faut défendre la société', Foucault (1997) defines this perspective, as I have already recalled, the 'retournement de la présupposition de Clausewitz'.

3 The politics of the governed

Governmentality, forms of life, subjectivation

The objective of this chapter is to analyse how, from the end of the 1970s, Michel Foucault radicalizes his analytic of power by modifying the schemes and interpretive categories of *Surveiller et punir*. On the one hand, in those years he introduces the terms 'biopower' and 'biopolitics'. This happens specifically in the fifth chapter of *La volonté de savoir* (1976) and in the *Cours* at the Collège de France at the lecture of the 17th of March 1976 titled 'Il faut défendre la société'. By doing so, he emphasizes the ways in which the non-disciplinary technologies of power that invert the codes of sovereignty-centred thanatopolitics entrap the phenomena of life. These are ways that target population as an object of care and management that is hazardous, random, unpredictable because of the autonomy of dynamics that affect population by deploying legal webs that provide its conditions of possibility. These ways disclose the transformation of a power that turns out to be more and more de-territorialized, de-sovereignized, de-juridicized vis-à-vis the processes that it has to govern. On the other hand, from the fourth lecture of the 1977–78 *Cours* 'Sécurité, territoire, population', and in shorter but fundamental contributions dated 1978–1979, he coins the term 'governmentality'. It denotes a much more complex phenomenon whose genealogy can be traced back to before the nineteenth century. At the same time, he discovers the "social" as an effect of the processes of population, and once and for all dispels the equivocation that many of his readers are inclined to project on Foucault's entire analytic of power: "biopower" ' and "biopolitics" as terms that gesture to a further extension of the surface of domination (the amplification of its codes, the concretization of its effects, the refinement of its strategies with a view to a more effective radiation of his subjection devices on the whole field marked off by the trajectories of freedom and life). It is worth underlining that this is a misunderstanding, or a distortion, that I believe has beset significant parts of the Italian reception of the terms "biopower" and "biopolitics" until recently.[1]

What emerges from this reformulation of Foucault's analytic of power is his definite exit from the identification of the political and the state entailed in the modern concept of sovereignty. For Foucault, dealing with power as government means 'cutting off the King's head' in the field of theory, once it was possible to do that, at least from time to time, in the field of practice. There are two coordinates that reorient Foucault's research in those years. First, he takes the state as a mere 'peripeteia' of the fact of government.[2] Second, he regards the problem of freedom as the heart of a subject-making process different from disciplinary individuation – for it is produced as a reflexive fold of life, as 'care' and 'government of the self', capable of reframing the relation itself of the individual with himself and with the others.

Ludwig Wittgenstein once wrote that only those who prove to be able to revolutionize themselves can truly become revolutionaries.[3] 'Reread the Greeks because the revolution will be ethical', Foucault is claimed to have said, as he was aware that the Greek ethical-political thought was not reducible to the Christian pastoral power that he recognized as the engine of the fact of government.

From here, the path that I intend to follow in the subsequent pages is the following. First, I will attend to the problem of power and how its analytic has to be carried out. Second, I will discuss what it is that marks the irruption that prompts Foucault to rethink genealogy. Finally, I will examine what it means to 'evenementialize' liberalism in the way that makes it our present and therefore makes it what is to be thought.

1. In 1978, on the 2nd of June, Foucault (1978b/2001) gives a lecture in Tokyo which we can read in the second volume of *Dits et Ecrits*. I believe this writing to be particularly noteworthy. Here Foucault discusses the relation between philosophy and politics and clarifies in some detail the notions of 'power' and 'analytic of power'. Philosophy cannot be severed from politics, nor should it play a superordained role of guidance for politics. In Antiquity, this twofold impossibility – impossibility of severing and impossibility of founding – gave rise to the figures of the philosopher-legislator (Solon), the philosopher-pedagogist who teaches the tyrants against the possible use of the power conquered by the latter (Plato), and the philosopher *prima facie* anti-political who mocks power and measures the power of philosophy against its capacity to avoid politics (the Cynics). This inescapable intercourse between philosophy and politics, according to Foucault, is to be emphasized further. Indeed, philosophy still keeps a role vis-à-vis politics that it lost long ago vis-à-vis science. However, when the relation between philosophy and politics takes a directly organizational shape, it often eventuates in a catastrophe. This happened from Hobbes to Marx, as the human praxis was rendered dependent on a theoretical project aiming to justify it, thus radically modifying the framework of classical anthropology and the prudential, ethical schemes whereby politics had long been conceived.[4] This applies particularly to the modern trajectory of that relationship. The tone of resistance of philosophy, its taking a critical stance with respect to power – to correct the latter, to blandish it or to organize it in accordance with abstract ideals of freedom and justice – is definitely extinguished by its proximity with power. Philosophy, for example, turns into the terrorist outcome of Rousseau's theorizing, into Hegel's pan-Germanism, into the Nazi use of Nietzsche, into the Stalinist translation/betrayal of Marx's philosophy. Founding or contradicting power means postulating a direct link between philosophy and politics, squeezing together practice and theory. This first option, which we can call "modern", results in the rigid alternative between

reinstating the constitutive connection of philosophy and politics, thus entrusting the former with the legitimation of the latter,[5] and "rescuing" philosophy by breaking its compromise with praxis, thus giving it a theoretical, methodological or foundational role with respect to other knowledges and other practices.

However, this ever-possible 'retrait' of political philosophy proves to be but a further effect engendered by the particular framing of the modern relation between philosophy and politics. As often happens in Foucault, the bifurcation we are faced with can therefore be circumvented. For philosophy can be assigned a decisive role with respect to power – neither a foundational one, nor the pedagogical-prophetic-legislative one in the light of which between Antiquity and early modernity it was conceived as a corrective or restorative instance with respect to the field of practice. In fact, philosophy can bring power to light as a strategic plot, as a knot around which a battle takes place, an empty place in which freedom and control conflict, someone or something gets away, while someone else tries to entrap him/it.[6] This is the second option at our disposal, the one that, for Foucault, allows keeping and relaunching philosophy's political vocation at a moment when the specialization and autonomization of knowledges marginalize it once and for all within the other subject-areas.

This is a perspective that philosophy gets rid of only on the condition that it locates itself in a disenchantment that is able to deal with power outside and beyond the axiological connotation that qualifies it as "good" or "bad". Against Sartre, but indirectly also against Habermas and the utopia of the "smooth", transparent, boundless communicative relationship, some years later Foucault will say that 'le pouvoir n'est pas le mal. Le pouvoir c'est des jeux stratégiques'.[7] Power should not be understood as a thing that can be kept, conquered, eliminated, founded or refounded. Instead, it has to be assumed as a bare fact.

Philosophy has to dispense with the ghost of Leviathan, with the spectre of sovereignty, through an exorcism that frees philosophy from the obsession with power as well as the latter's influence on the philosophical potential for the imagination of freedom. This is possible only on account of a consideration of things that easies itself from the moral and legal overload that forces philosophy to think of itself as corrective or as a formalization of reality. Instead, philosophy simply has to adhere to the surface of reality. Its task is not to discover what is hidden as a secret; nor is it to pit an alleged truth of things against the mystification that makes it an ideology; nor is it to assess the imperfection of things against the model that philosophy permits us to think for them. Rather, the task of an analytic of truth is to make visible what is so close to us, what is so intimately tied to us that it becomes almost imperceptible. This is the operation that can rescue us and at once rescue philosophy itself.[8]

What is philosophy, then, for Foucault, as far as its relation to politics is concerned? A relation that places philosophy beyond the interpretations that time by time have turned it into word-law, word-prophecy or word-pedagogy. Philosophy is a *reagent* in the first place – just as freedom and resistance are. Philosophy, freedom and resistance are in the position to bring to light the relations of power that constitute us, that traverse us, and within which philosophy itself is trapped without any claim to overstep the threshold of regularities, of the quotidian within which power materially works, acts and circulates. Philosophy is a *thickener*, a *catalyst* and an *intensifier* in the second place. While dwelling on those that Foucault, with a blatant and justified reference to the analytic philosophy of power, calls 'power games' as 'linguistic games', he does not only bring politics, to employ Wittgenstein's terms,[9] back to its 'everyday use', to the system of movements that mark an irreducible, daily confrontation between freedom and domination, between resistance and power. He also multiplies, amplifies, disperses its stakes and battlefields. Finally, philosophy can re-determine itself, exactly on account of the above, as an '*analytical-political philosophy*'. A philosophy that takes it upon itself 'ce qui se passe quotidiennement dans les relations de pouvoir', as Foucault writes. It gives up definite, global, unilateral, absolute judgements, like those that it has long supported. The real is polemical, and philosophy is involved in this battle.[10] Philosophy cannot set itself up as the judge of reality, as an "object" isolated from the outside. If this is the case, the power which engages this battle is to be analysed in the games of tactic and strategy by which it moves as an always precarious, contingent, random logic of connection between elements characterized by constitutive and irreducible heterogeneity.[11]

Based on this, we can get to three crucial axioms concerning the meaning of philosophy. First, philosophy does not have to understand anything, because also the philosopher's gaze is traversed by relations of power. The philosopher's eye is not the sovereign's eye – one that hovers over things from an absolute exteriority. The philosopher's is a gaze that is capable of walking through the world and its things by totally immersing itself in their vicissitude. Second, truth belongs in *this* word.[12] It emerges as the tensor of the relation between its components. Third, philosophy is not meant to understand, to capture reality with the structural delay of the concept. Rather, it has to take a stance[13] – and this for Foucault is crucial to the ethic of the intellectual work.

2. Famously Foucault identifies the meaning of the philosophical work – in the sense of a radical Enlightenment – with the sagittal relationship that has to be established, in genealogical terms, between the present and its history (Foucault 1984b/2001: 1500). The philosopher bears the specific responsibility to say what is happening, why it is possible to take a stance on it. Foucault takes this responsibility so seriously that he goes so far as to bring into question his closest friendships. There is a story that is particularly telling in this regard. In the years in which Foucault works on the courses on biopolitics, after a decade-long friendship, he fell out with Gilles Deleuze. This occurred because apparently he refused to sign the petition that Félix Guattari had drawn up against the extradition of Klaus Croissant, a lawyer of the Baader-Meinhof Gang. In this petition, Guattari (and indirectly Deleuze, who signed it) still pitted – *et pour cause* in the end – "human rights" against the "fascism" of the German state and its special laws. But this was not an issue Foucault concerned himself with. The battle that was taking place around the Croissant case was certainly "a real battle", on which Foucault took a stance so much so that he joined the demonstration outside la Santé Prison, which was aggressively dispersed by the police. However, it was at the same time a battle

that signalled a decisive shift, one that could not be grasped with the categories applied by Guattari.[14] Croissant is a figure of diaspora and exile, like the dissident of the Soviet bloc or the subjectivities of the new social composition of labour freed as protagonists of the radical of the 1960s and the 1970s. Foucault identifies Croissant with something radically new. Contrary to what some of his interlocutors believed, Croissant was not the negative side within a dialectic between constituted power and revolutionary counter-power. Rather, he was the element that *exceeded* all of the various forms of that relation, always looked at through the prism of a sovereign law.[15] Croissant was not the militant of a possible revolutionary overthrow of power, the 'future governor' destined to take over the place of the enemy. He was the 'perpétuel dissident' who radically refuses the system of rules in which he lives. He was one whose very existence defies the legal centric, who defects from the imperative of power and is guided by a claim to freedom – a 'droit à vivre, à être libre', whose grammar cannot but be thought of as a withdrawal and as an exodus.

What is at stake in the Croissant case, Foucault avers, is the 'droit des gouvernés': a right that exceeds any strictly legal definition, that evades the chains of sovereignty, that revokes the 'survalorisation' of the state which (also) infiltrates radical thought as the latter identifies the state with a detested object that has to be wiped out and that, above all, still lacks theorization.[16] It is exactly this lack of theorization that leads Foucault to focus his attention on the fact of government. This passage marks a radical turn in the Foucauldian analytic of power and gets to a point in which it ties up to the future study of Ancient ethics.[17]

It is a double movement. On the one hand, within the perspective of *La volonté de savoir*, he integrates the Political with the dynamics of regulation whereby power intercepts and subsumes life phenomena. The anatomo-political discipline of the human body (docility, productivity, empowerment of its attitudes) along with the biopolitics of population (the controls that do not affect the individual body but the species-body to optimize the cycle of social reproduction) invert the thanatopolitical code of sovereignty and get rid of the character of pure extraction. On the other hand, in connection with the first movement, the self-referential perimeter of power is smashed. This exceeds the formal cycle of legitimation by which the subject is referred to the state and the state presents itself as the product of the will of incorporation of the subjects in accordance with the scheme of juridification of power typical of social contract theories that inaugurate modernity – the classical epoch of politics.[18]

By introducing the issue of government – whose genealogy gestures to Christian pastoral power and signals a type of relationship that Western politics incorporates, as it were, from outside[19] – Foucault breaks with the effect of reference between the fabrication of Leviathan and the fabrication of the individual in the mirror of discipline.[20] By doing so, he marginalizes the state along with the whole state monopoly on decision-making in the way it developed in the philosophical-political sequence of modernity from Hobbes to Weber.

But let me unpack these two points. As far as the first is concerned, it entails the despatialization, dejuridification and desovereignization of domination. It is a way to do history that rejects any temporal imputation – when history settles on our conscience and memory and employs spatial metaphors to chart the shifts and transformations in the relation of power with the objects on which it pivots in order to keep circulating.[21] In this sense, this is a radical change in the relation between space and power which articulates the genealogy of biopower. It is not the space in which a norm is binding in the binary relationship to which the underpinning notion of sovereignty attaches (legal/illegal; inclusion/exclusion; within/without). Rather, it is an environment of unstable, contingent, random relations of oversight and control over a territory which develops as a set of largely autonomous processes. Therefore it is a change that also affects dispositifs of power. It is a perspective of *regulation* – not simply prescriptive or pre-emptive. It is forced to relate to an outside that precedes it, to trajectories that power can neither pre-constitute in the form of laws nor confine to the schemes of discipline. It is a regulation *within* reality that *ensures* the exchange against the *risk* entailed by freedom itself – the risk that progressively emerges as the mobile field of social interests (Foucault 2004a: 48). Optimisation and growth instead of extraction and consumption. The redistribution of the relationship of sovereignty, discipline and security in the 'governmental' administration of population and society (Foucault 2004a: 111).

And this is the second point that interests me. As early as the fourth lecture of the *Cours*, Foucault introduces the term 'gouvernementalité' in lieu of the expression biopower. The integration of economy in the exercise of politics as an 'enjeu essentiel du gouvernement' (Foucault 1978d/2001: 642). More than that. This opens the state, through economy and what it entails, to a system of relations that definitively dislocates the Political. *Oikonomia*: structure of "government", in Aristotle. But even more so in the overall Christian theology where it is wedded to pastoral power.[22] It is a relation that involves human beings and things. It is a form of relation that traverses the individual – who has to be able to conduct himself – and that extends to the whole field of relations that he is called upon to administer and in which he is included as a living being.

It is well known that government is a marine metaphor. *Kubernein*, *gubernare*, to govern derive from the same Sanskrit root *kubara*, the boat rudder.[23] Now, it is evident that taking government to be the matrix of politics means radically dislocating politics from the neutralisation, administration and monopoly of decision that are typical of the modern tradition of the state.[24] Governing mainly means having to do, as Foucault points out, with the complex defined by the contingent, unstable and unpredictable interactions of human beings and things. Having to do with environmental factors (the conditions of the sea, the wind, the time, the load balancing).

Yet governing also, and above all, means partaking in a living relationship which includes the directive function of the captain and exposes the latter to a confrontation with those who are on-board with him (the resistance of the crew made up of free human beings who can always mutiny and whose desires, opinions, and living conditions on-board define a *risk* in the exercise of captainship).[25] The captain has first and foremost to govern himself in the relation with the series of social and environmental factors characterizing the exchange in which he partakes. He must be able to ***conduct himself*** to be able to pull off the navigation.

Foucault progressively reducing the centrality of the notion of biopower to the advantage of the notion of "governmentality" has to do with this. On the one hand, with an analytic that is increasingly attentive to the plane of immanence of power games, that is, to the divisive dynamics that traverse it and highlight its relational structure. On the other hand, with the possibility of thematizing the process of mutual constitution connecting technologies of power, forms of knowledge and practices of subjectivation, in the crucial intersection between pastoral power and counter-conducts.[26]

With a move that picks up the "fil du present" which is the engine of genealogy and prompts him to take a further leap forward – or aside, as he would have probably preferred – with respect to the critics of the society of the spectacle or mass society – 'nous n'en sommes plus là', Foucault (2004b: 154) warns – he speaks of a 'droit des gouvernés' apropos of Klaus Croissant. Here I believe the genitive is both objective and subjective.

The era of liberalism, historical universal to be dismantled along with the others,[27] is the era in which dispositifs of power slide towards the administrativization and the disinterestedness of command, that is, towards government. To prove this, one only needs to go back to Tocqueville.[28] Yet, it is also the era in which the governed become stronger thanks to a subjective freedom that acts in terms irreducibly *critical* towards command.

The ellipse of liberal governmentality focuses on two elements. On one side, the constellation of sovereignty, discipline and dispositifs of security, oriented towards the centrality that these dispositifs have acquired. On the other, the system of contingent and random variables that is determined by the bundle of free conducts of subjects who pursue their interests, who claim to be free and claim that their freedom be constantly given back to them – a freedom whose trajectories always run the risk of escaping the criteria of an ordered socialization.[29]

3. 'Nous n'en sommes plus là'. Ours is not the society of the spectacle that situationists dealt with, let alone the mass society adumbrated by the members of the Frankfurt School. Where are we, then? This question urges the philosopher to interrogate his own discursive present – the philosopher who speaks, and only by speaking takes the responsibility that is foisted on him by his thinking. Speaking in the sense of mobilizing what appears to be crystallized and self-evident, by re-immersing what appears as universal and necessary in the flux of processual dynamics, by bringing to the surface the thud of the battle that traverses the laborious silence of categories and concepts. To make a difference: this is the task of the genealogist. More: the modern attitude, the ethos of thought. The emergence of the question of the 'pure actualité' as a constant *reactivation* of the problem of the present: its introducing, marking a difference vis-à-vis yesterday. 'Quelle différence aujourd'hui introduit-il par rapport à hier?'. It is the productivity of this difference that is crucial to Foucault (1984b/2001: 1383).

If there is anything that qualifies this difference, this cannot and should not be looked for in the place indicated by the critiques that refer to the evanescence of the political and to the immediacy and pervasiveness of domination. For Foucault, it is not the 'étatisation de la société', as it is the 'gouvernementalisation de l'État' that characterizes the present to which we belong. No functional, mythological unity can be assigned to the state, as well as to power, in spite of what its critics do. The state does not act by subsuming society from above or by integrally colonizing it. At most, what allows the state to "survive" is its capacity to exploit – as it intercepts them – the processes of government that have always been external to it, that have a precise theological-political matrix, that concern the way in which the order is achieved in a diminished form by passing through the free self-disposition of the subjects, the movement of their desire, the fibrillation of interests, the dynamics of oriented exchange whereby someone, or something, manages to produce effects, portions, folds, to others' ***anyway unavailable*** action or will (Foucault 2004a: 112).

Passing through the processes of governmentalization of the state therefore means moving away from a position that "overvalues" the apparatuses of the latter based on the abstract personification that assigns the state a will. It really means killing the black-hearted cold monster, the big Leviathan theorized by Hobbes and Carl Schmitt – that monster whose image is so powerful that it continues to exercise 'its effect even when it appears as a wall painting' (Schmitt 1982) and thus conditions political imaginings, even subversive ones. But it still means accepting to confront dynamics, tensions and processes that cannot be translated into a linear, ultimate transformation of the state settings. I think it is also to clear up this misunderstanding that Foucault dispenses with the terms biopower and biopolitics.

Biopower and biopolitics are not the ultimate custodians of a framework of categories and concepts that can be related to the experience of state politics. They have to be taken as indexes of transition that opens the state to its *outside*; which is to say, to processes of government in which life folds onto itself, becomes subject, and can be captured as a (political) relation.[30] The concepts of biopower and biopolitics play out as placeholders, signs that gesture to something else, to allude to an order of discourse within which the panoptical figure of the state as a grand machine of neutralization and subjection can finally be dispossessed of its centrality. The dispositif of liberal governmentality is reconstructed as something that corresponds to the processes of subjectivation and resistance of the "epoch" to which we belong.

The term "governmentality" is used by Foucault to refer to three different things. The ensemble of procedures, analyses and reflections, 'the calculations and tactics' – as he writes – that allow exercising this specific form of power. Its target is population, its principal knowledge is political economy, its key technical instruments are security dispositifs, Foucault says in the first place. With "governmentality" Foucault alludes to the 'tendency', the 'ligne de force', that in the West has never ceased operating on the pre-eminence of government and its knowledges vis-à-vis other dispositifs of power (Foucault 2004a: 112). Both the Orient and Ancient Greece are exclued from this genealogy, it is worth noting, as they are focuses of practices of subjectivation that neither involve nor tolerate subjection, as we will see later. And, in the end, a further meaning of "governmentality" is the procedures of "governmentalization" that mark the overhaul of the state apparatuses up to the transformation that renders them into nodes of processes which exceed it and traverse it. Always partially and hazardously can these processes be territorialized, controlled, filtered, administered or handled (Foucault 2004a: 111–112; importantly, see Sassen 2006). Their excess can at most be ***normalized***, to put it otherwise.

We live in the era of governmentality, Foucault writes (Foucault 2004a: 112; see also Lemke, Krasmann, and Bröckling 2000). Again: ours is the epoch of the governed, as he said with regard to the Croissant *affaire*. On the one hand, it is an epoch of the "survival" of the state, of the reconfiguration of its dispositifs on the verge of a relation that opens the government up to the market as an ensemble of social processes. It offers a surface of inscription to the market dispositifs, while the latter at the same time screen off or bar definitively the access to the Political as a would-be 'thing-in-itself' (Foucault 2004b: 47–48). On the other hand, it is an epoch in which the governed are identified by their own interests and are able to conduct themselves within autonomous networks of cooperation, marked by the unavailability of desire and passions, by dynamics of subjectivation that can hardly be confined to the filter of political representation. The governed demand more and more freedom with more and more strength. Thus, they claim to be governed on condition of expanding and increasing their own autonomy.

For Foucault, liberalism is not a political theory. Rather, it is, concretely, a "technology" – the way in which the existing configuration of the relation between the governors and the governed came about. A configuration that allows placing government – its function of protection and promotion of the exchange – in the hazardous, inhospitable, *soziale Umwelt* of market cooperation and the conflict of interests. Yet, government is not just that. It also corresponds to the just as hazardous process that opens it to the ethical relation with the others. Government is the practice of a subjectivation that is an ongoing relation with the Other-than-self. The becoming that acquires its rhythm from a relation freely inferred from the contingency of immanent relations between the individuality and the world.

Foucault points this out in one of the few contributions where he tries to account for his own research path by casting a retrospective light on it. He writes that he never meant to lay the foundation for an analytic of power and its "types". Although this is a question I cannot tackle here, this is symptomatic of a Weberian tinge that is at work in the framing of the issue of *Lebensführung* within, through and beyond the questions of power and discipline (see Chapter 5). 'J'ai cherché plutôt à produire une histoire des différents modes de subjectivation de l'être humain dans notre culture', Foucault writes, 'J'ai traité, dans cette optique, des trois modes d'objectivation qui transforment les êtres humains en sujets'.

Foucault sought to study the "objectifying" torsion whereby life – the pure biological determination of the human being as a political and speaking animal, to draw from Aristotle – became subject, as it were. And he identifies three different modes. First, the one that was brought about through knowledges – one that

Foucault addressed in *Les mots et les choses*. The objectivation of the subject as a speaking animal through grammar, philology and linguistics. That of the ***animal laborans*** through the economy. The objectivation of "bare life" ('du seul fait d'être en vie', he had already written at the time) within biological sciences or natural history. Afterwards, Foucault's research centred on the partition, on the decisive logic, that traverses the subject or separates him from the dark background on which subjectivation rises and connects to the dispositifs of discipline: the separation between the subject responsible for himself and the fool, the sane and the insane, the criminal and the citizen. Then, in the third phase – one to which he committed before being definitely and all-too-soon interrupted – 'la manière dont un être humain se transforme en sujet'. Therefore, the general theme of my research is not power, 'mais le sujet', he concludes (Foucault 1982a/2001: 1042).

Working on the scenario of subjectivation certainly means working on the dispositifs of power – on the way in which power cuts in the living matter and gives it a form by rendering it into a normalized, perfectly representable subjectivity. But it also means allowing oneself to go beyond the perimeter determined by the 'moment cartésien' of which Foucault (2001a: 19) speaks in the course of the *Herméneutique du sujet* and that still marks the modern mode of individuation. The modern mode of subjectivation – an upshot of the administrative state appropriation of the fact of government – is marked by a guidance, an orientation, that operates on the "containment" of the dynamics of freedom in the form of an individual and collective responsibilization with regard to its use. It postulates an access to freedom that concerns the form of "knowledge" and thus of normalization. Nevertheless, if the task we are confronting is not that of discovering, 'mais de refuser ce que nous sommes' (Foucault 1982a/2001: 1051; see also Luce 2009), to follow the trace of the 'fil du présent' that unfolds as the moving away from, the refusal, a leap outside the womb of Leviathan and the subjectivation that it safeguards through the legal dispositif and that of sovereignty, then this genealogical approach to the government has to be mobilized again and relocated.

The themes of counter-conducts, anti-pastoral revolts, care of the self, articulate this perspective. That of a free subjectivation, an ethical one, as necessarily referred to the world and to the Other, including that Other-than-self that each of us turns out to be if we tie our own self to the practice and the becoming of truth: 'Il nous faut promuovoir des nouvelles formes de subjectivation *en refusant* le type d'individualité qu'on nous a imposé pendant plusieurs siècles' (Foucault 1982a/2001: 1051; emphasis added).

It is a refusal again, then, but one that articulates the breaching of the very background on which the scene of power is displayed. Refusing that which we are entails moving beyond the forms of individuation "governed" by a divisive production of truth. It entails finding the place of truth in one's own heart. And also articulating, in the practice of an immanent freedom that becomes research, *curiositas*, recognition of the temporal and relational constitution of the subject, the modes of a production of the common, of forms of life, ultimately subtracted from the spectre of the sovereign.

4. Foucault's writings and lectures of the early 1980s head towards this direction. On the one hand, they advance a specific ethic of the intellectual work. They relocate the role of critique – its specific "attitude", its ethos. On the other hand, they cut deep into the problematization of the subject, as he reads the processes not from the angle of "subjection" but from that of the practice, activation.

In an interview with François Ewald dated May 1984 – shortly before he died – Foucault puts these two questions together. It is a general appraisal and a sort of response to those who failed to understand the meaning of the last phase of his research and got disoriented by it. He relocated it in a sort of long duration and placed it, at least apparently, in an academically sheltered field, bounded by a canon of texts, interpretations, technical lexica, modes of writing that seemed to abandon the vibrancy and experimentalism of the 1960s to approximate to the much more traditional practices of the history of ideas.[31] But this does not look particularly relevant to me. On the contrary, as Gilles Deleuze pointed out, what was at stake was a further operation of problematization – an arguably even more radical one. On the most immediate level, going from the permanence of the codes of morality. Ruptures, discontinuities, short durations are made to accommodate the articulation and rearticulation of powers in relation to the historically concrete modes of their exercise. But what is at stake is the type of relation that the subject has to himself, especially in the epoch of the "governmentalization" of power, one in which the old schemes of pastoral conduct operate for the recomposition of one's freedom with an eye to the general order by infiltrating the most private, intimate core of the self. This means that the processes from which the subject is relieved prove to be the effect of much broader cycles. What Foucault works on is a genealogy of morality. To this end, he goes back to late Antiquity and early Christianity to find the torsion that the theme of the law – the norm, more than the prohibition; the deciphering, more than the exercise; the confession, more than the hermeneutics – imposes on the structures of classical ethics.

However, this is not the end of the story. For Deleuze, the deepest reason why Foucault re-orientates his research on the long duration concerns the topics of subjectivation and memory. Memory is the real name of one's relation to oneself. Not in the sense of a reflection – Plato's anamnestic process that ties memory to knowledge – but in the sense of an activation of philosophy as practice (ensemble of short aphorisms to be learned by heart, admonitions to repeat to remain on track, *hypomnēmata* as props to concentration). It has to do with the action and the navigation of time that anybody can potentially avail himself of as the route to free subjectivation.[32] 'If you want, you are free' is Epictetus' motto (*Diat.*, I, 17, 28), it is worth recalling. For Foucault, recovering the long duration, radically changing his own work and writing "style", not only means getting rid of the analytic of power through the genealogy of power dispositifs (as these are utterly modern, since within modernity power represented the most effective solution to the problem of human conduct). It also means recovering the core itself of temporality as to that which takes it out of the operativity of dispositifs. Time can be memory as the retrieval of the question of the subject at the heart of philosophy after a century-long "oblivion", as Deleuze maintains. It can serve this purpose because of the ways in which the living being becomes subject – this is the outcome of the Foucauldian interpretation of Stoicism – through a process of appropriation of the self that works with memory. Here duration is not the duration of the history of ideas. Instead, it is the duration that actualizes one's work on oneself which takes hold of time as a possibility as well as a potential. Memory, then, is not merely historical memory. For it is the reactivation of the care of the self as a task and as the responsibility of the event that each one finds out he is by answering to himself as to the choice of a philosophical life he has conducted and continues to conduct (Deleuze 1986: 114–115). Memory is practised time as appropriation and reinvention of the self, as a relaunching, as imagination. And this also applies to Foucault.

'J'avais commencé à écrire deux livres conformement à mon plan primitif', Michel Foucault tells François Ewald as he speaks of his works after *Volonté de savoir*, 'mais très vite, je me suis ennuyé. C'était imprudent de ma part et contraire à mes habitudes' (Foucault 1984c/2001: 1487–1497). Only when one is very tired or very old, or even tremendously conceited, can one interpret one's intellectual work – a term which Foucault reclaims with pride – as the linear development of a project clearly foreseen in its fundamental lines. Or as the ongoing tilling of a well-defined field of academic competences. 'Travailler', Foucault says, 'c'est entreprendre de penser autre chose que ce qu'on pensait avant'. This *thinking otherwise*, this valorization of a mismatch, concerns an *ethic* of the intellectual work. The way in which, that is to say, a man faces his own limits and the limits of his own present through that which he did, thought and wrote. This is critique: a work carried out at the edge of what we are, Foucault wrote in the same period while talking about Kant and a hypermodern 'attitude' of thought – an attitude so paradoxical that retrieves a classical 'style'.[33] By doing so, a man enters into an intense relation of problematization with the world that coincides with the act that frees his creative potential of thought.

'Qu'est-ce que peut être l'éthique d'un intellectuel sinon cela: se rendre capable en permanence de se déprendre de soi-même (ce qui est contraire de l'attitude de conversion)?' (Foucault 1984c/2001: 1494).[34] Moving away, breaking loose, freeing oneself from the disciplinary and pastoral forms of individuation. This is the ethic of the intellectual. The modern attitude to critique. Working on the modification of the others' thought and, in doing so, working on one's own. Double inversion of the pastoral code of conversion. It does not repress the *curiositas* by trapping it and holding it in a distressing work of 'deciphering' meant to mould the coherence of an authorial profile, in Foucault's case. It does not exert this on the others to have them undergo a change, a transformation, which we do not want for ourselves in the first place. It is impossible to gain access to the *déprise*, which is the element that dynamizes subjectivation, by means of an enlightenment. Let alone by conceding with no reservation to any fibrillation of the conjuncture. It takes all the time that is needed. The tension and the constancy of memory, which continually brings us back to that which we actually decided to be.

It is true that the modern attitude to thought is critique and that critique cannot be exerted but in terms of problematization of the present to which we belong. Yet, what Foucault calls ethic of detachment, ethic of *déprise*, can hardly coincide with one's simply tracking down the processes that time by time define the very edge of the present. Such a 'se déprendre de soi-même', such a refusal of the disciplinary individuation that pins the subject to a register of births, identifies him with a *curriculum*, binds him to a bibliography, can only be interpreted as an 'élaboration de soi par soi', 'une transformation studieuse', 'une modification lente et ardue par souci constant de la vérité' (Foucault 1984c/2001: 1494). These are the exact terms of the philosophical *ascesis* of the Ancients, with which Foucault deals in the lectures he gives in those years at Berkeley and the Collège de France. It is not an ascesis, but a rigorous work of handcraft production within the immanence of a practice, *ergon* (Foucault 2008a: 202; see also Mcgushin 2007). It is this constitutive relation between truth, problematization and subjectivity that lies at the heart of the later Foucault's work – even that performed on himself in the first person.

5. What is a subject? A subject is not a substance. At most, it is a 'form', and a form can never be identical to itself. This is what Foucault pointed out a few months before, during an interview (Foucault 1984f/2001: 1537). One of those interviews that – as Deleuze (1986: 122) rightly noted – are part and parcel of the Foucauldian oeuvre. For they take his research beyond the "historical workshop" of his books to make it affect reality as they try to materialize the effect of dynamization that pertains to Foucault's research. On his account, saying that a subject – just like power – is not a thing, let alone a substance, does not only mean sidestepping the line that, in the tradition of philosophy 'à la française' (as Pierre Macherey (2013b) refers to it), weds Descartes to phenomenology. Hence, it does not simply mean vindicating once again Foucault's moving away from Sartre as well as from what the latter represented as the bearer of an intellectual function. Rather, it also means claiming the reasons of multiplicity, the temporal, the heterogeneous, in the field of immanence within which the subject is produced.

Nobody has the same relation to himself when one gets constituted as a political subject, when one votes or speaks in the assembly, and when one gets constituted as a subject of desire within a sexual relation, says Foucault. And the same goes for the *multiversum* of affective, linguistic and relational functions through which we have relations to others and to the disciplinary codes of the power dispositifs that stabilize an experience of the world, although in a contingent, partial and always revocable form. It is certainly true that there are many effects of interference, exchange and passage between the multiple forms taken by subjectivities in relation to the various centres of gravity of their field of expression. Yet it is just as true that 'dans chaque cas, on joue, on établit à soi-même des formes de rapport différentes'. And it is precisely 'la constitution historique de ces formes différentes de sujet en rapport avec les jeux de vérité, qui m'intéresse' Foucault (1984f/2001: 1537–1538) concludes.

On the external side, Foucault is evidently influenced by the polemic with the Cartesian notion of subject.[35] He intends to circumvent the foundational event of modern philosophy; which is to say, the point described by Descartes where thought and reality interact, regardless of the personal qualities of the utterer of the true proposition. It is a rationality that unfolds with claims to universality. It validates its own setting without getting embodied in any concrete consciousness, in any texture of life.[36] On the external side, instead, Foucault sets out to identify the torsion point where the webs of power and knowledges that traverse and constitute the subject (what he himself defines as 'memory') get bent not to efface interiority (an "I think" that precedes reality or gets rid of it . . .), but to transform the superficial effect determined by the disciplinary dispositifs and to reinvent the consciousness' relation to itself and thus to 'free' the subject from the historically limited scheme of subjectivity produced in the classical era of European politics.

A decisive consequence ensues from this. The subject – simple form and not substance, as I recalled above – is only ***one of the possible ways*** in which the 'consciousness of the self' is actualized or organized. The subject is neither the foundation nor the last refuge of an 'authenticity' that might rescue the space subtracted from the invasiveness of disciplinary machines or the law of value. Most of Foucault's bad feeling concerning the Frankfurt School in those years – although there are circumstances in which he admitted that knowing it better would have saved him much work – derives from this stance.

Subjectivity is a process that takes place within (not in an "elsewhere" with respect to) the circuits of knowledge and powers that constitutively intersect life and language. Neither subjectivity nor those circuits pertain to universal conditions. Knowledge is the form taken by the diagram in which – in a particular moment – the visible and the utterable relate to each other. Power is the variable, contestable and always reversible relation of force, which crosses the singularity and gives it the (always partial and provisional) order of regulation. And the "subject" – or better, the 'soi', l'être soi' – is nothing other than the effect of the process of subjectivation through which the 'dehors' in which life gets caught (labour, reproduction, language, to draw from the division of *Les mots et les choses*) cannot be moulded to stitch an identity, but to ***unfold*** a possibility, a potential. A "subject" does not have anything universal: it only marks a constellation of (historically) singular positions from within which 'One speaks', 'One confronts', 'One lives' (Deleuze 1986: 122), which marks off a pure section of immanence.

'J'appellerai subjectivation le processus par lequel on obtient la constitution d'un sujet, plus exactement d'une subjectivité, qui n'est évidemment que l'une des possibilités données d'organisation d'une conscience de soi' (Foucault 1984e/2001: 1525).[37] Remounting the whole process of disciplinary individuation, organizing the resistance to the techniques of pastoral government, means moving beyond the history of power, reactivating the memory of "life" that is constantly interfaced to it, 'branchée' as that which has always forced power to transform and readdress its dispositifs. What interests Foucault in his later research is not the access to a vocabulary and a "knowledge" so different from ours that it represents a possible resource or escape route – 'aucun penseur grec n'a jamais trouvé une définition du sujet, ni n'a jamais cherché', he explicitly says, 'je dirai tout simplement qu'il n'y a pas de sujet', in that phase of Western culture.[38] Rather, it entails the identification of a further contested field – one that pertains to the 'soi' and its elaboration – where the modern system of knowledges traces a pacified frame of objective individuation.

6. The Greeks did not even have the word "sujet", as in Greece – which in relation to the operation that Michel Foucault conducts on it does not express any philosophy to "rehabilitate" or "restore"[39] – the living being was qualified by drawing from Aristotle as 'zôon politikon kai logon echon'. It is political speaker spatialized in the relation of truth, discourse and the fact of government. The living being did not yield to the illusion of a self-knowledge sedimented in a form and severed from the "koinon", from the *common*, from the relation. It is worth recalling again that what modernity calls "sujet" is the effect of an integral "assujettissement" to the code that universalizes it as an abstraction – a pure *in-difference* that emerges as something correlated to modern technologies of law and clinical, psychological and moral normalization. In the Ancient ethical and philosophical thought, this "sujet" was located in the multilateral system of practices through which it is reflectively *folded* into a "style", a freedom that continues to *unfold* its potential in a context that is crossed by other forces and other trajectories of the singularity. 'La liberté est la condition ontologique de l'éthique' (Foucault 1984f/2001: 1531).[40] 'Mais l'éthique est la forme réfléchie que prend la liberté'.

Obviously, what interests Foucault is not the relation that traditionally exists between freedom and ethics. In the end, Christian morality was a solution to this problem. Rather, he is concerned with the way in which the degree zero of problematization – that part which generally triggers it and takes refuge in its 'dehors' – is integrally problematized in its turn. Thinking, for Foucault, amounts to experimenting, putting to the test: 'Je suis un expérimenteur et non pas un théoricien', he repeated many a time (Foucault 1980d/2001: 861). And problematization – as he notes in the conclusive lines of the lecture he gave in Berkeley in the autumn of 1983 – is a response to a concrete situation, one that is real (Foucault 2001b[41]).

What is it then that urges Foucault to work on Ancient and late Ancient ethics? Many observations could be made in this regard. At its simplest, the most recent transformations in the technologies of power. The fact that they directly take root in life. The way of exercising governmentality is how it speaks to the will of the subject, what in the modern form of individuation coincides with the "free" self-disposition of one's will.[42] Therefore it is evident that the work of problematization that has to be conducted on the field of these new modes of exercising power tends to target the subject, the form that the process of subjectivation assumes within the framework of liberal governmentality, the abstract, subjective and formal, or, vice versa, inventive, creative notion of freedom that corresponds to it.

In other words, the classic type of individuation is never passive, pacified or objectual. It arises in an agonistic and contested field, within which each one exists on account of the others, under the gaze and through the eyes of the others. In this frame, the more stable a person's foundations, the broader his reputation.

True death, for a Greek, does not amount to the physical extinction to which all living beings are destined as mortal beings. Rather, it is the oblivion, the silence, the lack of fame. As Jean-Pierre Vernant noted, if it is true that the Greeks – both in archaic and classic Greece, as the latter depends heavily on the former – had an experience of the self, of their own person, of their own body, their experience was articulated differently than ours. The Greek self is neither delimited nor unified; it is not "subjected" to the sovereignty of a formal synthesis. The self is an 'open field of multiple forces'. And, far from coinciding with a protected interiority, sheltered from social factors, its experience is integrally oriented towards the outside. It is tied to agonistic fields in which social and political practices take place.

The individual looks for himself and finds himself in the others, in those mirrors that reflect his image that his *alter egos* are: parents, friends, children, comrades, rivals. The subject does not circumscribe any sealed-off inner world, in which he dives to find himself or to discover himself. The subject is *extroverted*. As an eye cannot see itself – this is Plato's famous argument in *Alcibiades*[43] – so does the "individual" to experiment itself look at somewhere else, at its "outside".[44] It *unfolds* in existential terms and never *re-folds* in consciential terms, I may say.

The 1982–1983 course, the one that attends to the issue of the *Gouvernement de soi et des autres*, revolves around this dynamic. In order to govern the others, one cannot stay in the isolated, sheltered position of the *nomothetes*. Governing the others requires one's working hard on oneself and taking the risk this entails. Conquering the relation in the agonistic game of recognition puts philosophy to the test of reality. Its truth, in Greece, is the stake not in a propositional setting, but in a serious confrontation where it is the exemplarity of life – not a given system of rules – that predetermines the possibilities of a circle of veridiction.

In his comment to Plato's *Seventh Letter* (328c) – here it is not relevant whether or not this text is authentic – Foucault brings this out very clearly. First of all, he insists on the insufficiency of the *logos* and the rejection of writing. Plato owns up to his 'feeling of shame with regard to myself, lest I might some day appear to myself wholly and solely a mere man of words', as the disclosure of a philosophical-political horizon that rejects a type of knowledge only grounded on names and definitions. Then, he stresses the risk of practice. The denunciation of the limits of the *logos* (and therefore, of turning politics into logics, that which will actually constitute the distinctive trait of modernity from Descartes to Hobbes) and the fact that one cannot swing into action by convincing one's interlocutor on the basis of a discourse that claims to be "truer". Practice is first and foremost prompted by *tribé*, by the hard work that the subject conducts on himself, by the practice of truth as the diagram of subjectivation, by the exemplarity of a life that confers authority, by the risk the speaker has to take while dealing with his own inclinations and the resistance of the others. I believe Foucault (2008a: 235) returns to the prior discussion with Derrida in another form:

> Ce n'est pas du tout l'avènement d'un logocentrisme qu'il faut déchiffrer dans ce refus de l'écriture, c'est l'avénement de tout autre chose. C'est l'avènement de la philosophie, d'une philosophie dans laquelle le réel même de la philosophie serait la pratique de soi sur soi.

Finally, the verification of what philosophy is: it is not a discourse, but a form of life, a practice of the self, an exercise in which knowledge and power, the "being able" and the "saying", the frames within which any living-political being moves and breathes, are employed – never transcended, discarded, upturned – as instruments, technologies of the self, as Foucault dubs them. A subjectivation that is a force among forces, an event of truth.[45] The "serious" game of philosophy does not consist in saying or instructing human beings in how they should conduct their relationships in keeping with an ideal scheme of socialization – Plato's *kallipolis*, for example. Rather, human beings should be constantly reminded (the activation of a circuit of memory, again; this marks the continuity with Socrates, up to the Cynics) that what in philosophy is real is practice: 'ces pratiques que l'on exerce sur soi' and on the others, when one has the courage to take the test of listening (Foucault 2008a: 236). The risk of relationship.

7. For Foucault, what gives philosophy reality is, as I pointed out above, its capacity to meet with, and feed, an attentiveness, to place itself in a listening. The capacity – which is also one's material acceptance of the risk to fail – to address someone or something that in their turn are able to get in touch with that piercing sharpness of which philosophy's veridiction is capable. 'La réalité, l'épreuve par laquelle, à travers laquelle, la véridiction philosophique va se manifester comme réelle, c'est le fait qu'elle s'adresse, qu'elle peut s'adresser, qu'elle a le courage de s'adresser, à qui exerce le pouvoir' (Foucault 2008a: 210.).

What scrapes inoperosity off philosophy – empty chat, erudite speculation, waged academic performance, to recall the way Joseph Ferrari (1983) in a famous text gnaws at Victor Cousin's eclecticism and the Sorbonne academic philosophy – is its capacity to determine the conditions of its own correlation to the field of politics. It is true that a discourse characterized by the sign of intervention, as philosophy ought to be, has always to oppose power, the regime of discursive normality – 'un dire-vrai irruptif', as Foucault defines it, a form of discourse that effects a discontinuity in the middle of the enunciation. Yet, if one's speech lapses into "cry", "contestation", "protest", to draw on Pierre Rosanvallon's[46] terminology, it is no longer able to keep the specific tension that qualifies philosophy.

The reality of philosophy lies in the circle of listening – the performative potential of a concrete word, capable of triggering reactions, intersecting practices, co-determining "government". 'Art stochastique, art de conjoncture', as Foucault (2001a: 368) calls the latter, as he never got tired of emphasizing the tie between government and the art of navigation as well as with medicine, the invincible relation that government has with the occasion, with the 'kairos'. At the same time, that circle of listening is capable of resisting its tendency to eventuate in adulation, empty rhetoric, thin thinking. It also lies in the courage with which the philosopher puts himself to the test in order to acquire that degree of incandescence, the coherence of his own discourse on the field of political decision – first and foremost his own decision and then the one of those whose responsibility he takes on himself.[47]

Philosophy belongs to the *pragmata*. It can hardly be considered pure *logos*. It is a *practice* that ties to a specific form of life, where the speaker takes the test of listening and where the game of truth and veridiction primarily occurs as one's hard work on oneself. It therefore becomes courage, responsibility for truth in one's own eyes and of those who govern. These are the considerations that progressively urge Foucault to get down to his studies on *parrhēsia*, on 'franc-parler' and the 'courage de la vérité' (Foucault 2009).[48] These considerations have a series of decisive consequences.

The first concerns the relation between politics and philosophy. A relation of *correlation* and *exteriority*. Philosophy is alien to the field of illusions, delusions, *doxai* – things that challenge philosophy to constitute itself as true discourse in the philosopher's life. It follows that philosophy is not called upon to say what one ought to do. Its veridiction does not belong to the order of project or ideology. It should not – and cannot, if it aims to continue to be at the start of a game of veridiction that correlates it to the Political – align with the discourse of those who govern. 'Elle a à être dans une extériorité permanente et rétive par rapport à la politique, et c'est en cela qu'elle est réelle', says Foucault. It has to be permanently exercised as a critique 'à l'égard de ce qui est leurre, tromperie et illusion' (Foucault 2008a: 326). Only in this way can it support the achievement of truth's dialectic role. The form of correlation determines a figure which we have already come across: the ellipse – no superimposition, capture, linear organization between a theory, proper to the philosopher, and a practice, entrusted to the politician. The ellipse is a figure where the two focuses face one another, and within which a tension gets spatialized.

The second consequence, which is just as relevant as the first, has to do with the ontology of the true discourse. The true discourse organizes itself as a practice. Practice of word, a style of philosophical life, the risk of listening. An uninterrupted series kept in movement by freedom, the matrix of ethics. Freedom gets forwarded in the form of one's opting for a philosophical life. One's philosophical life is truly such if it exhibits the courage of truth. And the courage of truth can be exhibited by facing the risk of the free, frank speech, open to those who have power, while it is up to the latter whether to listen or not to listen. Those who have power can push their indifference to the extreme consequence, to such an extent that they can persecute, exile, sentence to death – which is Socrates' destiny – those who are up to the challenge and thus live this challenge as an opportunity for philosophy. The conjunctural characteristics of the fact of government – in other words, the fact that that ellipse can never be undone – make sure that the relation between philosophy and government, between *parrhēsia* and "power", is thought of as a singular invention and that freedom is never stylized as a "right"; it is lived as a potential, 'une capacité de faire' (Foucault 2008a: 286).

Finally, the third consequence looks decisive to me. Not only is that which Foucault describes a dynamic of freedom, a process of subjectivation that is tied to a form of life, to the practice of relation. But even if we admit that the Greeks had some notion of subjectivity – though we know that Foucault denied that possibility, and with good reason – he does not utilize the materials of Ancient philosophy to carve out the space for a new "theory" of the subject.[49] As Gilles Deleuze (2003b: 127) tellingly noted, 'il n'y a [pas] de retour au sujet chez Foucault'.

Foucault does not use the word "subject" while interpreting the Greeks. This is not because he has difficulties finding an adequate form. In other cases, for example, he had no qualms about speaking indifferently of "government" or "power" even in relation to the Greek *poleis* or to Rome, in whose institutional settings there was nothing anywhere near what modernity identifies as "power". Foucault speaks of a "process", a process of "subjectivation", in this case, and speaks of a "self" that is invested and that delineates the form of a relation. A 'rapport à soi', evidently. But what does this mean? Deleuze explains this very clearly: that process and that relation draw the curve of a torsion, the line of a fold, of a force. The way in which the living being's free creativity devises new modes of existence in new possibilities of life.

This all clarifies the "why" of the later stage of Foucault's research path and explains why he returns to Kant's writing on Enlightenment in *Le gouvernement de soi et des autres* (Foucault 2008a). He has no penchant for restoration, as we know. Nor is he nostalgic or defensive of a backward "movement" that is able to go against the grain of modernity. What is at stake here is the present. What becomes visible with the Greeks is a mode of relation to the self that emphasizes the creative aspect of freedom. It does that not in the "retrait" of a private style – many a time did Foucault have to stave off the charge of being prey to a fascination for the Californian cult of the self[50] – but in the practice of a relation. By obeying voluntary, revisable, adjustable rules that enable one to escape captivation, this practice generates forms of life, inaugurates new existential possibilities, opens up gateways heading to other forms of relation, other forms of the common.

Ethopoiesis is at the heart of the present: this is how Foucault combines Plutarch and Kant, as it were. If subjectivation is a process, evidently this process is not individuation. To quote Deleuze (2003a: 127) again:

> les modes d'existence ou possibilité de vie ne cessent de se recréer, de nouveaux surgissent, et s'il est vrai que cette dimension fut inventée par les Grecs, nous ne faisons pas un retour aux Grecs, quand nous cherchons quels sont ceux qui se dessinent aujourd'hui, quel est notre vouloir-artiste irréductible au savoir-pouvoir.

While concentrating on the process of subjectivation of the Ancients, what Foucault has in mind is the possibility of reinventing this process in the conjuncture of the present. Not as a "private" style, as an escape from the political, but as radical politicization of one's relation to oneself and as a vehicle for radically new forms of life. 'L'on doit s'autogouverner comme un gouverneur gouverne ses sujets', says Foucault. And thinking of the 'culture de soi' – again: the specific torsion that the technologies of the self impose on "knowledge" and "power" as it takes hold of its impossible transcendence in view of the process of subjectivation – as 'une sorte de rapport politique permanent entre soi et soi' (Foucault 1983a/2001: 1222–1223).

8. Arguably it is the sense of this "politics" of the self that most of the time has escaped the attention of those commentators who were led astray by Foucault's use of terms drawn from aesthetics.[51] The 'stylistics of existence', the 'ascesis' of the self, does not have anything to do with a 'retrait' from what we are, from the

power relations that involve us; nor is it a romantic search for authenticity. On the contrary, I believe it is a way for Foucault to begin to think of the possibility of a 'politics of the governed' – to get back to the issue with which I commenced.

As Foucault himself underlines while talking to Hubert Dreyfus and Paul Rabinow, his investigation into Ancient ethics is meant to show that the long Christian detour led us to believe that morality is something that merely concerns the individual. A code of control coupled with introspection, guilt and confession. This however has nothing to do with ethics. 'Je veux montrer que le grand problème éthique grec n'était pas une technique du soi', says Foucault. 'C'était une *technē* de vie, la *technē toû biou*, la manière de vivre'. What is at stake for the Greeks is not monasticism, the individual ethics connected to self-discipline and interiority of late Antiquity.[52] Rather, the scrutiny of Ancient philosophy casts light on the way in which a practice is organized – one that innovates and creates its own forms of life, that imposes new modes of relation with oneself and with the others, which impresses new forms on single and collective experiences.

On one side, the *bíos*, the immanence of life as a basis for the creative process. On the other, the idea that ethics, the structure of regulation and "government" of subjectivation, can be a decisive structure for one's existence with no need for any ties with a legal or disciplinary core (Foucault 1983a/2001). Which is to say, ethics does not have to depend on sovereignty or on a code or on one's being habilitated – as happened many centuries after – by a bunch of rights.

I believe this is a decisive passage. First of all, Foucault emphasizes once again his moving away from Sartre and his ultimate break with Heidegger, despite elegant concessions to the latter. What is relevant in Ancient thought is exactly the possibility of upturning the canon of authenticity. Foucault upturns that which Sartre operates in his analysis of Flaubert and Baudelaire, to wit, the establishment of a connection – also in relation to the aesthetics of dandyism and *flânerie* – between the inventive job of writing and the subjective-authorial dimension. In the process of subjectivation, what is central is not the circle of authenticity that goes from subject to subject, the mechanism that unveils a truer "self" lying behind the inauthentic or not-yet appropriated self. Rather, it is the creative activity, the force that dispossesses the subject and includes him in a form of life: 'Nous ne devrions pas lier l'activité créatrice d'un individu au rapport qu'il entretient avec lui-même, mais lier ce type de rapport à soi que l'on peut avoir à une activité créatrice' (Foucault 1983a/2001: 1211–1212).

The second conclusion Foucault arrives at is even more important. As I noted, a subject is not a substance. At most, it is a form, the effect of the technologies, knowledges and powers that surround and constitute him. For him, there is no sovereign, founding subject to be discovered as a universal. The subject can be constituted through practices of subjection, as was the case with the juridical and disciplinary modernity of the state. Alternatively, the subject can constitute himself autonomously, as was the case with classic Antiquity, by creatively working on himself and by unfolding the rules, styles, conventions that all individuals acquire from their own culture (since there is no freedom without government) (Foucault 1984g/2001: 1552). Establishing a link between the self and this productive, immanent dimension of freedom means constructing the subject through the fold that one can give a force. A fold that relaunches freedom and neither ever morphs into anything else nor transfers it to anything else.

As an aside: when Foucault speaks of the gay movement, he is utterly coherent – but what he says does apply to the whole set of social movements of the 1960s and the 1970s with which Foucault sides and which he considers as an absolute novelty that marks a whole epoch ('distinctive trait', 'Auszeichnung', Kant would have said) at the time of the *affaire* Croissant. Couching the homosexual question with recourse to the lexicon of rights means curbing the potential of that situation as well as reinforcing the mechanism of sovereignty that those rights are able to grant and to make available. Rather, what one has to do is subjectivate the homosexual condition by creating new forms of life, established through free ethical, sexual and political choices. What one has to do is ignite free processes of radical transformation with no need to take a defensive stance to claim rights that are not recognized. What is at stake is a *power of affirmation*, a 'force créatrice' that irreducibly extends the ellipse between freedom and government and thus advances a problematization of what exists and is backed up by the processes of subjectivation that underpin it. 'Nous devons non seulement nous défendre, mais aussi nous affirmer, et nous affirmer non seulement en tant qu'identité, mais en tant que force créatrice' (Foucault 1982c/2001: 1555).

The analysis he conducts of the developmental phases of the 1960s and 1970s that led to the era of the governed is quite clear. And it does not end with sexual liberation movements. The ellipse of government stabilizes a relation between resistance and power that for Foucault represents the only way out of the mirror effect whereby liberation tends to mime domination. For him, it is neither a matter of counter-power nor class autonomy. Nonetheless, that elliptic relation cannot be dissolved through an immediate liberation from government that finds place in one end of the ellipse. In this regard, Foucault moves away from democratic and liberal irenicism. He makes quite clear what he thinks is particularly relevant as he takes a position against Habermas. He believes it is ingenuous or utopian to think that the games of veridiction can freely circulate in the circuit of communication 'sans contraintes et sans effets coércitifs'. Or rather, that there can be truth without power. The problem that we have to face is not so much that of dissolving government 'dans l'utopie d'une communication parfaitement transparente', but that of 'se donner les régles de droit, les techniques de gestion et aussi la morale, l'*ethos*, la pratique de soi, qui permettront dans ce jeux de pouvoir, de jouer avec le minimum possibile de domination' (Foucault 1984f/2001: 1564).[53]

We should not treat power as an evil, but as a strategic game in which we have to take a position on the other end of the governmental ellipse. It is the lynchpin of an ineliminable resistance that is able to cross both the individual and the pure multiplicity of his relations. We should thwart domination by facing it in the diagram of forces within which struggles take place along with the dynamics that feed the processes of subjectivation. We should minimize the invasiveness of power and make it stick to its regulatory task.

We cannot expect the government to speak the truth. Rather, we should urge it to account for the ends it pursues and how it pursues them. We should interpellate it, force it to face us. We should impose on those who govern the priorities and the political agenda of the governed by expressing in these terms the destituent and constituent power of freedom. To this end, we have to amend once and for all the ideas of subjectivity and political agency. Nobody any longer represents anybody. It is no longer possible to think of the decision as something that falls from above, through an executive hierarchy, onto society and its processes without incurring any resistance or objections.

'Je pense que l'un des grands constats que nous avons fait depuis la derniére guerre', Michel Foucault tells Gallagher and Wilson in Toronto, in 1982, 'est celui de l'échec de tous les programmes sociaux et politiques'. There is no political programme or administrative plan (and this also applies to progressives) that is not fallible or does not try to impose the hegemony of an apparatus or a bureaucracy, says Foucault. He goes on to say: 'Mais l'une des réalisations des années soixante et soixante-dix, que je considère comme une réalisation bénéfique, est que certains modèles institutionnels on été expérimentés sans programme' (Foucault 1982c/2001: 1565).

Obviously, such a *programmeless action* – which in those years is the innovative practice of social movements in Continental Europe, Eastern Europe and the USA – does not amount to an unorganized action. And yet, this practice of there being no programme, as an organized practice, can be useful, original and extremely creative exactly because it is punctiliously interpolated in the strategic game of the present and is loaded with a courage of truth that does not care about the impossible. 'L'une des choses qu'il faut préserver, à mon avis', Foucault continues to say, 'est l'existence, en dehors des grands partis politiques et en dehors du programme normal de l'ordinaire, d'une certaine forme d'innovation politique, de création politique et d'expérimentation politique' (Foucault 1982c/2001: 1565). The latter is an effect of innovation that is produced outside the schemes of political representation and their reference to sovereignty.

The courage of truth that Foucault speaks of is a function that gets ignited as a specific form of the "politics of the governed" – one that is able to nudge power in a period in which it decentres, decreases its sovereignty, becomes flexible, "governmentalizes" its dispositifs, also in response to the excess of claims that are addressed to it.[54] It is the courage of a frankness of speech and action that Foucault himself was able to embrace on several public occasions while siding with political prisoners, detainees, migrants, the dissidents in the Eastern Bloc, the anticolonial insurgents in Tunisia and Iran.[55] In the epoch of the anonymity of the multitude, *parrhēsia* does not only belong to the philosopher. What Foucault speaks of 'c'est la *parrhēsia* du gouverné' (Foucault 1982c/2001: 1553). To put it otherwise, the way in which the governed interpellates power for the bare fact of being involved in the relation of government.

It is not the governed who is called upon to say what to do. It is a specious objection to claim that this way the governed ends up being the one who takes it upon himself to give solutions, thus temporarily swapping his place with the governor. It obliterates in one stroke the informational and positional asymmetry that characterizes political communication in the era of postdemocratic governance (see Crouch 2004). Furthermore, it is the objection by which the inventiveness, potential and creativity of the governed gets caught in the canon of quite a cynical political realism.[56]

What the governed, as such, has to do – if we take it for granted that we can speak in terms of a duty when we are in the field of a creativity that directly spawns its own institutions – is bear the subjective right to raise 'questions of truth', as Foucault dubs them. They defy the bureaucratic routine and break into the operational circuits of government. It is a task that concerns the ethic of the intellectual work. Its position within the realm of freedom rather than power. A position that rescues philosophy from the ideological torsion that turns it into political theory, knowledge available to the Prince, empty ideal legislation. This is a task that is assigned to all those who face the government by forcing it to account for the meaning of its actions and the strategies it pursues and by obliging it to recognize the governed as a subject who resists.

I do not think this is an easy political stance. It is not a rhetoric of political engagement that exceeds its proper time. Instead, it concerns the end itself of philosophy. Let's reread Paul Veyne (1986), then. What is philosophy for? Does it have to be persuasive as to that which human beings are not persuaded about? Does it have to provide guidance to those who govern for them to make more effective decisions in a way that might also appear more acceptable to the governed? In spite of what the irenicism of philosophy teaches us, the spectacle of the past provides no historical reasons other than the conflict of what, neither true nor false, comes across as the truth that has to be spoken. Foucault's is really an *ethic*, we might comment – a philosophy with no happy end.

The conflict that inaugurates the era of neoliberal politics is that between the governors and the governed. This lucid conclusion is not an option for "liberalism" on the part of the later Foucault. It is the way to continue to stay, with a partisan perspective, in the strategic game marked off by the ellipse constituted by the practices of freedom and the trapping dispositifs of the post-sovereign and post-representative time of 'governmentality'. Choosing sides means having the courage of truth. It means locating oneself in the 'devenir' of a transformation that concerns, even before power and its dispositifs, the subject and his capacity to take care of his own desire. If this is the case, then I think it is difficult to maintain, as Foucault (1984e/2001: 1515) himself once did, that he made a mistake in studying Antiquity.

Notes

1 Cf., despite their respective differences, at least Agamben 1998 and Esposito 2008. More in general, see Cutro 2004; Cutro 2005.
2 'Mais l'État, ce n'est qu'une péripétie du gouvernement et ce n'est pas le gouvernement qui est un instrument de l'État. Ou en tout cas l'État est une péripétie de la gouvernementalité' (Foucault 2004a: 253).
3 Wittgenstein 1977. The aphorism is dated "around 1944".
4 Duso 2003a, 2004.
5 It does not matter if this happens directly, as is the case with a good deal of bourgeois or revolutionary political theory, or indirectly, by assigning critique a normative value on whose grounds one can imagine more just and more inclusive power structures.

6 It is worth recalling how Foucault's analytic of power builds on the presupposition that power becomes visible only where something resists it. Resistance as a "chemical catalyst" of power. See Foucault 1982/2001: 1044. Revel (2005: 204) properly emphasizes the 'antériorité non seulement chronologique, mais onthologique de la résistance au pouvoir'.
7 Foucault 1984e/2001: 1546.
8 Foucault 1978b/2001: 540–542.
9 On the relationship between Foucault and Wittgenstein, which I believe to be foundational to the former's analytic of power, now see Gros and Davidson 2011.
10 Foucault 1978c/2001: 633.
11 See Karsenti's (2006) observations in this regard.
12 Foucault 1976b/2001: 112.
13 Foucault 1977a/2001: 158.
14 See at least: Miller 2000: 296; Oksala 2012: 150-ff; Hannah 2012.
15 On this topic, see Chevallier 2014: 171–187.
16 On the centrality of Foucault's position as to its relation with Deleuze, see Eribon 1989: 276, but above all see the important Artières and Potte-Bonneville 2007.
17 Cf. Cesaroni and Chignola 2012 and Lorenzini, Revel and Sforzini 2013.
18 Cf. Duso 2003b.
19 I'm drawing again on Bruno Karsenti's take on this, which I agree on.
20 On this issue, in a not entirely dissenting perspective, see Schiera 1999.
21 See Foucault 1976a/2001: 28–40. Famously, on Foucault as a 'nouveau cartographe' see Deleuze 1986.
22 See also Richter 2005; Agamben 2007.
23 Arienzo 2004. On the metaphor of gubernare rempublicam and the government as navigation of the state, see Rigotti 1989: 41 ff.
24 Cf. Duso 1999: 55–85. Also see Chignola 2008: 117–141.
25 On this constellation, beyond "classic" references, I would like to mention an important history book: Rediker 1987.
26 This point has been recently raised by Lemke (2007: 85–107) in a way that I concur with.
27 See Veyne 1971.
28 I tried to make this point in a long detour of mine. See Chignola 2004a and Chignola 2011.
29 For a thorough analysis of the notion of liberalism in Michel Foucault: Bonnafous-Boucher 2004; Reinfeldt and Schwarz 2004. More in line with my reading, Bernini 2006 and Bernini 2008.
30 For a deft and innovative analysis of Foucault's latest writings as a "rewriting" of the Hegelian dialectic of self-consciousness in *The Phenomenology of Spirit*, see Fimiani 2007.
31 This criticism was raised with vigor by Narducci (1985) and reiterated by Vegetti (1986). More in general, see Moss 1998. For a comprehensive account of how Foucault dealt with classic thought, Cremonesi 2008.
32 The topic of the dislocation of memory (from Plato's anamnesis to the "practical" activation) is investigated in Foucault 2001: 246 ff.
33 'Par attitude je veux dire un mode de relation à l'égard de l'actualité; un choix volontaire qui est fait par certains; enfin, une manière de penser et de sentir, une manière aussi d'agir et de se conduire qui, tout à la fois, marque une appartenance et se présente comme une tâche. Un peu, sans doute, comme ce que les Grecs appellaient un ethos' (Foucault 1984b/2001: 1387) (emphasis mine).
34 On this theme, Cesaroni (2010) makes very significant considerations.
35 See Guenancia 2002.
36 Foucault 1985, in particular: 1586.

37 On this topic, see Gros 2002a; Revel 2005: 207 ff.
38 Foucault 1984e/2001: 1525. For a comprehensive account of Foucault's reading of Antiquity, see Daraki 1985; Gros and Lévy 2003. More specifically on the topic I am dwelling on, see Devos 2002; Hahn 2002: 176–212.
39 About that which in the early 1980s explicitly comes across as a "rehabilitation" of Greek practical philosophy, with some influence in Europe, see Riedel 1972–1974. On the meaning of this overall work, see Volpi 1986 and Volpi 1999.
40 Pandolfi (1998) usefully develops this point.
41 Foucault's lectures are transcribed and published with this title and are available at www.lib.berkeley.edu/MRC/foucault/parrhesia.html.
42 In the end, the same applies to governmentality, as it represents a diagram of orientation of will, of valorization that makes it compatible with general ends, but at the same time, as we have seen, has nothing to do with the sovereign dispositif of interdiction, prohibition and control.
43 Platone, Alcibiades I, 132d-133c. On the complexity of Foucault's reading of Plato see Wolff 1989.
44 See Vernant 1989. See also Fränkel 1962; Snell 1948; Redfield 1985; Vernant 1979.
45 G. Deleuze, Foucault, cit., p. 124
46 These forms of "protest" have been valued by Rosanvallon – and I believe this is of some interest – as pillars of a possible institutionalization of 'counter-democracy'. See Rosanvallon 2006.
47 See in particular Foucault 2008a: 223.
48 On this issue, see Gros 2002b.
49 On the contrary, this hypothesis is quite widespread and debated among scholars. See Evrard, 1998; Dews 1989; Devos 2002. For a different account, see Hebel 1990; Allen 2000; Nehamas 2000.
50 Yet see Foucault's reply to this objection in Foucault 1983a/2001, particularly at p. 1222.
51 See e.g. Wolin (1986). Against Rorty's (1981) interpretation, analogous to Wolin's, expressed in a review of (among other things) *Volonté de savoir*, see Taylor (1985). On this topic, see Abrams 2002.
52 See Brown 1978 and Brown 1982. On the issue I am dealing with, see Gros 2002a.
53 On the discussion between Habermas and Foucault, see Aladjem 1995.
54 In this light, it might be worth rereading Crozier, Huntington and Watanuki 1975.
55 On this wavelength, for a broader analysis of Foucault's intellectual trajectory, see Carnevale 2005. But see also Young 2001: 395–410; Artières and Potte-Bonneville 2007: 189 ff.: Veyne 2008: 185 e ss.
56 See Sloterdijk 1983. Sloterdijk's work is probably influenced by the contemporary Foucauldian analysis of ancient cynicism.

4 *Koinōnikon zôon*

Stoics and the other modernity

Jeder sei auf seiner Art ein Grieche!
Aber er sei's

Goethe, *Antik und Modern*

1. As stated in the Goethian quotation that appears in the epigraph of this chapter, Antiquity is surely necessary. Obviously neither as an expression of the idea of a politics that has to be redeemed, nor as a constant, as the *everlasting* eternity of the "philosophical", destined to remain within and beyond the break determined by the state form of politics. The disquieting presence of the idea, whose excess allows destabilizing and understanding the real, cipher of the speculative. Rather, Antiquity is necessary for us for what is not visible in it. It is necessary as far as it pries the specular (and speculative) glare whereby modernity ties itself to the retrospective projection of its own history, that is, to a selective reading of what foreruns it.

In a text that, although not overtly, resonates in the opening lines of Foucault's *Les mots et les choses*, Nietzsche writes: 'Wenn wir von den Griechen reden, reden wir unwillkürlich zugleich von Heute und Gestern: ihre allbekannte Geschichte ist ein blanker Spiegel, der immer Etwas wiederstrahlt, das nicht im Spiegel selbst ist' (Nietzsche 2006: n. 217). The history of the Greeks is a mirror that always reflects something that is not in the mirror itself. What it gives back to us is not only a word that talks about 'today and the past' at the same time. A word that shatters the crystal of a 'passive resonance' (as Nietzsche calls it in *Second Untimely Meditation*) within which the shallow philology of the historical objectivist isolates and exerts itself. Instead, it gives back something more than what such a history contains. For speaking of the Greeks means listening to something that at the same time produces and destabilizes the mirror effect between Antiquity and Modernity. It means, according to Nietzsche, demobilizing the linear game of difference. Modernity is not the mere displacement of Antiquity, nor is Antiquity the specular reverse of Modernity.

Natural law theory determines the juridification of power, the individuation of a subject around the knot of will, the necessity of a decision capable of reincorporating the (otherwise irreducible) conflict between passions and interests, the representative retrieval of dominion as a form of free self-obligation of singularities to the universal of law.[1] This does not corroborate, at least not exclusively, a reading of what antedates Hobbes in terms of a valorization of pluralities and differences, of prudential logics of government, of harmonization of the effectual based on the 'gauge' of the idea of justice.[2]

This Antiquity, recovered as the specific difference of Modernity, as that which the modern scientification of politics removes, is the reverse image of Modernity. Its specular double. It remains internal to the effect of truth that the latter is able to project as the spectrum of its own history.

Nevertheless, the history of the Greeks always reflects something more, 'something that is not within the mirror'. Nietzsche (2006: n. 218) goes on: 'Wir benützen die Freiheit von ihnen zu reden, um von Anderen schweigen zu dürfen damit jene nun selber dem sinnenden Leser Etwas in's Ohr sagen'. We make use of the freedom to speak of the Greeks to pass over others in silence. Only in this way does something reach the ear of the thoughtful reader.

What Nietzsche has in mind is not easy to tell. A dispute with the dusty powers of academia, in the first place. And with how they set the conditions for meeting with Antiquity that defuses its destabilizing potential. However, what else does the Ancient suggest to the modern reader? Not the *other of its own history*, an alterity captured in the specular mirroring that isolates in Greek culture the peaks, the emergencies that empower the displacement through which modernity is installed – a *given* Aristotle, a *given* Plato. Rather, *another history*. A history made of submerged series, unexpressed virtualities, underground archives whose trace remains active and actionable as a counter-hegemonic form facing the *récit* that – from Hobbes to Weber – modern political philosophy retrospectively constructs as the outline of the legal and institutional history of the West.

Probably, it could be said that what is not in the mirror, what cannot be reflected in it, is on the one hand, the representative instance, the historical-genetic dispositif of modernity. In other words, a philosophy of history that also operates in the works of authors, like Hobbes, who are usually not deemed familiar with it. On the other hand, it is what eludes the speculative instance, the way in which it faces the general process of the real in order to understand it. What distorts the transparency and peremptoriness of self-representation of Modernity.

It is the permanence of this Antiquity that interests me – the one that sets in motion other genealogies: *another Antiquity* and *another modernity*. An Antiquity that is not ensnared in the reflection of modernity and a modernity that is not reflected – and thus is not based on – the catastrophe of Antiquity.

2. Ch. XIII of Hobbes' *Leviathan* (1968: Part I, *Of Man*) can be presented as the deliberate inversion of the first book of Aristotle's *Politics* (I (A), 1252b-1253a.), at least for what concerns the 'natural condition of humanity'. This inversion engenders the mirror effect through which modernity differentiates itself from Antiquity. Enmity, not *philia*, is the natural relation between human beings. Unhappiness, and not the *eudaimonia* ("flourishing"), is produced in the encounters between humans. The highest harm to avoid, death, is the most probable risk for individuals in the war of all against all, instead of the highest good

that entails the natural tendency to the social valorization of differences, to the "living well" (*eu zên*) – one that can be achieved only in the city, as the fulfilment, the actualization, of the socializing potentiality that characterizes and defines the specificity of the human. Finally, a wolf, an animal that hunts, is the icon of an individuality irreducibly inclined to war. This wolf takes the place of the inherently political animal, ***kata physin***, disposed to symbiosis and relationality, with an attitude derived from the special property of having a language, the only animal that has a "voice" (*phōnē*).

A desert, at last, is the premise for the political renovation of the social process. The annihilation of freedom, in the vacuum of fear and misery of a basic view of human life as 'solitary, poor, nasty, brutish and short'. Because human life is continually exposed to the risk of violent death and is thus literally incapable of weaving the conditions for its own security, unless it turns to a power that is able to subject simultaneously everyone in the same way, by disciplinarily constituting subjects with the same coarse feral matter of wolves. This replaces the relational fullness that according to Aristotle makes politics the most authentic possibility of self-sufficiency for mankind, the felicitous fulfilment of what human beings are only in potency; what gods and beasts experience immediately, without undergoing the reciprocity of governance and dependence (Aristotle, *Pol.* I (A), 2, 1253a).

The human being as a *politikon zôon*, rather than a wolf, is the presupposition that Antiquity opposes to modernity. On this account, politics – action and interaction: *praxis* – is the natural environment of human beings, not the war of all against all that Hobbes takes as the precondition for the political artifice. Nor is it the *dissociation* that separates, isolates and opposes single individuals, which the moderns take to be the engine of the state legal machine. This dissociation appears, in modern thought, as the only condition that by *subject-ing* individuals to its dispositif provides them with an otherwise impossible freedom, as it turns wolves into legal subjects. This is the difference that the genealogy of the modern political form stabilizes on the basis of the Greek sources of Western political thinking.

And yet, what does it mean to take the human being as a political animal? What is the kind of relation that links the Aristotelian definition to the *polis*? Is it really true that Greek political thought thinks of anthropology on the edge of difference, on the rim of governed dependence (soul/body, man/woman, adult/child, free man/slave), on the relation between the part and the whole? Or rather, is not this view a product of modern totalization? Our representation of an Ancient political thought, univocally attested as differential in relation to the imagination that constitutes the juridification of the political relationship in an alternative way?

'Dominus non est in definitione patris', Thomas Hobbes (*De Cive* IX, I) writes. This statement not only confronts the entire paradigm of political patriarchalism that persists until the seventeenth century and founds a specific political theology on Aristotelianism, particularly in a Protestant milieu (from Althusius to Filmer – see Schochet 1975). At the same time, it also postulates the need to conventionalize the social bond. Natural dependence does not coincide with the legitimacy of a dominion where the conditions are set for a man to govern another – who in turn would be led to recognize this power as given "in nature". This does not only apply to the *dominium* of the father over the children, but also to the very relation between master and slave. This proves that Hobbes intends to criticize the Aristotelian *oikodespotêia*, that is, the kind of natural and naturally governed bond between free human beings and unfree ones that is determined in the *oikos*, the reproductive basis of the *polis*.

> I know that Aristotle, in the first booke of his Politiques, for a foundation of his doctrine maketh men by Nature, some more worthy to Command, meaning the wiser sort (such as he thought himselfe to be for his Philosophy) others to Serve, (meaning those that had strong bodies, but were not Philosophers as he) as if Master and Servant were not introduced by consent of men, but by difference of Wit: which is not only against reason; but also against experience.
>
> (*Leviathan*, Part I, chap XV)

These words from Hobbes clarify how the mirror reflection that I mentioned above is produced – since it is very difficult to think of Aristotle's *Politics* as anticipating the foundational logic that pertains to modern natural law theory.

Hobbes refers to Aristotle's *Politics* to debunk a notion of 'dominion' exactly based on nature. This notion draws the dynamic of an ordered exchange within which life itself is reproduced as a 'governed' process out of the difference between the wise and the unwise, man and woman, adult and child, free and slave. Furthermore, Hobbes makes use of this difference to juxtapose it to his own model, based on the pactional idea of covenant. In the *Commonwealth*, pacified by the sovereign's sword and administered by the web of rules that his apparatuses impose on the territory, the difference that makes possible a relation of authority and obedience cannot but be based on the artifice of the contract. It is based on consent, on the architectonical function carried out by free will, in the passage from the state of nature and to the civil or political state. There is nothing in nature that can be made instrumental in taming individual will. Nothing to which the human being could be reduced other than the element of empty volition, which is absolutely formal in that it is perfectly *indifferent*.

Hobbes polemically insulates in Antiquity what the scientification of politics that he takes upon himself requires in order to neutralize the destructive potentialities of academic disciplines.[3] He also intends to dismiss the idea that the field of action cannot be submitted to a geometrization or read in terms of a mere physics of forces. The is no exercise of 'power', dominion, that can be said natural and that cannot be contested. Likewise, there is no regime of competencies that can be immediately promoted to a function of govern. Furthermore: it is impossible to treat anthropology as the basis for a general notion of politics inclined to borrow from 'nature' – and not from mechanics – the system of constants that is able to explain how and in what forms human beings establish relationships.

According to Hobbes, the premise that empties out Aristotle's presupposition is necessary to infer the foundational logic of the body politic. The human being as *politikon zôon*, the *politikē koinonia* as the living nexus of relationships based on nature, the mutual dependence as "social" compensation of an otherwise impossible self-sufficiency that guides the parties within the *polis* and that sees the *polis* as the site in which the *potential* for relation and communication with the other human beings is realized and actualized; that is to say, where the ordered system of relation and communication that takes priority over all the others elements that are gathered in that relation is realized and actualized (Aristotle, *Pol.* I [A], 2, 1253a, 25). Modern natural law theory assumes as a premise for its re-foundation of the political the disarticulation of the active/passive relation of *archein* as the fabric of political life and its emphasis on natural differences. Equality, the conflict that derives from it in the absence of rules and a state of nature that overturns the Aristotelian presuppositions are Hobbes' starting points to create a gap between Antiquity and Modernity, before and after – a gap that allows him to assert the modernity of his "scientification" of politics.

That a human being is not the master of a human being, anyway, is not an exclusively modern idea. Rather, it appears already in a literal quotation from Epictetus: *antrōphos anthrōpou kyrios ouk estin* (*Discourses*, I, 29, 60). The quotation appears in an argumentation on the living testimony that the philosopher ought to give of philosophy (*labe hēghemonian* [*Discourses*, I, 29, 44], you take the lead of your life . . .) and how the liberation that this latter promises should be understood. In order not to resemble the fragile and fearful freedom of the slave on the run (the one who always watches his back and feels the shadow of the lord looming large over his movements), the freedom of the philosopher is the freedom of he who has no master. Not even death, as the extreme spectre of a power that cannot be acted upon.

And there is more. There is an Ancient thought that not only ridicules Caesar's vanity, dismissing from the inside the idea that anybody could think of himself as the lord, *kyrios*, of another human being. But it also opposes itself to the Aristotelian (and Platonic) code that turns difference into the principle of differentiation of living beings. In a passage by Chrysippus of Soli mentioned by Philo, it is possible to read something very similar to what Hobbes says against Aristotle: 'No man is naturally a slave'.[4] Nobody is, because only the foolish, the one who does not have the courage to lead a philosophical life, finds himself in a condition of slavery. Slave is the one who is enslaved to his passions and fears and not one who finds himself in a servile condition, in chains or in captivity due to contingent events or to an imponderable fate. Nor the one who, for the same reasons, comes to life with a gendered feature that assigns her, in Aristotle's perspective, a soul, and thus a nature, that differs from the one of the free adult man, that is, the only one to whom Aristotle recognizes the role of the citizen.

The Stoic position is radical. Not only is nobody a slave by nature, but everybody can pursue wisdom. The equality that virtue makes possible does not admit any difference. Not even between the human being and god. Virtue is in fact a perfect state and as such it recognizes no gradations, no thresholds of approximation or progress,[5] no differences – in Cicero's words: *est autem virtus nihil aliud nisi perfecta et ad summum perducta natura* (*De Legibus*, I, 8, 25). But if it is so, it is clear that every human has to turn to philosophy and the liberation that follows from it. Even workers, farmers and women (*opifices, rusticos et mulieres*), everyone who has human features (*qui humanam formam gerunt*), has in some way the "right" to benefit from an education to gain wisdom.[6]

The presumption of superiority that Hobbes find in the self-representation of the philosopher (either in Aristotle or in the philosopher elevated to a governmental function in Plato's *Politeia*) seems to crash under the generalization of philosophical initiation. An initiation that Stoicism considers open to everyone, at least as a possibility. And one might recall that possibility for Stoic logics is the most universal form of the necessary. As Boethius observes: *stoicis universalius videatur esse possibile a necessario* (*Ad. Arist, de inter.*, B.1, 201, 3).[7]

Many passages emphasize this principle. And the consequence we derive from them is at the origin of the Stoics "cosmopolitanism". The universal 'invitation' to philosophy – as Lactantius calls it, recognizing that not only Stoics, but also Epicurus practiced it – discloses a different perspective from cynicism. If the Cynic perspective is an anticonventional, negative, position, at least relating to the aspect that allows the foundation of a sort of philosophizing nomadism – Crates: 'my homeland is not one tower, nor one roof, but the citadel and home of the whole world is ready for us to inhabit'.[8] While this position recognizes no city nor homeland, the Stoic perspective is expansive and positive. If wisdom is a possibility generally available to humanity, then *populum [sapientum] ex omni lingua et conditione et sexu et aetate conflari*: a people of sages of every language, and conditions, and age, and sex,[9] as a people of a city that extends to the entire universe.

Zeno of Citium, the founder of the Stoic school and author of a *Republic* 'written on the tail of a dog', as accounted by reports that accentuate its affinity to Diogenes the Cynic,[10] by now lost, but in open discussion with Plato. He goes even further.[11] Human beings should not live in groups according to a territorial order that, spatializing them, would draw them closer and draw them away at the same time ('everyone taken apart from the other by its own laws' *idiois hekastoi diōrismenoi dikaiois*). Rather they should live as fellow townmen and citizen, according to a singular form of living and to a singular order 'based on a common law' (*nomōi koinōi*) (Plutarch, *De Alex. Virt. I, 6*).

The semantic of the "common" expressed by Stoicism is what interests me. If only for the shift that it makes visible in the qualification of a human being as a *koinōnikon zôon* and not as a "political" animal, *politikon*, as in Aristotle. And for what derives from it in terms of the capacity to trace back other possible histories among Ancient and modern. A non-formal equality that is not produced through subjection, as in state modernity. A logic and an ontology that do not know any idea, but virtuality and modulations. A politics that does not stick to the horizon of the *polis* and to its system of differences in order to infer an anthropology from it. Finally, a *systēma* (a word whose technical use derives from Stoicism) that does not separate physics, logics and ethics, but that draws its political consequences from their reciprocal interactions – Stoicism is a 'bulk-philosophy', as its most prominent interpreters observe (Brehier 1971).

3. It is possible to move from a distinction that we have already met: the one between the wise and the foolish. But for the wise man, every human being is foolish. And yet, the possibility of philosophy is opened indistinctly to everyone. While the wise, even if he necessitates many things, does not need anything; the foolish lacks everything, even if he necessitates nothing since he cannot take advantage of anything (Seneca, *Ep.* 9.14). From Chrysippus' differentiation an important series of consequences arises: the wise man is rich, even if he owns few things; only his life is happy because it is self-sufficient and free ('the wise man's life is a feast' [Philo, *De sept. et fest. diebus*]). The wise man docilely follows the leader, yet he has a natural inclination to authority that can find expression in all the main administrative and political positions of the *polis*. Among wise men goods are commons, life is fair. Until here, on the path drawn by Zeno, Chrysippus seems to move in the orbit of the stoic "correction" of Platonic *Politeia*. A republic of philosopher, within which every man and every woman can become a citizen, and a regal science (*basilikē epistēmē*) that coincides with the wise man's wisdom (Proclus, *In Plat. Alcib. Pr.*; Philo, *De nominum mut.* § 152). However, we can derive more from it. Far from chasing a dream of perfection that draw him away from the masses, the wise Stoic (in complete opposition with the ascetic figure of Christianity that will come after[12]) knows no loneliness (*erēmia*), because its nature is sociable and active (*koinōnikos physei kai praktikos* [Diog. Laer., VII, 123]).

The definition is interesting, but not univocal. It should be clarified how a series of apparently discordant positions on "political" engagement and "ethical" features of the stoic wise man can be grouped together. (He must *politeuesthai*, participating in political life, taming the vice and improving virtue. However, a kind of withdrawal from political roles characterizes early Stoics, even if they prompt their disciples to take them up).[13] But this is not the problem. What is relevant, at least for me, is to understand in what sense the wise man is *koinōnikos*. And even more, what do we mean by saying that human beings as such are "living" animals naturally *koinōnikoi* and *philallēloi* (Epictetus, *Discourses* III, 13, 5).

In addition to Epicurus' works (see Epictetus, *Discourses* I, 22), the term *koinōnikon zôon* also appears in Aristotle. Particularly it appears in the *Eudemian Ethics* (VII [H]], 10,1242-a-b) with a sense that interests us. Aristotle devotes a passage to a differentiation among forms of bonds, particularly to the different modalities of friendship that are actualized within the *oikos*, in a "social" or "political" domain. If the family friendship (*syngenikē*) is differentiated according to proportions (the relation of the father with his offspring) or number (the relation among siblings), the "civil friendship" (*politikē synestēkē*) is rooted in a particular form of utility. The one that prompts the process of socialization. That prompt to live together (*syzên*), then, to compensate the need that troubles the single man, due to his unbearable lack of natural self-sufficiency. It is at a "political" level that arises the problem of justice. The relationship of reciprocal utility is the basis of a "commonality" of aims, which curbs out the unilaterality of the performance. The carpenter's relation to his saw – as well as the bond between a master and a slave – is a relation of use and does not raise the question of justice, which is only meaningful in one's relationship to a friend (*Eudemian Ethics* VII

(H), 10, 1242 a 20). From this follows that justice only applies to associative relationships, those that concern community, lineage or the way of living. Further, this also determines the attention that Aristotle devotes to the use of terms that define the levels of this natural associative inclination. The human being is not, in fact, only a ***politikon zôon***. He is also defined as ***oikonomicon zôon***, since it has the capacity to found and keep an 'oikos', avoiding casual and intermittent reproduction, which characterizes other animals. And ***koinōnikon zôon***, since he tends naturally to establish relationships with alike people, since a human being is by vocation non-solitary. The link that exists among justice and association-bond testimonies that there will be 'commonality and justice' even if there were no *polis*, or other earlier forms (*Eudemian Ethics* VII (H), 10, 1242 a 25).[14]

The Aristotelian tripartition, through the inclusion of a ***koinōnikon zôon*** between the ***oikonomic*** and the political, multiplies and differentiates the features and forms of an associative instinct that finds its fulfilment in the *polis*. The ***koinōnia*** is valorized as ***politikē koinōnia*** only when it proves its capacity to channel single forms of relationship into the "good life" that is actualized only in the self-sufficiency of the *polis* (Aristotle, *Pol.* 1 (A) 30 1258a). For this reason, in the synoecistic Aristotelian sequence,[15] the human being is defined as a ***politikon zôon***. The very modalities in which the human being unfolds his associative instinct are described by referring to the system of politically oriented relations that produce the ***koinon*** as the other side of the political, assimilated to the 'institutional' system of the city (Weber 1985: chap. VIII, in part. § 2).[16]

In this sense, linguistics provides us with precious evidence. In his analysis of the four circles of social belonging, Émile Benveniste comes to very similar conclusions. In its fundamental terms, which in Greek are Aristotle's ones, the political vocabulary refers to a cluster of functions that pertains to the city. *Dominus* is not the lord of the ***domus***. Rather, his title derives from the authority that comes to be recognized within the system of relations that belongs to the 'house'. Relations that exclude strangers, that close the circuit of recognition by separating the inside from the outside and that cannot be referred to ***domus*** as to a building. *Domus* and ***dominus*** refer one to the other and indicate a narrower social group. They belong to the root, otherwise obscure, of the archaic compost ****dem(s)-poti***, "landlord". This root is maintained in the Greek word ***despotēs***, but its originary meaning is kept only in the Attic ***oikodespotēs***, an expression used by Aristotle to indicate the 'political' function related to the internal management and government of the 'house'. Following the trace of a progressive 'territorialization' of the social bond, something similar is determined at the highest levels of the organization of the city. From the forms of the nominal root ****weik***, ****woiko*** originates the series of terms that defines the unit formed by several families: ***uicus***, hamlet, village, for example, or much later, ***ciuitas***. In fact, new territorial divisions take the place of blood relationships, while belonging to a territory acquires a wider relevance than stock (Chignola 1993). Chance or war, or whatever reason urge men to convene in the *polis* or in the ***kōmē***: this is the term used by Aristotle to define the intermediate associative stage between the natural community (the ***oikos***) and the city of free men, and it is therefore the sate that the Stagirite refers to when he speaks of the *koinōnikon zôon*. According to Benveniste, what Aristotle codifies in the beginning of the *Politics* is nothing but a situation settled long time ago – an opinion shared by Manfred Riedel himself. The 'genetic' description of the urbanization and civilization places in the *oikos* (the community of husband and wife, of the lord and the servant; daily community where food and cult are shared) the furthest unit. Then, he considers more differentiated or wider cells of socialization, such as the village, to finally come to the *polis*.

However, according to Benveniste, the process described by Aristotle offers a 'false representation'. From the beginning, as demonstrated by the tight root of the Indo-European vocabulary 'social', society is a web of relationships of belonging, segmented into units that encompass one another. The anteriority of the city on the *oikos* and its single members (Aristotle, *Pol.* I (A), 2, 1253a 18–26) is not contingent only on the logical and metaphysical precedence of the whole vis-à-vis its parts. Rather, it depends on the Aristotelian transposition (in a philosophical and universal sense) of what his culture presented as a repertory of associative circuits, all referred to the *polis* as a politic-territorial dominant unit. Thus, Aristotle systematized the wealthy Greek social life of the Attic democracy through the projection, in absolute sense, of a determinate historical stage of Western civilization (Benveniste 1969; Riedel 1975). The Aristotelian *politeia*, intended as the cluster of citizens who operate politically, constantly reproduces the *taxis* – the order – of its institutional and social parts; whereas this very *taxis* of relationships can be what configures the specific 'political' arrangement, the 'consititution', of a specific city (Ventura 2009). The definition of the human being as political animal (and prior to this, as oikonomical, communitarian) meets the need to keep the subject within this circle of general finalization – one that borrows from *polis* its formal cause.

Stoics reject precisely this formal principle – and this also applies to the Platonic paradigm of politics as the relation between the whole and its parts in which 'each of the principles within him does its own work in the matter of ruling and being ruled' (Plato, *Rep.*, IV, 443b.). The definition of human being as *koinōnikon zôon* does not derive from the crisis of the urban element – it would be an oversimplification (Kelsen 1937: 21). Rather, what is important in this definition is a whole set of assumptions radically addressed against Aristotle and Plato.

Stoics' Cosmos is a reasoning living being, endowed with soul and intelligence.[17] In turn, every single being (whatever it might be) is sought as a living being who has in itself its own principle of activity. This is held together by a *tonos* of the *pneuma*, a dynamic, whose specific force gives it the irreducible features of a qualified individuality (*idiōs poion*). It is the individuality of the being – which coincides with the body itself, since Stoics only recognize the body and the soul itself is a body – what justifies its evidence. The qualification of the being does not proceed from a cause that operates on the matter in a relation of participation with the idea (as in Plato); nor does it derive from a system of final causes (as in Aristotle [Brehier 1971: 108–109]). Stoics replace the Forms and the Prime mover the world as a finite, living, eternal, and divine *beatum animal* (*Chalcidium in Tim.* c 292; Arius Didymus, *Apud Eusebium praep. evang.* XV, 15). In doing so, they not only substitute the body for the idea, the movement for the final cause, but also disable the very notion of 'project', with all that it means in terms of devaluation of the finite, the corporeal, the contingent in favour of dynamism and of the primacy of action: 'Stoics believed the primal cause to be a being in motion (*kinēton*)' (Aëtius Plac. 11, 7). In Stoic physics, movement is not the shift from potentiality to actuality, but a pure, integral act (Goldschmidt 1977: 48, 63). The transformation of forms (transformation of the ones into the others, an action of reciprocal variation) is not dependent on an external action. While in the case of inanimate things (*apsychēn*), transformation happens 'as a result of a transformation of the matter carried out by a demiurge', here it is immanent to the process of things, 'as if things were taking part in a real and important competition and were fighting for victory' (Dio Chrysostom, *Or.* XXXVI §51). Since Stoics do not understand matter as inanimate or inert, it is not possible to consider their position as materialistic in a modern sense. Body is active in itself – a *tonos* is active also in the *hexis* that defines the cohesive principle of a stone. Virtues are bodies. The soul is a body (Long 1982: 34–57; Brehier 1962: 8–9). The process of 'apparition' of beings is given as an immanent and immediate process. It is a rhythm of effects-events that is produced on the surface of the being. 'It is as if some magician were to mould horses out of wax, and then, subtracting and scraping off the wax from each, should add a little now to this one and now to that, until finally, having used up all the horses in constructing one from the four, he should fashion a single horse out of all his material' (Dio Chrysostom, *Or.*, XXXVI § 51). A dissolution of substance is not possible, as it is impossible the dissolution of the driving principle of substance. It is necessary that substance remains in the moving realities, because it has the natural capacity to receive all modifications as well as the action of all that nature itself uses for creating. Generation is impossible, since substance is inborn and undestroyable (Arius Didymus, *Epit. phys.* fr. 37 Diels). The Cosmos is eternal if it is conceived as a substance. It is born and perishable, only in accordance with the 'period' that establishes its end in the fire (*ekpyrōis*). Which is to say, as *diakosmēsis* – that is, the unfolding of the substance in the actual variety of forms (Pohlenz 1949: I, 149).

The debt of Stoics physics to Heraclitus is evident. Still, the former place a stronger attention to the stability (and mutability) of individual things. The *pneuma* flows in the entire universe – as Tertullian (*adv. Hermog.* Cp. 44) writes: *stoici enim volunt deum sic per materiam decurrisse quomodo mel per favos.* It establishes the qualitative essence of individual beings. Each of them is an individuality (*idiōs poion*) characterized by the cohesive force that piece its parts together. In addition, it is not limited by other bodies, since Stoics do not consider space as a reality. On the contrary, space is created by the movement of beings that "carve out" the place to which they belong. They do so by expressing the tension (the "tonal movement") they are capable of in the *krasis di'olōn*, from which individual forms emerge (Goldschmidt 1977: 96; Long 1986: 157-ff). The corporeality of single beings – even of the piece of wood, of the stone – is determined by the twofold tonal movement that goes from the centre to the periphery and from the periphery to the centre once it reaches the "limit" of their surface. The solidity of things and living beings is given by the pneumatic tension that confers to the substratum unity and consistency. It is given by the static effect that is determined in the game of conflicting movements. It is an apparent immobility, like the one of a bird that is poised in the air (Pohlenz 1949: 143).

What is conceptualized by the Stoics with the technical term *pneuma* is the materialization of a force. Through this term, they try to trace all the events back to one, continuous, immanent, rational cause, able to make corporeal and to form individual substances by altering the degree of their own tension (Long 1968). For according to Stoic ontology and cosmology there are only 'happenings' and not 'events', as Ammonius observes: 'what terms do the Stoic use? They call events happenings (*tynchanonta*) because their aim is to happen' (*tychein*) (Ammonius, *In Arist. Analyt. Prim.* [Comm. Graec. IV 6]). In the rhythm that the god plays in everything, like Apollo who touches the lyre strings with his plectrum, this tension takes different features and names according to the being that it modulates in the incessant flux of being. It is called *hexis*, in the case of inorganic bodies; *physis*, in the case of plants; *psychē*, in the case of the human being. *Psychē* confers the status of a linguistic animal on the human being. It shapes him as a free concomitant cause of the causal immanent nexus that Stoics indifferently call nature, destiny, god, through which the general *oikonomia* of the universe unfolds (Plutarc. *De Stoic. Repugn.* Cp. 34 p. 1049 f).[18] However, within it no hierarchies or differences are established, since limits are nothing but modulations of the same substance, and contact lines between beings are only variations, ripples, immediately and simultaneously produced on the surface of being.

'Nature endowed us with a soul and gave us a body and predisposed us for the perfection of both' (Alexander of Aphrodisias, *De anima libri mant.*). Living in accordance with nature means living in the perfection of both. Not only within Stoic psychology the soul has no parts, but there is not even the paradigmatic function of government that, according to Aristotle and Plato, the soul governs the body – what made available the difference between the two, which is necessary to think of the relationship of command. For the Stoics, being a living being endowed with psychic and (as is the case for the human) linguistic functions entails being a body endowed with a sense of the self that derives from his being at one and the same time a subject and an object of impulse (*hormē*) (Long 1986). The 'self-appropriation' that every living being carries out is an act of assent (a central term both in Stoic's logics and in their ethics: *synkatathesis*) and implies a conciliation with what we are. It is a commitment to safeguarding ourselves by choosing what is useful to our conservation and avoiding what is dangerous, escaping death.

4. *Prima est conciliatio hominis ad ea, quae sunt secundum naturam* (Cicerone, *De Fin.* III, 20). Cicero translates the Stoic term *oikeiōsis* with *sibi conciliatio.* This is a crucial turning point for the Stoic ethics and politics. For it is exactly the path of physics, its centrality in the stoic cosmologic *systēma*,[19] that grants the recognition of the separation between Stoicism and cynicism. The idealization of the Cynic in Epictetus' III *Discourse* demonstrates that otherwise there would be

no difference between the stoic *sophos* and the cynic philosopher in a phase of the late Stoicism in which physics loses its importance. In either case, anyway, it is not *sophia* that qualifies a man as wise – this would be impossible, given the non-predicative logic of the Stoics. Conversely, it is the testimony of the wise man's life, his consistency, that gives values to wisdom (see Rist 1977).

The human being differs from the plant in that he has a soul whose first manifestation is perception. At the moment of birth, in the particular form of a living being that the human is, the central organ of the soul resembles a blank wax tablet, ready to receive the imprints (*typosin*) supplied by the senses. These perceptions are recorded as representations (*phantasiai*). Then, these become notions or 'concepts' after having received the assent – a process only anticipated in children as *prolēpseis.* This is what concerns the theory of knowledge and, namely, the alteration (*alloiōsis*) through which perceptions modify the hegemonic part of the soul. Like a spider on his web, the soul, body among bodies, vibrates with the vibrations conveyed by the senses and is activated by them. While in the *sibi conciliatio* the sensorial imprint of the 'external' world produces in the living being an internal 'co-perception' that drives the subject towards his own being.

The principle that every living being loves his own nature can be also found in Aristotle's *Nicomachean Ethics* (IX, 9, 1170 a 26): 'Life is by nature a good, and perceiving some good thing as present in us is pleasant'. Anyway, what differentiates Stoics from Peripatetics is the way in which the former roots this principle in an hylozoist ontology. Here, beings are not distinguished according to species and, thus, the good to which each of them aims is not specified on the basis of a specific nature. The *sensus sui* is a perception of the being's sense and self-love and it manifests itself as a self-preservation instinct – thus as expansive 'potentiality', a search for everything that is capable of favouring and increasing the singular being. As a nature that does not coincide with a logical universal, but with the distributed intelligence of the matter.

One of Cicero's (*De Fin.* V, 14, 39) arguments demonstrates how far from the academic-peripatetic compromise the Stoic position is. It concerns the issue of vegetables. According to Cicero, inferior natures have 'little strength to find themselves in the best situation'. He recalls the example of the vine, a climber that needs supports to develop properly and thus legitimates the external mediation of the art of cultivation, the 'care' that the farmer gives it with a view to the achievement of its end.[20] It is worth noticing that Cicero offers the further example of sheep farming and the 'good' of the flock. It is not difficult to grasp the political consequences of this position: a form of government is necessary in order for the living being to reach their wellbeing.

However, according to Stoics, nature determines itself, it is its own immanent causal connection, the activity of living matter, the pure act of its potency, what *necessarily* and *immediately* achieves its own end. The obstacles that the single vine shoot faces in the process of its expansion do not affect the living matter (which *also* took the form of a vine shoot) in its tension and the orientation of its development towards wellbeing. The active subject of the *oikeiōsis* is not the single individual, but nature, which is active in every being. This self-consciousness (*sensus sui*) is also present in vegetables. Soul, in the living beings who possess it, coincides with the bond produced between *systasis* and *syneidēsis*, that is, with the reflexive co-perception of one's own physical structure (flesh, nerves, muscles), taken into account in the stage of development in which all beings find themselves. 'The things that every living being feels as his own are his constitution and his consciousness'.[21] This is what leads a newborn baby to move and find pleasure in his movement or a duckling to toil towards water after coming out of its shell. 'What the animal feels as its own' is nothing more than its own self (*prōton oikeion einai tō zôon hautōi*[22]). Through the functions of its senses, the living being epitomizes an 'extra-ception' with an equally decisive 'proprioception' (Radice 2000: 191–192).

In principle, then, there is no difference (*ouden diēllaxen*) between plants, animals or rational beings. The appropriation through which they feel themselves, 'sense' what favours and what damages their self-preservation, through which they get pleasure from their existence, is the same in all living beings. Such appropriation is a fact that urges them to live 'in accordance with nature', whether or not they are rational. The precept of the Stoic ethic is a linear emanation of physics. Contrary to animals, a vegetable does not have 'impulse' or 'sensation'. However, it has the capacity to live and develop according to the modalities through which nature cares for itself. These modalities realize the series of symbioses and selections that allow the bees to pollinate flowers, the plants to tend towards the light or to avoid dry or rocky soil. This part of nature exists, without any gaps, also in human beings. It regulates some basic biologic-vegetative functions. The "impulse" (*hormē*) is what pushes the animal to live in accordance with its nature, since it loves itself and takes pleasure from its body and, thus, is 'reconciled' with its own being. Before it can experience pleasure and pain, the animal aims at self-preservation. He looks for what agrees with him and avoids what cause him troubles, since he loves himself and takes pleasure from his body and, thus, he is 'reconciled' with his own being. The existence of a rational soul in the human being does not add anything to this series. The human being is a living being too. He 'loves' his own being in his own body and in his vital *systatis* before everything else. Even for him, to live 'by reason' means to live 'by nature'.[23] To live in accordance with the event that he is. The 'happiness' that he can reach – and that Stoics, from Zeno to Marcus Aurelius, indicate with a peculiar term: *euroia biou*, the happy, smooth, flowing of life[24] – coincides with the flow and the expansion of the processes triggered by this original 'amorous' and natural appropriation of the self. Which is an event among events in the vast and calm flux of things.

5. There is in Epictetus a curious dialogue. The tyrant speaks out against the philosopher, asking him to be recognized: 'I will show you that I am master (*kyrios*)'. 'But you are master of my carcase: take it', answers the philosopher, whose expression sounds familiar to the modern reader of Spinoza. 'So when you approach me, you have no regard to me?' the tyrant goes on, even if his splendour flows over those who are (as Stoic ethics had it) 'indifferent'. For this splendour can be exercised only in destructive ways. And only on what is, in any case, perishable and

mortal, rather than on what is 'incoercible' and 'invincible', that is, on freedom, which is the most typical trait of the rational animal. 'No, but I have regard to myself', the philosopher answers 'and if you wish me to say that I have regard to you also, I tell you that I have the same regard to you that I have to my pipkin'.

The tyrant's power makes no difference at all to the Stoic, but this is not the most relevant trait in Epictetus' passage quoted above. And this is because the stoic notion of freedom as *autopragia*[25] (independence in action) is one of the consequences of the denial of the system of differences and dependences that marks the Aristotelian and Platonic *taxis* of political positions. What is really important is the way in which Epictetus substantiates his position. The philosopher's attitude against the tyrant shows derision, intolerance, refusal of his (as of every sort of) power since nobody can proclaim himself the master of another human being. This attitude should not be considered 'egoistic' (*philauton*), 'since this is the nature of the living being: to do everything for himself' (*hautou hēneka panta poiei*). However, in doing so, he cannot but benefit the 'common good' (*to koinon*). By following the original impulse of *oikeiosis* and the positive, natural inclination to self-love, which is at the basis of the very philosophical choice of liberation from subjection, to do things for oneself is not to be considered as *akoinōnēton*. Which is to say, as an action that damages the 'community' relation that includes all living beings, human beings and gods, who have been endowed with a rational soul (Epictetus, *Dialogues* I, 9–15). Individualization, the conferral of a subjective sense on life with an authentically free gesture, is not an "antipolitical" gesture.

Thus, there is no contradiction between *philautia* and *philallēlia*, between selfishness and selflessness, between "individualization" and "reciprocity". The natural drive to the *sibi conciliatio*, to the appropriation of one's own *sytasis* and *syneidēsis*, equates to the confirmation that the human being (given his animal constitution and the cognitive-symbolic sphere where he finds himself) is a social, relational and communal being. Not a "political" animal, because his being taken in a web of governed relationships is not contingent on the qualified differences of the *polis*. Rather, a *koinōnikon zôon*, whose socializing process is an improvement and expansion of the original self-appropriation/apprehension and proceeds from an inclination that is naturally present in all human being.

In the Stoic view, nature is an entire system. And it does nothing without purpose. The very understanding of bodily *systasis* is an understanding of the necessary coordination of limbs, the *inter se congruere*. As we are made to avoid pain, so are we made by nature[26] in a way that does not allow us to avoid the *co-perception* of the relational, communicative, "social" world. A world to which we are linked and that prevents us both from cutting ourselves off from others and from treating them as strangers. The potency (*vis*) of this communal, selfless nature also expresses itself within beasts if we think of how they beget and takes care of their offspring. *Ex hoc nascitur, ut etiam communis hominum inter homines naturalis sit commendatio*, as Cicero (*De Fin*. III, 62) writes.[27]

The "communal" inclination that orientates both human ontogenesis and phylogenesis are the results of a kind of equality and solidarity that not only overcome the differences politically established within the *polis*. Rather, on the contrary, they exceed every "space" created to govern them. What is common is the reason in which we communicate. The *communis ratio* (Cleanthes refers to it as *koinon logon* [Stobeus Ecl. I, I, 12]), that precedes every individuation. Individuation that can operate only in the *coniunctio* with other individuals, in which the same conjunctive process takes place.[28]

This is what the very definition of the human being as a *koinōnikon zôon* reveals. The adjective expresses neither a predicate nor a definition. In the Stoic logic, an attribute expresses neither a being (let alone participated by the idea) nor a non-being. It indicates a way of being (*pōs echon*), in which the relationship between thought and object, between *noēma* and *pragma*, is abolished. In a universe where everything is corporeal and where the body itself is active, predication is a *lekton*, a discursive event that "indicates" a fact as the performance of an action. Each body operates on other bodies. The interaction of bodies places one of them in an active position (*to poioun*) with respect to another in a passive one (*to paschon*). What *lekton* "means"' is the incorporeal and verbal modulation of a relation of causation. Here the copula "is" comes to be dispossessed of its role. This copula leads to a dispossession of the reference to the world of the essences and of the formal or ideal dimension of concepts and categories that it produces. In the relation between *poioun* and *paschon*, there is no need for an 'impact, a contrast or a contact' (Proclus, *In Plat. Parm.* vol. V.). What the action of one on the other determines is a real event, which accounts for a mode of being. This however cannot be accounted for in the classical terms of a cause-effect relation. Because, in the general merging of elements, the space does not exist as a functional category to represent the causal relation, nor is there any an idea of limit as that which separates bodies from one another. The verb "to be" then, simply indicates the way in which the substance operates by performing the "chain" of events. It indicates the way in which it activates a series of sense on its surface. A chain that does not invent anything new, but unceasingly develops what already existed (*nihil novi efficientis et primum replicantis* [Cicero, *De divinatione* I, 56, 127]) and that refers to the inborn being-active of substance (Goldschmidt 1977: 22-ff).

Thus, the function of the *lekton* is purely expressive. The Stoic dialectic is overtly anti-Aristotelian, in that judgments have no reality, do not express the being, and what they do "indicate" are attributes, *lekta*, which only exist in language or in thought (Brehier 1962: 24). It is the science of incorporeal events as they are expressed in sentences and in chains of events, as they are "built up" in the relation between sentences. The stoic dialectic is the art of conjugation (Deleuze 1990: 4).

The knife, that is a body, is the cause in the flesh, that is a body, of the incorporeal predicate (*asōmatou katēgorēmatos*) of being cut (Simplicius, *In Arist. Categ.*, F 77 B). "Being cut" is not referred to a state of the being, but an effect of sense produced in language to express the interaction of objects, that is, the relation that exists between bodies. According to the Stoics, the content of a proposition, its meaning, never amounts to the reference to an object (defined or conceptualized – as is the case with the universal of thinking, a reference to Form). Rather, the meaning is the *relationship* expressing an activity or an action. A tree, to give an oft-quoted example, "is" not green. If this were the case, the judgement would derive from the application of categories or concepts in which being is predicated. The "tree greens": a conjugative expression that indicates, through an incorporeal *lekton*, a mode of the being in the immanence of its activity.

From this a series of consequences ensues. The exchange between wisdom and wise life mentioned above, for instance. This is the way in which a life is actively made consistent in order to be qualified as wise, instead of being the participation in an – eternal – idea that would allow the classification of this life as wise. It is not the precepts of a morality but nature that prompts a natural body (though endowed with a soul) to conform to nature. But, then, what does Epictetus' *physei esmen koinōnikon* mean? What does it mean to say that the human being "is" a *koinōnikon zôon*? We have already said that he does not belong to the space of the *polis*. A body produces his "place" in the *krasis di'olōn* of elements and has no limit with regard to his expressive possibilities. The "social" qualification of the human being does not derive from the ascription to citizenship. From a sort of "natural place" of politics. The human being is a social animal *ad coniunctionem natus*, because nature initiates him – from his birth – to a relation with himself and the world. This relationship is made of a co-perception of himself as a *zoôn* endowed with a *systasis* and a *syneidēsis*. The former is backed by altruism and solidarity (no new-borns, particularly if humans, could otherwise survive on their own); while the latter pushes the human being outside himself, granting him the resistance of the exchange between inside and outside, between himself and the others. The human being *is* a *koinōnikon* animal, in the conjugative relation that connects him to relationships, as well as to the series of knots, circumstances, events that can reinvigorate his *autopragia*. The expansion of the causal link that includes the human being, the potency of a social "mode of being" that every individual of the species exhibits. Precisely as in the case of the tree, the human being *is* not a *koinōnikon* animal, according to a logic of attribution. For he is an animal who *kōinōnei*. In virtue of a drive that pushes him from the bottom of his *systasis*, the human being makes the common. He extends, institutionalizes, juridifies it, according to a multivocal and active perspective, in which humans are taken to be equal (whether men, women, workers, slaves). All of them being driven to a socialization of the self by the impulse that incites them to look for what is beneficial, like potential natural philosophers, in the process of the universal cosmopolis.

6. I can thus go back to the first part of this chapter. What cannot be seen in the mirror effect between the Ancient and the modern is a *forclusive* effect. The other Ancient as well as the other modern are included and neutralized in the history of Western politics, in its being entirely related to state institutions and citizenship – whether implicitly or explicitly. However, politics is much more than that. It is connection, *agencement*, de-saturation of the "sites" of politics. It is the invention of relationships, expansive multiplication of subjectivating processes. It is becoming, unbroken and autonomous construction of the convention of the common action. Law itself is natural, not because it expresses a universal law. On

the contrary, it is natural because we are ***natura coniuncti et consociati ad civilem communitatem*** (Cicero, *De fin.* III,65).

Another history of the political. The history of another *praxis*. Maybe, more useful for the tasks that we have to face than the glimmering (and thus dazzling) specular mirroring between Hobbes and Aristotle to which the history of the state and of its institutions is connected.

Notes

1 See Hobbes 1998, Part II, Ch. XX: 'Free-Man is he, that in those things, which by his strength and wit he is able to do, is not hindred to doe what he has a will to'.
2 See Duso 1999, a key reference for the issue that this contribution problematizes.
3 This potential has to do with a fascination that classic Antiquity, the "republican" myth, exerts on English intellectuals – a fascination that leads them to see monarchy as a form of tyranny. But it also has to do with the idea of politics reproduced within universities on the basis of the centrality of Aristotelianism. See Hobbes, *Behemoth*, Dialogue I. On classical republicanism, see Skinner 2014. For a less oppositional reading of the relationship between Hobbes and Aristotle, see Strauss 1977; Skinner 1996; Skinner 2008.
4 All Stoic texts are quoted from Radice 2002 (English translations from Italian are generally the translator's or reference to other translations).
5 The question of the progress of virtue will reach its peak only in middle and late Stoicism.
6 The passage is mentioned in Lactantius, Inst. Div. III, 25, where he records that also Epicurus called to philosophy also the most uneducated human beings (***rudes omnium literarum***).
7 See also Stephanus In Arist. Rhet,: 'According to Stoics "mostly" and "necessarily" have the same meaning' (***hoi stōikoi to epi to poly etautizon tōi anagkaiōi***). For, once established that everything that happens is necessary (***panta kata to anagkaion ginomena***), they exclude contingency (***to endechomenon***). That is, they exclude what remains contingent, both if something happens, or if its contrary happens. Thus, it is possible to say that what is contingent, as the "mostly", simply does not happen. Or better, always and necessarily does not happen. While unanimously the Stoics assert in their definitions'. Clearly, this is an anti-Aristotelian position. On the importance of Boetius' notes for the interpretation of Stoic logic, see Reesor 1972.
8 Paquet 1992. On negative cynic cosmopolitanism: Tarn 1939; Montiglio 2000; Moles 1983.
9 On this topic Baldry 1983; Scuccimarra 2006: in particular 45-ff.
10 Sellars 2007: 1–29.
11 Baldry 1959; Devine 1970; Erskine 1990. And more generally Graeser 1975.
12 On early ascetic Christianity see Brown 1982.
13 Stobeus, Florileg. 45, 29; Seneca, *Ad Serenum de Otio*, 8, I. The fact that Stoics 'speak' a lot about politics but prefer inactivity to concrete engagement will attract Plutarch's bitter irony, see *De stoicorum repugnantia*, 2.
14 See also Finley 1970.
15 That is, in the scheme that connects the 'city' to its territory and associative relationships existing within it to a reciprocal integration governed by a mutuality that keeps being differentiated on the inside and in which the very idea of justice registers and reproduces a proportionality.
16 On the question of the limits of the Western discourse on citizenship see also Isin 2002.

17 Diog. Laert. VII, 142–143: *zôon ho kosmos kai logikon kai empsychon kai noeron.*
18 On the topic of immanence, Long's interpretation is opposed to Pohlenz's and Edelstein's ones. See Edelstein 1966.
19 As Radice (2009) defines it.
20 Radice (2009) shows how Cicero's position in texts more influenced by Stoicism leans towards a general finality of nature that will, anyway, be fulfilled by itself. See Striker 1983; Pohlenz 1949. For another, less interesting, perspective on Stoic *oikeoiosis*, Chang-Uh Lee 2002.
21 Diog. Laërt. VII, 85: *prōton oikeion legōn einai panti zôō tēn hautou systasinkai tēn tautēs syneidēsin.*
22 Alexander of Aphrodisias, De anima libri mant..
23 See the fragments [C e] 178–183 in Radice 2002.
24 Stobeus, Ecl. II, p. 77 20 W: tēn de eudaimonia ho Zēnōn ōrisato ton tropon touton: eudaimonia d'estin euroia biou.
25 On *autopragia* as a neologism and on Plato's *Republic* as a 'catalyzer' of stoic critique, see Erskine 1990: 37–40 ff.
26 A nature whose 'communal', altruistic, potency (vis) finds an expression even among feral animals, as the way in which they reproduce and take care of their offspring reveals.
27 See also De Fin. III, 65: *Facile intelligitur nos ad coniunctionem congregationemque hominum et ad naturalem communitatem esse natos.*
28 See Cicero, *De Legibus* I, 10, 28: *nemo ipse tam similis [est], quam omnes sunt omnium.*

5 'Phantasiebildern'/'histoire fiction'

Weber, Foucault

In the lecture of the 5th of January 1983, which inaugurates the course he gave in that year, Michel Foucault makes a startling statement. In the contemporary scene of philosophy – one that he integrally situates in the wake of Kant's legacy – there are only two options available. First, a work on the conditions of possibility of the true judgement, an analytic of truth which he believes is carried out within Anglo-American philosophy. Second, a political philosophy that takes the present as its problem. Nothing new, in many respects. It comes as no surprise that Foucault sides with the latter, if one only thinks of how much, in many other places, he praises Kant's essay published on 'Berlinische Monatsschrift' (*Was ist Aufklärung*? 1784). It was the bicentenary of such an inaugural act of a thinking of the present day (Foucault 1984b/2001). What looks somehow eccentric in the light of Foucault's trajectory is not the fact of the modern "attitude" of philosophy, in the field of the mobile forces of a present in an ongoing loss of balance with respect to the syntheses achieved time by time; nor is it the interrogation of the status of reason – its autonomy or authority over other knowledges. Rather, what is altogether striking[1] is this sequence to which Foucault connects his own work – one that, through Nietzsche and Weber, begins with Hegel and ends with the Frankfurt School (Foucault 2008a: 22).

Indeed, in many contributions of the preceding years, Foucault was very cautious and explicit in differentiating his position both from the Frankfurt School's and from Max Weber's. As far as the Frankfurt School is concerned, which Foucault almost metonymically identified with *Dialectic of Enlightenment* by Adorno and Horkheimer (1972), he chastises the connecting link at the basis of the upturning between reason's emancipative instance and its morphing into the domination of technique. In the same wavelength, he thought that Weber had identified modernity with one process of rationalization. 'Je ne crois pas que je sois webérien' – he said only a few years before :

> car mon problème n'est pas, finalement, celui de la rationalité comme invariant anthropologique. Je ne crois pas qu'on puisse parler de "rationalisation" en soi, sans, d'une part, supposer une raison absolue et sans s'exposer, d'autre part, à mettre un peu n'importe quoi dans la rubrique des rationalisations.
> (Foucault 1980b/2001: 845)[2]

Foucault often associated Weber with the Frankfurt School, as the epitome of a theoretical exercise irreducible to the French philosophical style, which was essentially imbued with phenomenology even when it dealt with the history of sciences[3] The gap between these two authors was due to a double order of problems. First, (what at least Foucault perceived as a) radical methodological difference: Foucault deems Weber's notion of "ideal type" to be untenable. Second, the reference of historical and social processes to a univocal line of transformation and assessment invested with 'valeur raison' that he thought utterly contestable.

While in those years he was making his own project more rigorous and explicit, it is evident how badly Foucault misunderstood Weber. Partly because, as Foucault will tell a few years later, German critical philosophy and its foundational referents had narrowly penetrated French academia – he will regard the scarce influence of the members of the Frankfurt School, who migrated to Paris in 1935, on the intellectual debate in France as a fascinating historical problem. Similarly, none of the professors he met in the years of his formation ever happened to name any of the authors who would be warmly welcomed a few years later in the USA (Foucault 1983b/2001: 1275–1258). Partly because of the decisive passage he was engaging in: moving away, through the history of sciences, from the philosophy of the subject and the idea of rationality that stemmed from it.

Foucault's research project was a work of 'événementialisation' of history intended to debunk those schemes that pivoted on necessitating and general structures and processes. It aimed to draw attention to distinct practices, programmes and dispositifs as differentiated effects of the multiple regimes of juridification and veridiction which shored up the government of human beings. As he was clarifying this research project, Foucault denounced Weber as the buttress of a theory of history mostly 'désévénementialisée', one that was meant to congeal abstract events – such as Calvinism, the state, the capitalist enterprise – as essences that make sense of processes.

More than that. He could point to Weber's methodology as the background against which, by contrast, he could claim the specificity of his own research. In this sense, for example, he opposes his own notion of "programme" to that of "ideal type": the scheme of the prison, the clinic, the workhouse does not correspond to a category or a set of principles that explain the practices of surveillance or punishment. Rather, they are an ensemble of prescriptions and strategies that allow organizing institutions, imagining and controlling spaces, regulating behaviours, while each of these objectives is scrutinized in its singularity and the specificity that localizes it through a resistance that has to be defeated and overcome. Like "discipline" – which, as is known, is a Weberian key-term – this ensemble is not the geometric point of practices, indeed the "universal" to which practices have to be referred as far as the common and generalizable features they exhibit are concerned. Rather it is that which allows nominating the *mise en connexion* of the different techniques that traverse it as programmes and strategies. They get assembled in a contingent, random, sometimes contradictory form. The outcomes of these techniques do not necessarily pursue a genetic intention in compliance with which they have been put at work; nor do they directly pass on to institutions something that was initially pre-designed.

The solidity and flexibility of that which Foucault calls 'dispositif' exactly correspond to such a *dispersive* rationality of the real. It is not a uniform totality recapitulated in thought. It is an ensemble of positivities engendered by the 'effets permanents et solides' of anonymous practices that can be perfectly comprehended within the strategical designs that orientate them without them needing to be referred to what comes before them or what performs them as their overall 'reason' (Foucault 1980b/2001: 846–847).[4] Behind the rich facade of the system, one posits the rich uncertainty of disorder, Foucault wrote a few years before, and beneath the thin surface of discourse, the whole mass of a largely silent development (Foucault 2002b: 84). Those that Foucault implies as concepts or categories for a philosophical work wholly steeped in the immanence of history and life[5] are nothing other than grids, indexes, frames against whose background one can chart the lines of visibility and the emersion points that actualize, in a constantly changeable form, the possibles and the virtualities that inhere in the system of forces, tensions, actions and reactions that compose history (see Deleuze 1986: 43-ff.).

The notion of programme against that of "ideal-type"; multiple rationalities and local strategies – local in the sense of permanently contested and countered – against the idea of one process of "rationalisation". An extra-legal analytic of power that takes power to be located in the everyday and in the reversible character of the relations that go across the social body. These relations make it impossible to attach power to one institution or one dominant order against the 'monopoly on legitimate violence' which Weber ascribes to the state ('anders ist er nicht zu definieren', Weber pointed out to emphasize the mutual, circular relations between the two terms – Foucault 1977e/2001: 378; Weber 1986: 547). These are the main sticking points that make sense of Foucault's misgivings about Weber.

And yet, many years after, the startling statement that opened this chapter. Foucault locates his own work in the trajectory that goes from Hegel to the Frankfurt School, whose turning points are Nietzsche and Weber.

While one can hardly underestimate the relevance of Nietzsche to Foucault, it is more complicated to pin down the meaning of the change of mind he experienced with respect to Weber. For sure, it is something that needs deciphering. A decisive change of mind, I believe, given the passage that concerns Foucault's own research between the end of the 1970s and the first half of the 1980s. He was moving the analytic of power to the field of governmentality, while the issues of subjectivation and the techniques of the self were acquiring centrality[6] and were intersecting the issues of pastoral power and counter-conducts.

Although Foucault never openly discusses it, he does seize on Weber's contribution within the transition that links the claims of an ethics of research and a practice of philosophy, as materially inscribed in the immanence of history, to the problematization of the status of the subject within the framework of the governmentalization of power dispositifs. A philosophy of politics and history, an ethics of the intellectual work, of course, not a mere sociology of action. I would like to dwell on these issues in the following pages.

1. Let me resume, then. What is it that changes in the work that Foucault was carrying out towards the end of the 1970s? What is it that the issue of governmentality suggests? In a text of 1981 published in the *London Review of Books*, which I mentioned above, Foucault develops an argument of some interest, in this case with reference to Habermas. It is well known that Foucault always believed the pragmatics of communication and discourse ethics to be a sort of ingenuous utopia. On one side, because of its transcendentalism; on the other, because it postulates the possibility of an ideal speech situation able to free reality from power relations. That is, a reality which has no outside 'tel que les jeux de vérité pourront y circuler sans obstacles, sans contraintes et sans effets coercitifs', Foucault writes. By doing so, he makes a sensible point that is worth repeating to many of the protagonists of the contemporary philosophical-analytical and normative mainstream (see Foucault 1982b/2001: 1099; Foucault 1984f/2001: 1546). And yet, in those pages Foucault's reference to Habermas plays out as a pretext for that which Foucault conjures as a 'self-criticism'. Habermas identifies three fundamental typologies of 'technique', he says. Techniques that are instrumental in the production, manipulation and transformation of things; techniques that enable to utilize systems of signs; techniques whereby one can determine the conduct of individuals, impose objectives on them, or orientate their actions in conformity with specific ends. Therefore, there are production techniques, signification or communication techniques, and techniques of domination. Foucault never makes it explicit, but here it is evident that Habermas, as far as this aspect is concerned, is interpreted as thoroughly internal to the contradictions of the Frankfurt School. It is a reason that perverts its own emancipative sign and turns into an empty apparatus of control and manipulation. But this is not the matter I am concerned with here. What I am concerned with is the game of mirrors on which Foucault builds and articulates his self-criticism. The techniques that Habermas speaks of are the disciplinary techniques with which the subject has been historically produced; they are the representative techniques that trapped him in the cage of knowledges.

In what ways did Foucault actually think and organize his exit from the philosophy of the subject? First, in *Les mots et les choses* (1966), through the construction of the subject as a speaking, living or working being, in what Foucault had conceived as an archaeology of human sciences. Second, and especially, in *Surveiller et punir* (1975), he studies the institutions and technologies for the subjection of human beings as the target of knowledges and powers that design nursery schools, prisons, barracks. What triggers Foucault's self-criticism is the somewhat unreflective, or not yet clear, use of the term "technique". In a way that resonates with the use made by the members of the Frankfurt School, this term tends to be employed as the expression of a project or an apparatus of domination. 'Ce dont je me suis rendu compte peu à peu', says Foucault (1981b/2001: 989–990) :

> 'c'est qu'il existe dans toutes les sociétés un autre type de techniques: celles qui permettent à des individus d'effectuer, par eux-mêmes, un certain nombre d'opérations sur leur corps, leur âme, leur pensées, leurs conduites, et ce de manière à produire en eux une transformation, une modification [. . .]. Appelons ces techniques les techniques de soi.

The topic of the technologies of the self is introduced as the outcome of a thorough reorientation of Foucault's research. I believe it denotes a radical problematization of its basic structure. It allows disambiguating the reference to the idea of rationality that orients the deployment of strategies and technologies of power. It also re-articulates the latter around the notion of government. If it is true that the 1976 and 1977–78 lectures at the Collège de France can be viewed as "anti-Hobbes",[7] it is also true that Foucault's idea of governmentality hinges on a dynamic of individuation that de-multiplies, fragments, superimposes or pits against each other specific and differentiated forms of rationality. At least, that which expresses the function of government (intended to totalize the effects of its own action) and that which is meant to express distinct interest and needs – as an absolute limit to the former – which subjectivate individual positions (Foucault 1981b/2001).

This complicates the bifurcated scheme of reason that Habermas actually takes from the Kantian tradition: on one side, a technical reason; on the other, an ethical-practical one (see Habermas 1971). What is at stake, for Foucault, is the incessant ramification (he calls it 'embranchement foisonnant') of reason, not its technical perversion.[8] For he tends to dissolve on the surface of everydayness and on a pure disenchantment relations and relationships, "games of power" and "games of truth" which have no highest points or radical turning points. Those who work on the genealogy of the subject[9] come across a use of "technique" that does not coincide with the structure or the deployment of domination and does not envision freedom as an unchallenged exteriority vis-à-vis. A "technique" where one can make use of conventions, rules and styles to constitute the subject by employing those conventions, rules and styles in a creative way – what others could ingenuously identify with the forms of "power".

There is more. Simply recognizing that power is a regularity, an instance of pure circulation that permeates the whole field of social relations,[10] prevents thinking of the subject as other than a formation – a fold, not an interiority – of that very "raison". Neither a fundamental establishment nor an axiological connotation pertain to the latter. It proliferates as a structure of allocation that is internal to the games of veridiction and the games of power.

> Je pense qu'il y a une autocréation de la raison et c'est pourquoi ce que j'ai essayé d'analyser, ce sont des formes de rationalité: différentes instaurations, différentes créations, différentes modifications par lesquelles des rationalités s'engendrent les unes les autres, sans que pour autant on puisse assigner un moment où la raison aurait perdu son projet fondamental, ni même assigner où on serait passé de la rationalité à l'irrationalitè.
>
> (Foucault 1983b/2001: 1260)

Therefore, what moves Foucault's geological project is an integral historicization of reason and the subject, a map of the unreflective and folded junctures that trigger the series – processes of subjectivation and subjections, isolation of "objects" within the field of knowledges, strategic lines of rationalization, practices that the historical analysis re-presents as "positivity".

Speaking of governmentality not only means bringing to light that the subject is constituted by – and is not the constitutive foundation for – the relations that encompass him. It also, and above all, means laying emphasis on the processes of subjectivation and continuous transformations that power is confronted with when it is at work, as well as the processes that limit, modify, modulate, relaunch or reinvest it.

Not only does this job of "événementialisation" have the effect of disrupting the borders between philosophy and history. It also integrally dismisses and debunks all perspectives that claim to defend "reason" by recovering the bifurcation that perverts reason into technique. The theoretical reflection of this job affects both the disciplines of philosophy (which are taken out of the self-referentiality of their own archive and are dropped in the low territories of the concrete organization of knowledges and "programmes") and the historians' history (one made up of continuities, linear causalities, invariants, universals).

For Foucault, "evenemenzializing" means finding beneath the transparent surface of evidence the points of connection, the footholds, the impediments, the relations of force and the strategies that gave shape to things that at one point have begun to be emphasized as universal and necessary (Foucault 1980b/2001: 842). And this not only means placing history back within the possibles that history itself has selected, but also retrieving all the virtualities that have not been actualized into possibles. This occurs in the framework of an integral historicization of reason within the system of practices that singularized it and made it plural. Not only, then, is there no process of rationalization in itself as the lynchpin of Western history (and this is, it is worth recalling, one of the stakes in Foucault's polemic against Weber). More importantly, there is no criterion of rationality based on which one can assess the success or failure of a given praxis that tries to conform with its alleged premises (Foucault 1980b/2001: 845–847).

Without a doubt, Foucault cannot be charged with "irrationalism" on account of his integral historicization of reason. On the contrary, as noted by Paul Veyne in what I believe to be one of his most important essays, Foucault openly enters a field exclusively circumscribed by positivity. History is not comprised of universals, let alone natural objects. Objects are related to practices that "objectivate" them and are to be studied at the level of the discursive regularities that organize the field of enunciation. What we "see" in history is discourses on sexuality, on the subject of punishment, on language, on mental illness, as far as Foucault's investigations are concerned; but this also applies to other signifiers that some authors deem to be transhistorical, such as the state, society, power. What Foucault calls 'discourse' is not the thin contact area between a thing and language, 'the intrication of a lexicon and an experience', as he writes. Instead, it is the regime of formation of objects – their trim, working phases, modes of government (Foucault 2002b: 48–49). He wants to 'de-presentify' things, to take objects out of their immediate completeness and to refer them, by way of a process of rarefaction, to the system of conditions that oversees their coming into sight. This does not imply neglecting the 'pre-discursive'. Yet – and this might be perceived as paradoxical – it implies placing it in a thoroughly material universe, one that is composed of virtualities that still lack a face or a "name", and forces that have not yet been actualized. Each practice depends on all the others and on their transformations. All is historical and all depends on all – a philosophy of relations, not of objectuality, therefore. And in this sort of act-like materiality,[11] nothing is inert and nothing is inexplicable. The world is not the reverse side of consciousness, what the latter has to master, but, quite the opposite, what determines it.[12]

I retrieved the notion of the 'prediscursive' in *The Archaeology of Knowledge*. What did Foucault refer to? The integral historicization he pursues is so intense that it jeopardizes the separation between 'philosophy' and 'history', given that reason speaks from within discourses that the philosopher usually ignores, dusty and spurious archives, reserved to professional historians, where the 'mole-like perspective' cannot make them speak on its own.[13] Yet, such an integral historicization does not obviously intend to abolish reality. It is worth recalling now, once the tiring debate on "new realism" has risen. The fact that genitals exist does not imply that sexuality is not constructed as a discursive effect. The inexistence of natural objects does not get one to downplay data, things, thresholds to which a discourse refers as supports for practices. What matters is that the existence of the prediscursive does not entail the existence of a teleological target to assess the proximity or the "value" of a discourse. Truth undergoes transformation along with practices, as well as the games of veridiction around which practices revolve. There is a radical discontinuity that is also an unceasing transformation/ramification of rationality and the dispositifs that organize, ignite and relocate discourses.

The human being is a sexuated body and a cognitive-linguistic attitude. Whether he is addressed as a subject of law, a sick, a lunatic, a lump of desires, as governed or as subject depends on the system of rules that traces and resignifies him within the discourse. The historical discourse is amenable to radical variations due to law, medicine, psychiatry, psychoanalysis and politics. This is what makes the field of enunciations not a surface, but a volume (Foucault 2002b: 42). It is determined by the thickness of discursive practices, by the systems that instantiate enunciations as events and things. And by their positivity.

Therefore, there is nothing outside the discourse. Nothing precedes it and nothing ensues it. If anything remains invisible, it is only because the conditions that make it visible have not yet obtained. In other words, the rules that govern its emergence as a singularity or an archaeological layer have not yet been isolated. Foucault's fundamental principle is that all is always integrally said – in every epoch, in every series – because every enunciation is readable or speakable only in relation to that which makes it so, and in this way also constitutes speakers and addressees as its own internal variables (Deleuze 1986: 60–61). Needless to say, this changes radically the definition of truth. In every moment the world is what it is: objects and practices are not surrounded by a further truth on which one can cast light, nor are there, which respect to them, messages that can be retrieved (Veyne 2002: 422). History takes over from philosophy, and this history allows no way back. 'L'histoire nous protège de l'historicisme', Foucault could say, and in particular, 'd'un historicisme qui invoque le passé pour résoudre les problèmes du présent' (Foucault 1982b/2001: 1099). The variation of truth in the interplay of practices is just as historical: every figure that emerges out of the process of rarefaction whereby enunciations, organized in discourses and practices, are made visible is no "truer" than another. There is no criterion of hierarchization or principle of validation. And yet, this is not nihilistic relativism. For there is no permanent object – an identical – as the referent of variable propositions in which truth gets dissolved. For example, politics is not a permanent "substance" with reference to which two thousand years of political theory align as it is treated in a diversified, opposed and often contradictory way; nor are the "objects" around which the field of enunciation organizes (the individual, the market, society, and so on).

Each truth is the truth of a game of veridiction (which is always a game of power) that the analysis "evenementialises" in its singularity. 'On peut aborder ces jeux de pouvoir par bien des angles', says Foucault.

> Plutôt que d'étudier le grand jeu de l'État avec les citoyens au avec les autres États, j'ai préféré [. . .] m'intéresser à des jeux de pouvoir beaucoup plus limités, beaucoup plus humbles et qui n'ont pas dans la philosophie le statut noble, reconnu qu'ont les grands problèmes: jeux de pouvoir autour de la médicine, autour de la maladie, autour du corps malade, jeux de pouvoir autour de la pénalité et de la prison.
>
> (Foucault 1978b/2001: 542)

Is this all about a mere 'preference' – curiosity, case, personal obsession? Or, rather, is it about the relevance of what is at stake in the daily fabric – no relevance is assigned to the state of exception, in Foucault – of an extra-juridical exercise of power that constantly re-describes the status of life and death, of crime and law, and, through them and beyond them, even 'le statut de la raison et de la non raison' (Foucault 1978b/2001: 542)?

Let's go back to the text I started with. What happens in that section of modern philosophy that is inaugurated by Kant and culminates in the Frankfurt School's critical philosophy passing through Nietzsche and Weber – one that Foucault takes to be the horizon in which his own research is inscribed? Kant's *Was ist Aufklärung?* marks a fundamental break in the archive of philosophy. At the very moment in which reason gets out of the system of tutelage that imprisons and constricts it and gains autonomy, it can hardly get away with questioning – according to Foucault – the value that is to be assigned to the penetration of the domain of rationality into the domains of science, technique and politics. Reason has to question its own movement, then, at the very moment in which it emerges from its self-imposed nonage; and also the "sense" (simple provenance, direction, tendency) of its own history. The task of philosophy becomes an ethics – elsewhere Foucault speaks of modernity and the philosophical ethos that it entails as a specific 'attitude' whereby the practice of thinking ties up with an 'ascétisme indispensable' (and here again he uses another term that is certainly not neutral when it comes to Weber – Foucault 1984b/2001: 1389). Philosophy has to disseminate 'une question inquiète' within the domain of reason (Foucault 1983b/2001: 1257).

The disquietude I just mentioned is coupled with a critical function. Not the critique that proceeds from a transcendental of reason, but the critique that radically historicizes the reticular process whereby its domain expands and that questions its own status and forms. The philosophical ethos of modernity, reactivated by Nietzsche and Weber as well as critical theory, and that Foucault embraces as the engine of his own research, is to be understood as a 'permanent critique of our historicity' ('critique permanente de notre être historique') (Foucault 1984b/2001: 1390). A permanent critique that does not assume any point of relevance in the present – in no present, given that each day is "a day like any other", since there is no speculative Good Friday. Rather this critique exalts the decentring movement that places "reason" in the flux of practices within the moving kaleidoscope of the forms and discourses that are organized as games of truth and games of power. As reason becomes subjectivation,[14] it only turns out to be possible as an ethics, an 'asceticism'. Like a torsion, the use of history and the discursive conventions that traverse it also dissolves the 'réel' of rationality, its comeback as a transcendental or as a 'value' that triggers and reproduces critique. One has to locate oneself in the immanence of the world and its 'reasons' to 'accepter', Foucault writes, 'cette sorte de spirale, cette sorte de porte tournante de la rationalité, qui nous renvoie à sa nécessité, à ce qu'elle a d'indispensable, et en même temps aux dangers qu'elle contient' (Foucault 1982b/2001: 1098).

2. But what sort of "history" of rationality is it when Foucault speaks of madness, penalty, sexuality, pastoral power, governmentality or hermeneutics of the subject? What happens to the "truth" of representation, of the concepts employed, of the account of contexts and the visits to the archives that are mobilized? Does it make sense to criticize Foucault's genealogical project on the part of historians once its radical immanentization of truth and its reproduction in situated practices and knowledges have been lambasted by philosophers who regard it as an inflation or dissipation of truth, as the latter gets dispersed on the broad surface of history? Or is it the case that both criticisms in reality are off the mark and what is at stake is something else? 'Je ne suis pas véritablement un historien', Foucault declared more than once, 'd'une certaine manière, je sais très bien que ce que je dis n'est pas vrai'. I am not saying the truth, says Foucault, not because there is no truth,[15] but because drawing a genealogy can scarcely be compared to the 'objectivism' conjured up by the most ingenuous among historians.[16] What I practise is a 'fiction historique' (Foucault 1978d/2001: 859), he writes. A *fiction*, then.

We should try to pin down what he means. Obviously, Foucault does not want to say that his inquiry has nothing to do with truth; let alone that it is pure forgery. The Latin etymon of fiction only refers to simulation, imitation or forgery in a figurative sense, as it connotes a material creativity in the first place: to give shape, to cast clay or wax, to mould. In the legal lexicon, the *fictio* is, again in a creative sense, the technique by which a concrete fact is subsumed under a disposition that, according to its usual meaning, cannot be applied to it, or else to grant legal personality to an entity or to subjects that lack pre-normative ontological substance.[17] In both cases, a *fictio* denotes a *transformation*, an action whereby something affects something else and modifies it, a shapeless matter that is made instrumental in a project.

It is more than obvious that Foucault's inquiry into madness, the clinic or the prison is not concerned with discovering an underlying truth. Foucault's is a *partial* practice of history. Nothing prevents advancing alternative practices that make use of the same archives in a more complete, pacified, or "professional" way. And yet, this is not the core of the matter. What Foucault's inquiry aims to produce is a shift effect: it is not concerned with the past, but in line with Nietzsche's second *Untimely Meditation*, the future and the actual, vital needs where it is prefigured. That inquiry had an immediate impact on the practices and knowledges, Foucault remarks, as they modified the social perception of the phenomena to which they were applied. If those books have any truth, this truth lies not so much in the light they shed, as in the present that they are able to set in motion: 'Mon espoir est que mes livres prennent leur vérité une fois écrits et non avant' (Foucault 1978d/2001: 859). In other words, what they would do if they claimed to record a hidden fundament-truth, found(er)ed in the dark of the archive. Foucault works with a different notion of truth and a different notion of temporality. Truth does not coincide with a 'vérité-ciel', drawn out of things and projected beyond them as a criterion of fit. It coincides with the 'vérité-foudre', which as a particular streak of light illuminates the production of an event that unites the *future anterior* with the time of philosophy.

On this field, the "disquietude" that I conjured earlier as the sense of critique takes the aspect of an *interference* between past and future that productively short-circuits the relationship between theory and practice (Foucault 1980d/2001: 861)[18] – for sure, critique is the meaning of the intellectual job *sans phrase*, if, like in the lecture Weber gave in Munich, one's initiation to research coincides, for those who are preoccupied with it, with an ethics of radical problematization, along with the capacity to impact and endure 'inconvenient facts' vis-à-vis what one believes to know ('unbequeme Tatsachen anerkennen zu lehren') (Weber 1919/2002: 499). The truth of a story resides in the effects it produces, not in what it records, unearths or brings to the surface. The engine of a historical research is the urgency of the present. Its truth is the power to transform that which it proves able to trigger by evenementializing the whole chain of temporality and by mobilizing not only the past, but also the present and the future. 'J'espère que la vérité de mes livres est dans l'avenir', Foucault writes with reference to *Histoire de la folie, Naissance de la clinique, Surveiller et punir*.

Should we come to the conclusion that history conceived as 'histoire-fiction' does not have anything to do with history? I do not think so. Rather, I think that we are faced with the re-elaboration – maybe not conscious, certainly not declared, probably taken from Aron and Veyne, more than Weber[19] – of a Weberian theme. Paul Veyne was the first to note the proximity between Foucault's schematization of the singularity of historical formations and the notion of ideal-types (Veyne 2008: 57). What Foucault dubs 'discourse' is transported by the tectonic movement of a 'silent' and heterogeneous becoming within which it is the genealogist's decision that frames what emerges as meaningful. Foucault's intentional attempt to minimize this gap by dispersing it in the infinitesimal positivity of the 'petits faits vrais' that challenge the general[20] does not solve the problem of an indispensable constructivism. Such a constructivism is required for one to locate oneself within a belligerent historicity where truth is the stake and the problem is the present – its derivation, the way in which it selects its own actualization, the field of virtualities that cross it. 'Il n'y a pas le réel qu'on rejoindrait à condition de parler de tout ou de certaines choses plus "réelles" que les autres', Foucault writes (Foucault 1980a/2001: 834). This is the premise for *another use* of history.

There are no "universals", I said at the beginning. This means that one has to write stories, while the validity of a discourse or a practice can be isolated only by subsuming the series of 'éléments pertinents' under an index or a scheme: 'un type de rationalité, une manière de penser, un programme, une technique, un ensemble d'efforts rationnels et coordonnés, des objectifs définis et poursuivis [. . .]' that, although they are actual and real things, never coincide with reality as a whole (Foucault 1980a/2001: 834). Moreover, what orientates the selection – the same criterion of *pertinence* employed here – cannot straightforwardly be referred to the immanence of practices or to the rules that govern the formation of discourses. In fact, what decides on the relevance of one story or another and what marks it as a mobile transformative potential is the present. It is the present that modifies the past (because there is no truth to the past), while it is the present that modifies the future (for the latter will not be what it could have been unless in the time that precedes it an intervention is produced that proves able to *alter* the past so as to open the future up to its own possibilities).

History as a *fiction* means representing it while being fully aware of the chasm that exists between representation and truth. What one represents is not *the* truth, while the distinct games of veridiction are affected by power and the ever-present possibility of upturning it. History as a *fiction* means selecting the elements and their pertinence; forming, by drawing from them, the concepts that make discourses speak whereas they would rather be silent or marginal;[21] constructing perspectively the derivation map, not the immobile persistence of an origin.

When Max Weber defines the 'ideal type' he does nothing short of this. Or better, though it is unnecessary to recall it, he puts a perspectivism at work that has the same Nietzschean matrix. Knowledge of cultural reality cannot be but a situated one – a knowledge that arises from particular points of view ('eine Erkenntnis unter spezifisch besonderen Gesichtspunkten') (Weber 1904/1922: 181) and isolates individual sequences in the flux of becoming. Here the possibility of an ultimate and 'true' knowledge of reality is disallowed. It is impossible to saturate reality with the system of concepts where the decision on what is relevant 'to us' is continually relocated. 'The stream of immeasurable events flows unendingly towards eternity', Weber (1904/1922: 184) writes, while the 'cultural problems which move men form themselves ever anew and in different colours, and the boundaries of that area in the infinite stream of concrete events which acquires meaning and significance for us, i.e., which becomes an "historical individual", are constantly subject to change' ('was aus jenem stets gleich unendlichen Strome des individuellen Sinn und Bedeutung für uns erhält, "historisches Individuum" wird').

In these pages of Weber's there are three things that I consider as particularly relevant. The first is the anonymous and silent forward movement in whose flux the researcher's subjective decision singles out an 'Umkreis' of meaningfulness. History is based on a detachment, on a selection that emphasizes a series as long as it gives it a meaning. The second thing is the limit. A 'systematisierende Fixierung' of questions as well as the domains of the sciences of culture is unattainable. For the fields that they mark off are characterized by a radical heterogeneity of "points of view" that identify a meaning, an intentional action. The third thing is that the subjective "points of view" necessary to the isolation of significant sequences denote a second form of infinity, because their possibility moves indefinitely forward. The 'points of departure of the cultural sciences remain changeable throughout the limitless future [die Ausgangspunkte der Kulturwissenschaft bleiben damit wandelbar in die grenzenlose Zukunft]', Weber writes, 'as long as a Chinese ossification of intellectual life does not render mankind incapable of setting new questions to the eternally inexhaustible flow of life' ('solange nicht chinesische Erstarrung des Geisteslebens die Menschen entwöhnt, neue Fragen an das immer gleich unerschöpfliche Leben zu stellen') (Weber 1904/1922: 184).

Endlessness of life, endlessness of problematization. This overlap is a crucial passage for Weber. It is ignited by a futurist perspective that retrospectively sets in motion the overall flux of becoming and radically un-determines the chains of historical causality. Not only is the subjective position – a 'feeling', a 'particular ought-to', a 'will' – necessary to construct the historical object by elaborating it as particularity – that is, as a meaningful 'portion of reality' ('betreffender Ausschnitt aus der Wirklichkeit') (cfr. Weber 1905a/1922: 253) both for the researcher and for the actors involved. In addition, any causal nexus one can infer between actions and reactions, albeit referred to objective connections, equally depends on a selection or a framing operated with respect to the act-like eternity of possibles. To understand real causal connections, 'we construct the unreal' ('um die wirkliche Kausalzusammenhänge zu durchschauen, konstruieren wir unwirkliche') Weber 1905b/1922: 287.

I think this is a crucial point. What does Weber mean by this? History is the realm of possibles. Not only because the indeterminacy of the future acts back on the past and liberates it from the enchantment of necessity (one to which the ingenuous historical consciousness is subjected), but also because an objective and deterministic representation of events, like those that characterize the domain of the sciences of the spirit, can hardly be attained. The action selects and actualizes possibilities. As the future is "open", so is the past – and continues to be open on account of the untameable complexity of causes that interact in every distinct historical "fact", as far as it involves a doing, the web of random conditions that include it, the unfathomable series of effects that keep producing it. Two consequences ensue. The first is the *un-realization* of the historical process.[22] Each sequence is internally started by decisions, contingencies, cases. They select the chances and to a certain extent orient the selection of opportunities. Weber's decisionism is no less vigorous than Foucault's. The very same decisionism that touches the last pages of the Munich lecture on 'Politics as a Vocation'.

It inscribes one's action in the 'dennoch!' of an ethics of perseverance and limit, one that gives shape to the possible precisely because it is staunchly headed towards the impossible.[23] History turns out to be completely evenementialized. The second consequence is that the concatenations that the historian singles out and constructs as causal sequences are the result of the selection of distinct series, 'regardless of one or various elements of "reality" that actually exist'. Moreover, these very series can be imputed to efficient causes only on the basis of an implicit assessment of 'irrelevance' that rules out the vast infinity of causal factors necessarily implied in every moment of becoming and in every stage of the historical process. Weber employs a judicial metaphor[24] to account for the mechanism by which the sciences of culture elicit the connections that are granted intelligibility from the pure multiplicity of relation. Although they highlight objective sequences, the general frameworks that subsume them under their selection and construct them by irrealizing them are *fictiones*, 'Phantasiebildern'.[25]

Contrary to what Foucault seems to believe, an ideal-type does not define an essence.[26] Quite the reverse, it has the meaning of a pure ideal limit-concept ('eines reinen idealen Grenzbegriffes', says Weber) that, as such, never qualifies a historical reality. It does not neutralize the complexities and contingencies through which history unfolds. Rather, it operates as a technique that subsumes reality as an example (*Exemplar*) (Weber 1904/1922: 195). Weber's insisting on a legal lexicon is telling: the ideal-type as a legal category ('fattispecie'), the technicality of the *fictio* as that which allows for an accommodation (an 'Einordnung') of the 'Wirklichkeit' to a casuistics. What the ideal-types contribute to constructing – as they are obliged by the 'discursive nature of our knowledge' – is a conceptual short-hand ('Begriffsstenographie') (Weber 1904/1922: 195). It serves to put to work difference in order to specify the structures of action in a more and more individual and particularized way. Therefore, far from isolating 'essences' – as Foucault appears to believe, at least initially – it serves to genetically construct concepts against which one can measure the proliferation of the multiplicity of the real, the infinitely self-differentiated system of the processes of action.

Weber does not attend to a rarefaction but to a *mismatch*. The ideal-type is not the output of a research, but what makes the latter possible. By using it as a hermeneutic tool, one can gain entry to the actuality of history so as to *identify* (viz., to specify, distinguish, isolate) the structures that go across it, with no intention of ensnaring it in the Procustean bed of developmental schemes, systematizations, universal concepts and legalities. Ideal-typical concepts, as Weber writes, do *not* make visible what already conforms to the general ('Gattungsmäßige'). On the contrary, they foreground the *specific character* of particular social phenomena ('die Eigenart von Kulturerscheinungen scharf zum Bewußtsein zu bringen') (Weber 1904/1922: 202).

What Foucault dislikes, particularly in regard to the history of Western rationalization, is that Weber failed to push this research of particularization to its extreme. Weber only announced it at a methodological level. However, the idea of a *histoire-fiction* arguably comes into light by dint of an "open" problematization that is not too far from, or too at odds with, the background noise coming from Weber's inquiry.

3. How can one walk through the "revolving door" of Western rationality? One should not yield to the temptation of an axiological assessment of the processes that underlie its technical "perversion" or to the sharp bifurcation that separates reason from the rationalization of domination. On this point Foucault is crystal clear. In two distinct contexts he moves away from Habermas and the Frankfurt School. As he points out in the 1982 interview I mentioned above, the 'spiral' of rationality – as the rational winds around the irrational that traverses it, the line that spins around the emptiness that grounds it, the cipher of the aporetic character of rationalization (see Owen 1994; Colliot-Thélène 2009: 181–197; Stimilli 2011) – is something that we have to 'accepter' on account of critique's *philosophical vocation* (Foucault 1982b/2001: 1098). I believe this is key to understanding the later Foucault. The final point I want to argue is that this has to be interpreted in the light of the sharp Weberian tone that inspires it from at least two points of view. The first point concerns the processes of subjectivation.[27] Which is to say, the way in which the issue of the fabrication of the subject forcefully gains centre stage in Foucault's research from the end of the 1970s. The second has to do with Foucault's own ethics of intellectual work, his own style.[28] If it is true that the modern attitude to philosophy, one that begins with Kant and that draws the borders of Foucault's research, consists in a problematization of the present,[29] we still have to grasp the far-reaching relevance of the designation of the epoch that begins with the eighteenth century and that still encompasses us as the 'time of governmentality'.

What does Foucault mean by governmentality? Let me start with his words:

> Par "gouvernementalité", j'entends l'ensemble constitué par les institutions, les procédures, analyses et réflexions, les calculs et les tactiques qui permettent d'exercer cette forme bien spécifique, quoique très complexe, de pouvoir qui a pour cible principal la population, pour forme majeure de savoir l'économie politique, pour instrument technique essentiel les dispositifs de sécurité. Deuxièmement, par "gouvernementalité" j'entends la tendance, la ligne de force qui, dans tout l'Occident, n'a pas cessé de conduire, et depuis fort longtemps, vers la prééminence de ce type de pouvoir qu'on peut appeler le "gouvernement" sur tous les autres: souveraineté, discipline, et qui a amené, d'une part le développement de toute une série d'appareils spécifiques de gouvernement [et d'autre part] le développement de toute une série de savoirs. Enfin, par "gouvernementalité", je crois qu'il faudrait entendre le processus, ou plutôt le résultat du processus par lequel l'État de justice du Moyen Age, devenu aux XVe et au XVIe siècles État administratif, s'est trouvé petit à petit "gouvernementalisé".
>
> (Foucault 2004a: 111–112)[30]

At first sight, Foucault might simply seem to be hinting at another mode of organizing power; or, more simply, at its steady *deconstitutionalization*. By referring to the governmentalization of power, he might primarily aim to foreground a series of processes. In the constitutional history of the West, these processes progressively marginalize the "classic" forms of statehood – those that link the state to sovereignty, representation and constitution – to the advantage of emerging institutions and administrative bodies. The latter are those that materially connect the state to the population as a thick mass of relations which evolve in keeping with an irreducible (and unavailable) randomness. Against the political view that runs from Hobbes to the French Revolution, the state does not create the system of conditions that turns the relations between subjects into abstract legal relations, prefigured in mandatory legal forms. Rather, the state releases its regulative dispositifs into a slippery and opaque environment precisely because it is linked to circuits of valorization that it can neither foresee nor control. The state can gauge its own legitimacy *only after* ascertaining the effects of its own action.

The evolution of contemporary state-forms could then be located within this tendency. And in particular the welfare, insuring, liberal state. For this latter type becomes more and more a technical-executive state as it is endowed with legal, institutional and administrative instruments that de-multiply the impact of its own apparatuses. These instruments make the state flexible, microphysically invasive, able to penetrate all the environments of individual and collective life. They do not repress, but maximize the forces to which they apply. The 'ligne de force' that imposes 'biopolitics' as the comprehensive cipher of economization and governmentalization; or better, the necessary relation that ties the fact of the government to the needs and interests of the population. However, there is more than that. Foucault is more and more concerned with the subject – particularly form the 1970s, when apparently his primary interest is the analytic of power and its forms. In particular, as far as governmentality is concerned, he homes in on the role played by the risky surplus of individual freedom, both at the level of the individual and at the level of the 'social' relations between individuals who interact both with each other and on the market (as the *other side* of the fact of the government).

'J'appelle "gouvernementalité"', Foucault claims in 1982 at the University of Vermont, 'la rencontre entre les techniques de domination exercées sur les autres et les techniques de soi' (Foucault 1982d/2001: 1604). Governmentality signifies the irreducible ellipse of a node where the processes of subjectivation play so relevant a role that they reorient Foucault's overall research – which always made sure to define power not as a thing but as a 'relation'. 'Governmentality' is what he calls the zone of indistinction where the difference between subject and sovereign, between power and subject culminates – insofar as one offers a genealogy of the subject that is not confined to the modern-juridical type of the legal subject. This is an extremely relevant move. In my opinion, it hallmarks the entire phase of the later Foucault. It is true that the subject was always at the centre-stage of his books – as *objectivated* in the knowledges and as subjected to the dispositifs of power. Yet, the processes of subjectivation *exceed* the field of citizenship marked off by the legal knowledge on which the state reached a compromise between its own sovereign competences and the self-limitation of its power, which is subjected to the forms of the legal order. And this is what matters to the genealogist.

A whole series of techniques – those that exceed Habermas' classification and complicate the interpretation of the Western rationalization offered by the Frankfurt School – come into sight as formulas of subjectivation and instruments for weaving 'governed' relations. Those relations cannot be expropriated or recovered, either linearly or integrally, in the panoptic and transparent space of the state. 'Je m'intéresse de plus en plus à l'interaction qui s'opère entre soi et les autres, et aux techniques de domination individuelle, au mode d'action qu'un individu exerce sur lui-même à travers les techniques du soi', Foucault (1982d/2001: 1604) writes in the span of time between the end of the course *L'Herméneutique du sujet* and the beginning of the first of the two courses devoted to *Le Gouvernement de soi et des autres.*

Here I cannot discuss in detail the motives – which as always in Foucault are both intellectual and political – behind this passage, which looks to me as anything but occasional. It favours the further transition from *La volonté de savoir* to *Le courage de la vérité*, Michel Foucault's last course at the Collège de France. Suffice it to say that the theme of the 'techniques of the self', as well as its ambivalence, is introduced as a new reference to Max Weber. Foucault (1982d/2001) writes:

> Max Weber a posé cette question: si l'on veut adopter un comportement rationnel et régler son action en fonction de principes vrais, à quelle part de soi doit-on renoncer? De quel ascétisme se paie la raison? À quel type d'ascétisme doit-on se soumettre?

He goes on to say: 'J'ai, pour ma part, posé la question inverse: comment certains types de savoir sur soi sont-ils devenus le prix à payer pour certaines formes d'interdits? Que doit-on connaître de soi afin d'accepter le renoncement?'.

Weber is then claimed to take issue with the topic of 'Lebens-führung', the conduct, as a matter of a renunciation. Foucault adopts this term and applies it to the definition of the 'government' as 'conduct of conducts'.[31] Unlike Weber, and although he was operating on the reverse side of the Weberian matrix, as is the case with the *histoire fiction*, Foucault focuses on how the subject works on himself to accept a truth that, *only after*, entails a renunciation.

A few preliminary questions have to be clarified. First, for Foucault, the subject is never original. The subject is the product of a reflexive work that the individual does on himself. The research Foucault is carrying out in those years, in particular on the Ancient ethics of sexuality, casts light on this point. There is no Ancient morality of sexuality, if by morality we mean a code of prescriptions, prohibitions, bans. What there is is an 'ars erotica', a practice of oneself within the framework of the *aphrodisia* by which the individual learns to self-govern in his relation with the others and to constitute himself as a subject (free, male, adult) in the ensemble of social and political processes (see Foucault 1984a). Second, as the subject is not original, so is the truth that is given him in the certainty of his own self-censorship – a truth that is given to him only in that particular 'moment cartésien' of philosophy that the course *L'Herméneutique du sujet* circumscribes, deconstructs and evenementializes (Foucault 2001a: 15–17). In this sense, bringing subjectivity into question means reconstructing the system or practices and self-reflection by which the subject governs himself as he takes his own conduct of life as the object of care and interacts creatively with the conventions, resources and 'styles' of the culture to which he belongs. The third, and maybe the most decisive, question concerns this relation of government. The government of the self is what matters in one's relationship with oneself and with the others. It is a form of subjectivity that is not guaranteed by any stability or formal characteristic. It is an initiation that is necessary to the political life where one is governed and in turn governs. It is the kernel of practical philosophy, at least from classic Greece onward, with respect to which the question of the conduct of life is the decisive one.[32] Therefore, the techniques of the self, understood in this broader and more adequate sense, allude to this ethics.

'Hier nicht einfach Lebenstechnik, sondern eine eigentümliche "Ethik" gepredigt wird': this is exactly what Weber (1988: 33) wrote in relation to Protestant ethics.[33] And it is exactly the problem of this ethics that qualifies the issue of 'Lebensführung' as something which has got nothing to do with 'renunciation'. It is an ethos of duty and accomplishment; an asceticism not of renunciation, but of commitment and dedication, where the paradoxical nature of capitalistic rationalism becomes evident as well as 'the host of the contradictions' that inhabits it. 'Der "Rationalismus" ist ein historisches Begriff', Max Weber writes, as he shows the ideal-typical character of a notion that, on the contrary, Foucault fails to understand, as the latter reads it in destinal, historical-philosophical terms ('der eine Welt von Gegensätzen in sich schließt' – Weber 1988: 61). It is true that the Protestant Reformation imposes itself as a discipline, as a 'ästige und ernstgemeinte Reglementierung der Ganzen Lebensführung' that replaces a weak and comfortable religiosity (that is to say, the Roman one) and pervasively penetrates all spheres of public and private life. What moves the Protestant Reformers is a defect in the religious hold on life, not its excess.[34] Nonetheless, we should ask ourselves if, again, here Weber does not help foreground the issue of the 'porte tournante' of rationality which Foucault talks about.

The Protestant ethic knows no guide of conscience. Or at least, not in the form on which Foucault builds his inversion of Weber. There are forms of knowledge of oneself that are necessary for one to accept interdictions and renunciations, as Foucault said above. What does he refer to? I believe he refers to a topic which he deals with in the course devoted to the *Gouvernement des vivants* (1979–80). He returns to this topic elsewhere, in the lectures he gives in the autumn of 1980 at Dartmouth College in New Hampshire (Foucault 2012a; Foucault 2016). What is in question here is the penitential practice and in particular the one that late Ancient Christian texts call 'exomológēsis', the *publicatio sui* that, among others, Tertullian speaks of. The sinner ought to make himself and his guilt public. To put it otherwise, he ought to show himself as a sinner by dramatizing death, as he proved to favour the latter over eternal life. He has to make up for it by giving up his flesh. He shows around in public as the penitent – he wears sackcloth and ashes, his face is emaciated – and confesses his sin. It is in this way that the manifestation of truth becomes preliminary to self-renunciation. Once one is dead to flesh, one abandons oneself to the grace of God. Reconciliation first and foremost requires an episode of dramatic self-revelation. Penitence is a *sacrificial technique* performed through one's obligation to show oneself.

However, there is a further penitential form that Foucault studies as a form of veridiction. A further technique, then. It is the "exagoreusis", what Foucault defines as 'exhaustive verbalization'. It represents the governed form of the examination of conscience. A permanent mobility of the soul – 'polykinetos' and 'aeikinetos', in Cassian's terms – forces one to subject one's thoughts to one's spiritual director (also the unreflective ones, the constant variation of *cogitationes* that cross one's mind and rouses one's conscience) for them to be examined, selected and verified. Cassian draws from the old Stoic and Cynic metaphor of the money-changer who tests the good quality of coins. One has to decipher oneself by telling without hesitation or censure one's thoughts, even the most tacit or hidden, to one's spiritual director. Indeed the spiritual director, in a position of superiority on account of his experience and sanctity, is able to separate the good fantasies from the bad ones. By doing so, he can bring the monk or the penitent back to obedience. Here the price of truth on oneself is the fullness renunciation to one's will (Foucault 2012b: 87).

This does not happen within Protestantism. Its main characteristic, according to Weber, is that no 'Entlastung', *unburdening*, is available. 'Exagoreusis' and the examination of the soul are not techniques that infiltrate the context of the Reform. 'Whereas the keeping of a diary in Catholicism served to insure the completeness of the believer's confession or to offer to the 'directeur de l'âme', Weber (1988: 123) writes, 'the documents necessary for authoritarian guidance after the (mostly female) faithful, the Reformed Christian *himself*, with the help of these diaries, "felt his own" pulse' ('Aber während es im Katholizismus dem Zweck der Vollständigkeit der Beichte diente oder dem "directeur de l'âme" die Unterlage zu seiner autoritären Leitung des Christen bzw. (meist) der Christin bot, "fühlte sich" der reformierte Christ mit seiner Hilfe selbst "den Puls" '). A knowledge, the truth of oneself, is the price to pay for the renunciation to oneself which is implied in the absolute obedience that the Christian of the late Antiquity owes his director of conscience. So far, Foucault sides with Weber. But what Foucault seems not to realize is that the feeling of one's own pulse, whereby the reformed Christian constructs his own hermeneutics of the self, does not imply any mediation on the part of an external authority. The 'Lebensführung' of the Protestant is a form of asceticism that is internal to the world. A rational asceticism that enables the man to maintain his 'constant motives' ('konstante Motive') and to set them against 'affections'. In this way, he forms for himself a personality 'in the formal and psychological sense of the word' ('in formal-psychologischen Sinne des Worts) (Weber 1988: 117). The Protestant 'Lebensführung' coincides with a process of subjectivation that is performed as a counter-conduct against the pastoral power.

I believe this is an important passage. When Foucault raises the question of his inversion of Weber – 'j'ai pour ma part posé la question inverse', he writes, it is worth recalling – it is as if he set himself up to work on the trail of different options opened by Weber's sociology of religion. On the one hand, he seizes on the intuition of a capitalist relocation of authority of religion into the system of the factory as the notion of discipline becomes more rigid and technical;[35] on the other hand, he goes down the two roads opened by the issue of 'Lebensführung' in relation to the genealogy of the subject and to the technologies of the self. One concerns obedience, and therefore the governed subject; the other has to do with the forms of worldly asceticism as practices of veridiction and constitution of the self.

A few pages above I noted that Weber views the process of rationalization as replete with contradictions and paradoxes. It is clear that his problem – which after all is a problem that many of us face – concerns Western capitalism and its genesis. It concerns the 'light cloak' that ended up becoming the 'iron cage' that keeps us captive. The destiny that Weber introduces at this level has more to do with chance, one of those historical turns that lead history to randomness, than with a philosophy of history. Rationalization contains a mismatch, an emptiness. It is caused by the irrational[36] and gets valorized by functionalizing paradoxical heterogenesis of ends. 'The paradox of all rational asceticism', Weber writes, is that

> rational asceticism itself has created the very wealth it rejected ('daß sie den Reichtum den sie ablehnte, selbst schuf'). Operating in the world of the virtuous Puritan, with his methodical conduct being inspired by duty, is the way in which the contradiction is overcome – one that the monk could not solve, that is, the fact that his contemplative choice of poverty and obedience turned into the edification of monasteries as centres of enterprise and as fundamental cells for the organization of the 'rational economy'.
>
> (Weber 1986: 544)

Asceticism is definitely sent back to the world.

When Foucault, especially in the course *L'Herméneutique du sujet*, refers to the Stoic 'askēsis' as a practice of veridiction[37] he has already reoriented his analysis from the technologies of the self that are instrumental in the definition of a regime of obedience (the juridico-confessional practices of *publicatio sui* and of 'exagóreusis' of Christian monasticism) to the medical-therapeutic lexicon of the Weberian 'feeling his own pulse'. The latter is a worldly 'askēsis': spiritual exercises (meditation, writings, memory exercises) serve as practices that constantly allow one to verify one's own degree of self-mastery and self-government. These constitute the subject by moving his self-reflection away from self-consciousness. It is basically for this reason that Weber quotes Goethe, when the latter treats the old practice of 'askēsis' as something that survives as a technique of subjectivation. Accordingly, the issue of life as a 'Kunstwerk' becomes much more than an ingenuous aesthetics: 'How can a man come to know himself? Never by thinking, but by doing. Try to do your duty, and you will know at once what you are worth', Goethe writes. And he adds: 'But what is your duty? The claims of the day'.[38]

The goal of Puritan asceticism is not one's renunciation to oneself, but an aware, clear, clean conduct of life ('ein waches bewußtes helles Leben führen zu können') (Weber 1988: 117). In other words, one's relating to oneself as well as one's own daily tasks with the intention of continuously testing oneself, thereby testing one's ability of self-government, and therefore of being elected.

Asceticism concerns an ethics of action, because the relationship of the individual to oneself is a relationship that has to be continuously performed – a tension that can never be solved and that has to be continuously auscultated, assessed, felt.

These are the characteristics that Foucault emphasizes in the old "askēsis". The 'askēsis' is not a renunciation, but a principle of ***intensification*** of subjectivity. It is the ensemble of practices whereby the individual acquires and absorbs truth by transforming it into a permanent principle of action. It is in this way that truth becomes 'praxis', ethics: 'l'***alêtheia*** devient *ethos*', Foucault (1988/2001: 1616) writes. Such a worldly form of asceticism,[39] to which he refers a significant portion of the genealogy of the subject in the Antiquity, does not mutilate experience; nor does it imply abdications: 'elle ne réduit pas: elle équipe, elle dote'. It is on a par with one's preparation for life and the events that compose it (Foucault 2001a: 307).

This is the constitutive tension that Foucault's *histoire-fiction* of Antiquity is concerned with. A history in which what is at stake is not a pacified history of ideas – what some inattentive critics have failed to notice – but the crucial role of practices of subjectivation that are capable of forcing the 'porte tournante' of Western rationalism by detaching the monastic factory of the obedient subject from the Ancient laboratories in which a free government of the self is experimented. Also on this aspect Foucault does not appear to be far from Weber's style. Foucault fully shares – but this is a different matter – the intellectual tension of the truly 'musical' man invoked in *Wissenschaft als Beruf* (Weber 1919/2002: 507): the man, in the time in which he is fated to live, a 'godless time, without prophets', embraces as an everyday duty the courage of truth of the *parrhesiast*[40] and plays on the Doric chord of the *Laches.*

Notes

1 At least in the eyes of those who are acquainted with his overall oeuvre, which also comprises his many interviews, clarifications and positions, where he accounts, above all in his own eyes, for his own research path.

2 In 1978, maybe after reading Otto Kirchheimer and George Rushe's (1939) book on penality which he built on while writing *Surveiller et punir*, Foucault also starts changing his mind about the Frankfurt School. See Foucault 1980d/2001 (in particular: 891–892).

3 Foucault's opinion on Koyré is pretty explicit: 'Est-ce qu'un sujet de type phénoménologique, transhistorique, est capable de rendre compte de l'historicité de la raison?'. See Foucault 1983b/2001: 1255. On this issue see Paltrinieri 2012.

4 On this issue, see Fabiani 2004. More in general, Dean 1994. Much less useful, at least in this perspective, Szakolczai 1998.

5 A history which neither allows external positions nor acknowledges transcendentals and drags truth into the fragmentation and the antagonisms of this world. See Foucault 1976b/2001: 112. Nicely on this point, see Balibar 1989.

6 'J'ai essayé de sortir de la philosophie du sujet en faisant la généalogie du sujet moderne, que j'aborde comme une réalité historique et culturelle; c'est à dire comme quelque chose susceptible de se transformer, ce qui, bien entendu, est important du point de vue politique', Foucault (1981b/2001: 989) avers in those years to emphasize the ethical and political aspect of a philosophical position-taking against structuralism and phenomenology.

7 In effect these lectures detach once and for all the analysis of the political from the long shadow of the state and retrieve the idea of Christian pastoral power as the scheme of an obligation that pivots not on the sheer imposition of a regime of subjection and subjectivation, but – in terms that are not that far from Weber's – on the acquisition of obedience on the part of free agents, who are to be governed and guided based on a sort of matrix unavailability. See Foucault 1997 and Foucault 2004. Works that emphasize this passage are Karsenti 2005 and Büttgen 2007. The qualification of Foucault's genealogy of power as 'un contre-Hobbes' is proposed in Bert 2006. More in general, see Leblanc 2005.

8 Foucault 1983b/2001: 1259. See also, Foucault 1978b/2001, in particular pp. 540–542.

9 For Foucault (1982b/2001: 1099), this is the primer of a research that from the very beginning intends to free itself through history, but also to protect itself from historicism with history.

10 'Le pouvoir, ça, n'existe pas'. Foucault (1977c/2001: 302) puts it in more radical terms a few years before, 'le pouvoir c'est en réalité des relations un faisceau plus ou moins organisé, plus ou moins pyramidalisé, plus ou moins coordonné, de relations'.

11 One might recall Duns Scoto, *De rerum principio*, 9, VII: 'materia est in actu, sed nullius est actus'.

12 Cf. Veyne 2002: 415. Moreover, it is also worth recalling Revel 1975, as a sign of growing openness to Foucault on the part of historians.

13 As a consequence, 'la philosophie en tant qu'activité autonome a disparu'. Foucault was perfectly aware of this as early as the beginning of the 1970s. See Foucault 1970/2001.

14 A subjectivation that concerns the critical function, if it is true, as Foucault writes, that knowledge is not designed to understand, but to take a position towards a typology of discourses and programmes that one can hardly make visible from a bird's-eye view.

15 In one of the last interviews, he evoked, and hence reclaimed, his philosophical 'respect' for truth.

16 I do not think it necessary to point out the Nietzschean structure of Foucault's reflection: 'pure objectivity' only suits 'a race of eunuchs' (see Nietzsche 1954: II, 5; on this topic, see Berni and Fadini 2010).

17 For a history of the 'fictio iuris' see Todescan 1979 and above all Thomas 2011.

18 On this topic see the excellent Artières and Potte-Bonneville 2007.

19 Cf. Aron 1996 (on Weber: 497–574). See also Aron 1938. P. Veyne 1971, esp. 191–193.

20 'La poussière défiant le nuage': there is no real as a totality to record nor any Author as the responsible for its transcendentalization (Foucault 1980/2001).

21 After all, what are "governmentality", "biopower", "discipline", the "technique of the self" if not interpretative schemes applied to the sources to subsume texts, programmes, practices under their jurisdiction?

22 This is nicely illustrated – and it is highly unlikely that Foucault did not read these pages – Aron 1996: 516–518. Here Aron analyses Weber's theory of causation.

23 'Nur wer sicher ist, daß er daran nicht zerbricht, wenn die Welt, von seinem Standpunkt gesehen, zu dumm oder zu gemein ist für das, was er ihr bieten will, daß er all dem gegenüber: "dennoch!", zu sagen vermag, nur der hat den "Beruf" zur Politik' (Weber 1919/2002: 450). On the constitutive tie, in the sense clarified here, between epistemology and politics, see Veyne 1971: 76.

24 'Wie für die juristische', causal imputation in history is possible only insofar as one leaves out a good deal of reality: 'ergibt sich die Ausscheidung einer Unendlichkeit von Bestandteilen des wirklichen Hergangs als "kausal irrilevant"', he writes. Weber 1905b/1922: 273.

25 Weber 1905b/1922: 275.
26 Weber (1904/1922: 195) makes it very clear: 'Nichts aber ist allerdings gefährlicher, als die naturalistischen Vorurteilen entstammende, Vermischung von Theorie und Geschichte, sei es in der Form, daß man glaubt, in jenen theoretischen Begriffsbildern den "eigentlichen" Gehalt, das "Wesen" der geschichtlichen Wirklichkeit fixiert zu haben, oder daß man sie als ein Prokrustesbett benutz, in welches die Geschichte hineingezwängt werden soll'.
27 The issue is examined in Van Krieken 1990.
28 A style that by no means coincides with an "aesthetics", at least as it is understood, in Rorty's wake, in Gane 2002, esp. 98 ff.
29 Or rather, in bringing into question the difference that particularizes it with respect to the past and in freeing the ensemble of possibles that traverse it by projecting them as probes into a future freed from any teleology.
30 On the relevance of Max Weber on the topics of the course, see Gordon 1987: 293–316.
31 The lexicon of government is a lexicon of orientation and navigation, which cannot be reduced to the register of subjection. In fact, the government is always faced with the subjectivity of the governed, the latter's freedom being a centrifugal, unpredictable excess. On this, see Duso 1999: 55–85; Rigotti 1989 (on the metaphor of 'gubernatio rei publicae': 41-ff.).
32 See the excellent Pasquino 1985: 39–54.
33 On the problem of a décalage between 'technique of the self' and ethics, and thus between Foucault and Weber, see Essbach 1997: 2.
34 'Nicht ein Zuviel, sondern ein Zuwenig von kirchlich-religiöser Beherrschung des Lebens war es ja, was gerade diejenigen Reformatoren, welche in den ökonomisch entwickeltsten Ländern erstanden, zu tadeln fanden' (Weber 1988: 20).
35 On this, see O'Neill 1986: 42–60.
36 And what is more irrational than religion, ethics, a 'Bewhärung' of the otherworldly grace that triggers far-reaching processes of accumulation?
37 'L'askēsis n'est pas une manière de soumettre le sujet à la loi; l'ascèse est une manière de lier le sujet à la vérité' (Foucault 2001: 303).
38 J.W. Goethe, Maximen und Reflexionen, 30: 'Wie kann man sich selbst kennen lernen? Durch Betrachten niemals, wohl aber durch Handeln. Versuche, deine Pflicht zu tun, und du weißt gleich, was an dir ist'; 31: 'Was aber ist deine Pflicht? Die Forderung des Tages' (see Weber 1919/2002: 485). On Goethe and the tradition of spiritual exercises, see Hadot 2008.
39 Marcus Aurelius (*Ta eis eauton*, VII, 61) calls it 'hē biotikē'.
40 For an interpretation that glues the issue of *parrhēsia* with Foucault's preceding "archaeological" work by emphasizing Kant, see Revel 2013.

6 The courage of truth

Parrhēsia and critique

> As gold the Lydian touch-stone tries,
> So man-the virtuous, valiant, wise
> Must to all-powerful Truth submit
> His virtue, valour, and his wit.
>
> Bacchylides

That of *parrhēsia* is a complex notion. It is a term that has a long history that extends from Antiquity and early Christianity. *Parrhēsia* undergoes an unceasing process of re-semantization as it crosses different disciplines (philosophy, rhetoric, theology, for example) and historical periods. Because of the complexity of its semantic nature, Foucault (2008a: 45) defines *parrhēsia* as a 'spider-notion'.[1] In this chapter I want to give an account of how Foucault uses this notion and to explain why he attributes so much importance to it in his interpretation of Ancient and late-Ancient thought. Despite what the literature has maintained until recently, the interpretation provided by the Greeks was neither occasional nor unpolitical. Rather it inaugurates Foucault's lectures at Collège de France as it acquires importance on account of the light it casts on Foucault's whole analytic of power.[2] Although extremely significant, as I will try to show, seldom does the term *parrhēsia* appear in the conferences, interviews and the ensemble of writings that are now collected in *Dits et écrits*. Foucault devoted much attention to it in the cycle of lectures held at Berkeley in 1983 and in the courses he taught at the Collège de France between 1981 and 1984, the year of his death.

This final chapter does not simply discuss the way in which Foucault uses or puts at work the term *parrhēsia* within the scope of an interpretation of Ancient authors. Instead, it advances an interpretive hypothesis relating to the later Foucault. This can be summarized as follows: the deeper Foucault cuts into the meaning of critique (and hence what philosophy is) and the more intensely his analytic of power dwells on the theme of governmentality, the more important the term *parrhēsia* becomes. On the one hand, *parrhēsia* is a figure of philosophy and of critique when they are thought of outside the constitutive scheme theory/practice; on the other hand, *parrhēsia* is a central figure of the 'intransitivity of freedom'[3] that materializes the processes of political subjectivation in the ellipse that defines the fact of the government as an irreducible confrontation between the governing and the governed. By seizing upon an insight that dates back to the half of the 1970s, the later Foucault rejects both the idea of the Political and the foundational logic of Political Theology that at the time were making inroads into the debate: politics passes somewhere else. The modern state is interpreted as an organizational solution for politics that met with success but is outdated.

This chapter is divided in three parts. The first delves into the notion of critique in Foucault's work. The second offers an analysis of the fundamental threads of Foucault's interpretation of *parrhēsia* in the course he teaches at the Collège de France. The third deals with the relocation of *parrhēsia* in the scheme of governmentality and focuses on the '*parrhēsia* of the governed' of which Foucault speaks here and there.[4]

1. I am setting forth two hypotheses about which I have no conclusive answers. First, from the second half of the 1970s and in the years in which Foucault teaches at the Collège de France, he engages more and more with Max Weber. As I illustrated in Chapter 5, Weber's reading of Protestantism and the *Lebensführung* is key to the definition of the issue of anti-pastoral resistance. But the lecturers on the ethics of intellectual work and on politics as a vocation are key to Foucault's dealing (even personally) with the 'courage of truth'. For the latter is also a situated position-taking in which one's intellectual work is put to the test of reality as one takes responsibility for (to wit, the risk of) one's own work. I will return to this topic while talking about Plato. The second hypothesis concerns his relation to Kant, on which I would like to expand a bit. As is well known, between 1978 and 1984, Foucault multiplies his references to Kant (see Chapter 2). He does so not in the terms of *Les mots et les choses* (Foucault 2015) or the complementary claim that he elaborated with reference to *Anthropology from a Pragmatic Point of View* (Foucault 2008b). Rather, he takes issue with the notion of critique. And in an article signed with the pen name Maurice Florence that appeared in *Dictionnaire des philosophes* edited by Huisman (1984), he owns up to belonging to the Kantian tradition.

Here however I refer to another text, that is, to the lecture he gives on the 27th of May 1978 at the 'Société' titled 'Qu'est-ce-que la critique? (Critique et Aufklärung)' (Foucault 1990).[5] There are various reasons why I find this talk particularly relevant. These are the following.

The first has to do with the relationship between critique and "positivity" (knowledges are "positivity": the historical discourse of philosophy, morality, law, science, politics, and so on). Critique is not called upon to legislate – and I believe this is particularly important to understand Foucault's analysis of the governmentalization of power. Critique does not say what one ought to do. The decisive matter here is not only Foucault's polemic with Sartre about the role of the intellectual (indeed Foucault rejects a view of the intellectual as the spokesperson of the universal and turns it into the figure of the 'specific intellectual', situated in a context-specific confrontation between freedom and power). More importantly, the matter here is the withering away of the last defence of the political-theological lexicon of sovereignty. Critique is not a reasoning that has to provide a clarification of the sort 'therefore, this is what you ought to do'. 'Elle n'a pas à faire la loi de la loi', Foucault says elsewhere in the same year. If critique has a point, it does not restore from a bird's-eye view the subject as 'constituent' with respect to things. Critique cannot but express itself in terms of a challenge, a resistance to what exists: 'Elle doit être un instrument pour ceux qui luttent, résistent et ne veulent plus de ce qui est. Elle doit être utilisée dans des processus de conflits, d'affrontements, d'essais de refus' (Foucault 1980b/2001: 851).

This position is conditional on real processes – a tactical position, one that entails a particular attitude and, above all, a decision, a firm stand. One year later, Foucault will put this into clear words: no power is capable of making utterly impossible the resistance, ***disobedience***, 'soulèvement' by which a minority, a group or a whole people says 'je n'obéis plus' (and it is very significant that he writes this in relation to Poland and its dissidence against the Soviet bloc).

The relation between power and resistance is a matrix, subjectively conveyed by freedom, and it is 'irréductible'.[6] It is within this relation, which does not allow formalizing or juridifying that which Foucault (in opposition to the concept of the political) continues to call *politics*, that the intellectual work is to be rethought – politics is a 'champ d'expérience', a 'jeu politique indexé au dire vrai', which implies a particular relation to oneself and the others for those who are involved in it (Foucault 2008a: 146–147). While 'soulèvement', rebellion, ***withdrawal*** – not the Revolution as the appropriation and re-occupation of the sovereign's place – provide critique with a much steadier anchor pin than the rhetoric of human rights, that of the intellectual cannot but be defined as an *ethics*:

> Ma morale théorique est inverse. Elle est "antistratégique": être respectueux quand une singularité se soulève, intransigeant dès que le pouvoir enfreint l'universel. Choix simple, ouvrage malaisé: car il faut tout à la fois guetter, un peu au-dessous de l'histoire, ce qui la rompt et l'agite, et veiller un peu en arrière de la politique sur ce qui doit inconditionnellement la limiter. Après tout, c'est mon travail, je ne suis ni le premier, ni le seul à le faire. Mais je l'ai choisi.
>
> (Foucault 1979b/2001: 794)

The intellectual is answerable to himself about his own ***choice*** as well as his ***vocation***, as it were, as he answers to what interpellates him from the disquietude of history. This is the second important reason. In the lecture to the 'Société de philosophie', Foucault puts it very clearly: critique is a 'vertu', an answer to an 'impératif', much more pressing and radical than that of enunciating the mistakes and the mismatches that pollute the progress of things (Foucault 1990: 36).

The third and last reason – although this is a position that Foucault will revise later, exactly while reading Kant, to the advantage of critique as a modern attitude of philosophy – is how the issue of critique is connected to the issue of government. This is a famous claim of Foucault's. There is a double movement that orients the processes of governmentalization of power. On the one hand, the secularization ('laïcisation') of the Christian pastoral power which relocates it from the field of religion to the field of politics and its institutions. On the other hand, the dynamic expansion of the arts of government into the body of the civil society, which turns out to be completely infiltrated by them. What Foucault calls 'attitude critique' – one that finds its acme in Kant's writing on Enlightenment – unfurls hand-in-hand with the resematization of Christian pastoral power into a technique and an art of the government (see Senellart 1995). It is within these processes – administrative, institutional processes, which have a material impact and are not tied to the theological-political enchainment of sovereignty – that Foucault locates the emersion[7] of a complex relation between "politics" and "truth" around which the relation between governmentality and critique is pivoted.

As a quintessentially modern form of thought, critique is tied to the will 'to not be governed'. "Governed" not in an absolute sense, as this is impossible from a vantage point, like Foucault's, that takes Wittgenstein's disenchantment as the mainstay of an ethics of intellectual work (power, like language, is simply there, and one can just describe its games of veridiction – Foucault 1978b/2001: 542). Rather, the will to not be governed '*tellement*', that is, in the way one is *actually* governed. What in his lecture Foucault calls a game (*jeu*) of 'gouvernementalisation' and 'critique'[8] sets a threshold in the modern process of rationalization (the Protestant critique of the ecclesiastical biblical knowledge; the natural law critique of powers; the scientific critique of the government of knowledges) and methodologically inverts Weber, although it takes up Weber's question.[9] But more importantly, it plays out as a 'problematization' of the interplay of power, truth and the subject (which for Foucault is not only typical of modern Europe) (Foucault 1990: 39).

On this account, from this text onward, Kant is granted a central, strategic role. Although Kant never postulates the idea of a radical disobedience that challenges the fact of government as such, he assumes the 'courage de savoir' as a task with a theoretical and a political sides: de-subjugation, or rather, the institutionalization of an autonomy vis-à-vis those who govern with respect to the mutual implication of truth and power (Foucault 1990: 41). In the text that Foucault will publish in 1984, this aspect of the matter will give way to the 'attitude de la modernité', that is, the idea of a relation between thought and the present along with all that one has to think in order for him to locate himself within the present (see Chapter 1). And yet, even in this text, Kant is portrayed as the 'Weberian' icon of an ethics – an *êthos*, as Foucault calls it, and a few pages below an 'ascétisme indispensable' (Foucault 1984a/2001: 1387 and 1389) – of subjectivation. Critique 'comme travail de nous-mêmes sur nous-mêmes en tant qu'êtres libres' (Foucault 1984a/2001: 1394).

2. It is in this context, I believe, that Foucault elaborates on the growing centrality of the notion of *parrhēsia*. Which is to say, the question of the modes in which one can (and ought to) tell the truth. This notion surfaces in the course *L'herméneutique du sujet* (1981–1982) as the hallmark of the frankness and the openness that orients the relationship of 'maîtrise' between master and pupil. In this context, the distinctive trait of philosophy is to be found in a transformative,

ethopoietic function. In *parrhēsia* – according to how Foucault uses it as he first invokes late Antiquity – the type of knowledge in question is not that which subjects the individual to a truth that someone else owns over him, an abstract and 'objectivating' knowledge like those that fall under the scope of the primacy of representation. Rather it is a *relational knowledge*, a knowledge of the world, of becoming, of *interaction*, where a truth that 'affecte le sujet' is at stake. This truth forces the subject to adhere – to put it in improper, Deleuzian terms – to the event he is in his whole lifetime (Foucault 2001a: 233).

This is the point that leads Foucault to emphasize the Epicurean, Stoic and Cynic models (but also the Socratic ones) of the care of the self. Within these models, care is freed from the pedagogical scheme of one's preparation to adult life. They glue together the process of subjectivation and an immanent dynamic that is internal to the process of things, as they do not presuppose any division between the individual and the world. In the course *L'herméneutique du sujet*, *parrhēsia* – 'the naked transmission of truth' in the seductive and non-rhetorical relation between master and pupil – is bound up with a philosophical dimension that the successive courses will bring into question insofar as they trace its genealogy. However, it is instrumental in Foucault's elaborating on an ethical-political notion of philosophy – philosophy as 'philosophie en activité' (Foucault 1980e/2001: 929; 1984a: 1377) – in which he invests also personally at a time in which, in his writings, three concepts progressively gain momentum: 'problématisation' (in relation to knowledge and history); 'gouvernement' (in relation to politics); 'subjectivation' (in relation to the ethical and political problem of thinking of the de-subjectivation, viz. freedom, once the enquiry into the practices of subjectivation that mark individuation is over).[10] Therefore, it is my claim that it is in relation to politics, from *Hermeneutics of the Subject* up to the course *Le courage de la vérité* (1984), that Foucault constructs his history of *parrhēsia* (although it is always presented as a 'fiction historique', a genealogy that does not expose the objectivity of a development, but rather the fragmented frame of a series of problems that build on the question that is foisted upon us by the present. Which is to say, again, the "problematization" of the nexus between "governmentality" and "subjectivation").

Schematically: *parrhēsia*, broadly understood as "freedom of speech", coincides with the right to citizenship in classical Athens (*isonomia*, *isēgoria* and *parrhēsia* is what qualifies the relation between the *politēs* and the city). After the crisis of Athenian democracy, it gets appropriated and grafted onto another plane of philosophy. It then re-emerges as the form itself of the philosophical life in late Antiquity and in particular with Epicureanism, Stoicism and Cynicism. In very general terms, this is the history that for Foucault gets accomplished between Euripides' *Ion* and Diogenes and Demetrius, on which Epictetus draws as exemplars of the Stoic idea of the perfect philosophical life. Obviously, Foucault's analysis of the Ancient archive yields many lateral ramifications of this path. What I will say is likely to leave many things aside. But this is the price I deliberately accept to pay with a view to a somewhat univocal interpretation of Foucault's argumentative strategy as to the analytic and the use of the term *parrhēsia*, "speaking frankly".

Let me start from the beginning, however. *Parrhēsia* is a mode of speech. More precisely, it is a way of telling the truth, one that entails a risk for the speaker, exactly because of the fact that he tells the truth. While taking this risk, the parrhesiast freely ties himself to himself, *is* faithful to himself, exactly as long as he has the courage to tell the truth: 'La *parrhēsia* c'est le libre courage par lequel on se lie soi-même dans l'acte de dire vrai. Ou encore, la *parrhēsia* c'est l'éthique du dire vrai dans son acté risqué et libre' (Foucault 2008a: 64). Both with respect to the speaker, whose subjectivation coincides with the 'pacte' he makes with himself and with truth, and with respect to those who, along with him, enter what Foucault dubs 'the circle of listening', *parrhēsia* effects an opening, a disclosure of a situation vis-à-vis the codes and norms that shape it and the mobilization of the relation as it exposes it to an uncertain risk. The parrhesiastic utterance[11] constitutes the subject insofar as it refers it to freedom, truth and a dramatic enunciation (*drama*, from *draō*: I act, do, work, remember) in which the antagonist is the governmental institutions that guarantee the order of discourse.

Broadly speaking, what distinguishes the parrhesiastic utterance from a performative speech-act is that *parrhēsia*, on account of the unpredictable risk of the situation to which it is connected, is *a function of subjectivation*, not the 'performance of an act *in* saying' (Austin 1975) referred to an intentionality or a status that pre-exist the utterance.

In the course *Le Gouvernement de soi et des autres* (1982–1983), Foucault fleshes out this presupposition in two fashions. Firstly, Ion's whole story is read as the story of a recognition intended to affirm the protagonist's full citizenship through the complex game of three different forms of veridiction (that of the Oracle, that of Creusa's confession, and a political one, which in fact Ion establishes once he has ascended the throne as the founder of the Ionic people). Secondly, Foucault also retrieves a form of "true-speech" on which he confers a particularly demanding meaning. Here I cannot recall Euripides' play as a whole, let alone the entire system of movements through which Foucault's interpretation unfolds.[12] And yet, I need to briefly recollect the story line. Creusa, wife of King of Athens, Xuthus, secretly gave birth to Apollo's child, called Ion. Since her husband was ignorant of this, she left the child in a cave, expecting that he would die. However, Apollo sent Hermes to bring Ion to Delphi where he has grown up as an attendant at the temple. Years later, Xuthus and Creusa go to Delphi to ask if they can have children. The Oracle says that the first person he will meet will be his son. While getting out, Xuthus runs into Ion, and as he believes Ion is the product of a past affair, Xuthus takes him home to Athens to become the heir to the throne. Creusa objects to his husband's decision because she wants her child to be the heir to the throne and thus plans to kill Ion. The plan does not pan out and then the Pythia allows them to recognize each other. Finally, Athena appears *ex machina* and proposes a solution: to keep Ion as the heir to the throne and let Xuthus believe that he is his son.

It is evident that in the structure of Creusa's speech, as she reproaches Apollo for forcing her to expose Ion – an *invective*, the speech of the *weak*, a *challenge*, where the woman laments the *injustice* of the god – Foucault reclaims nothing short of the comprehensive 'matrice du discours politique' of the West – he calls it that way, and it is quite a demanding expression (Foucault 2008a: 126).

This looks to me as a decisive point to get to the conclusion of my argument, as I will show later. The speech of equality, an agonistic one, with which the weak, despite her weakness, takes the risk of reproaching the powerful for committing injustice, 'ce discours s'appelle précisément la *parrhēsia*', Foucault (2008a: 124–126) writes. It constitutes an inescapable point for the governmental rationality itself, which gets underway and stabilizes on this ellipse – that is, on the impossibility of undoing what others, in the historical-juridical field, recognize as the fundamental structure of the European constitutional history.

But let us see how Foucault develops his argument. It is interesting to note how loose his interpretation is. In Creusa's speech the term *parrhēsia* is nowhere to be seen. This means that Foucault is concerned with Euripides' argumentative form, as he finds in it much more than the use of speech, the occurrence of a word that could be put next to others. In that particular *structure* that the denunciation of an injustice is, Foucault concerns himself with the juxtaposition of speeches: 'Il s'agit de deux formes de discours qui se font face ou plutôt qui sont *profondément liées* l'une à l'autre', the speech of the powerful, who somehow holds the place where communicative normality is produced, and the speech of the weak, who challenges the former by subjectivating a courage of truth that the former cannot bear.

I do not think one can find a double-focus figure where a tie is expressed which is not that of the ellipse. The discourse of government and 'governmentality' plays a strategic role in this Foucault. In this case, it is what he calls 'couplage structurant', which later, and obviously not in Creusa's 'aveu' (a confession that is very different from the one that will become central in the guidance of Christian conscience), will give shape to the Western political discourse: on one side, the 'discours raisonnable qui permet de gouverner les hommes'; on the other, in a position that cannot be reduced to the former's, the 'discours du faible reprochant au fort son injustice' by indeed telling the truth.

This is a fundamental passage in Foucault's argumentation. At least on two levels. The first is that which allows the transition towards the philosophical *parrhēsia*. Those who govern are required to have wisdom, but this wisdom has to be formed, supported, advised. In order to be reasonable, the discourse of those who govern has to be founded on the discourse of another – an advisor, a minister, a master – who is necessarily weaker than him and has to take the risk to turn towards the powerful, to look into his eye, and to denounce the injustice (or the faults) that the former has committed (Foucault 2008a: 127). Also towards himself. It is worth highlighting a decisive point from this perspective. This passage is not only relevant to Foucault's exploration of Plato, or better, for the exhaustion of the political *parrhēsia* in the Athenian democratic crisis within which the principle of the equality un-determines and dissolves the agonistic game of ascendants that shores up the collective decision-making. It is also relevant to the construction of an analytic of politics, that of Foucault, that basically passes *outside* the state and that acknowledges the key role of institutional elements (broadly speaking: cameralistic, administrative, social ones) which the ideology of the Political conceals or confines to insignificance.[13] On another level, and I will return to this issue at the end of this chapter, the constitutive asymmetry of positions – that characterizes the 'couplage structurant' that Foucault talks about – becomes key to understanding the meaning he ascribes to the notion of critique.

Critiquing the government does not mean advancing 'reasonable' answers for its agenda. Rather, it means interpellating the ends it pursues, the general 'reasonableness' of its procedures and of the motives that surround its action. *Governing is not the task of the governed.* And this somehow marks the final exit from the lexicon – and the logic – of sovereignty and representation. Indeed, there is no identity between the people and the sovereign. This I believe orients the genealogy of governmentality that Foucault undertakes at the end of the 1970s starting from that which Crozier, Huntington and Watanuki's (1975) report to the Trilateral Commission calls 'the crisis of democracy', the post-representative technicization of politics and the design and implementation of technologies for a post-democratic governance (see Chignola 2008).

I spoke of a sort of 're-occupation', an *Umbesetzung*, of the issue of *parrhēsia* on the part of philosophy. This is the successive passage of Foucault's genealogy. It is true that the 'courage of truth', throughout a period that has not been completely analysed by Foucault in the last two courses at the Collège de France, sediments a series of figures that referred to just as many forms of life (the discourse of the advisor; that of the minister; that of critique, of which one should never tire of recalling the parrhesiastic core, that is to say, for Foucault, *never directly constituting or legislative*; the discourse of the revolutionary, as the "martyr"' of truth, etc.). Yet, what is particularly relevant here, exactly in the light of a definition of the technology of government, is the passage through Plato.

Also in this case, I apologize, I need to be very schematic. If philosophy takes up the legacy of "speaking frankly",[14] it fulfils this role only after a *structural impasse* of democracy comes into light during the Athenian crisis. I say "structural impasse" because in one of the few statements in which Foucault, albeit in the not-fully-controllable spoken language, goes so far as to directly emphasize one of his own textual analyses for the understanding of the present. Here he maintains that democracy – and he actually says 'this also applies to the present' – is at the same time that which cannot subsist, and cannot be governed, without true speech, and that, however, threatens with the possibility of there being true speech. I believe this is a further crucial passage. What in the structure of democracy jeopardizes the possibility of the true speech is the lack of the *difference*, which Foucault believes to be 'indispensable', in order that the true speech may be enunciated and may yield its effects.

In Ancient Athens, this basically means the explosion of "bad *parrhēsia*", the link between demagogy and rhetoric, the collapse of the agon in which the one who will be called upon to prompt collective decisions emerges – in virtue of the open recognition by his competitors, in a situation that Foucault calls 'supériorité permanentement contestée'. It is the same difference that nurtures other forms of speech moulded by *parrhēsia*: the speech of the physician, of the pilot, of the one who is actually called upon to govern. As regards the modern form of democracy, I believe, Foucault has in mind an *in-differentiation* of speech.

The difference between *parrhēsia* and a performative utterance lies in the lack of status that, in the case of the former, characterizes the speaker. If this is the case, the fact that in democracy *anybody* who claims to speak[15] by exercising a freedom of speech in which the subjectivity is *undifferentiated* ends up turning this very freedom of speech against himself and making the premises of democracy fade away. According to Foucault, the *parrhēsia* of the governed, as I will say in the conclusion of this chapter, stimulates processes of subjectivation that do not lay any claim to the universal, nor do they seek – and I think this is crucial – to reabsorb the difference between those who hold power and those who face it. The speaker is the protagonist of an irreducible speech – literally, an *antagonist* subject.

In Plato Foucault recovers the distinctive trait of philosophical *parrhēsia* and its being bound up with the form of the advisor's speech. More than that, because what in the Platonic dialogues becomes crucial is the line that runs from Socrates to the Cynics. Diogenes as a *Sokrates mainomenos*, 'a Socrates gone mad', after all, is a figure that comes back to the fore until Christoph Martin Wieland (see Niehues-Pröbsting 1993). I will try to proceed step by step. The first point is *Alcibiades*. According to Foucault's reading of this Platonic dialogue, there are at least two recurring themes that are key to understanding *parrhēsia*: *kairos* and *ergon*. Socrates takes the opportunity, as soon as he can, to establish a relation with Alcibiades not only to stimulate his awareness and self-government (which are the indispensable premise to aspire to the government of the others), but also and above all to *give shape* – to wit, meaning – to the same philosophical *logos* that only by virtue of the risk of frankness, that is to say, by bearing the risk of truth beyond itself, in putting itself to the test, finally meets with itself. The figure of the advisor's speech as a central figure of Foucault's analytic of *parrhēsia* stabilizes between *Alcibiades* and the *Seventh Letter*, in which, as is well known, Plato accounts for his own political missions in Sicily at the court of Dionysus. *Parrhēsia* 'est l'activité que Platon reconnaît et revendique à la racine de son activité de conseiller' (Foucault 2008a: 259). Whether it has to stabilize the 'circle of listening' in the erotic relationship with the young Alcibiades or with the tyrant in the political relationship against whose background one can literally *verify* the meaning and vocation of philosophy, frank speech operates by grasping the *kairos* of an occasion (one's being willing to listen as a further side of a parrhesiastic pact that the speaker forms, in this case, not only with himself, but with the other, and that can always be unilaterally broken; a pact that can always go disrespected), which is also an authentic move to action, 'ergon', of a speech that inscribes philosophy in the horizon of a *practice*.

Parrhēsia is different from rhetoric for other reasons. Mainly because it is a 'dire irruptif' – a speech that breaks the repetition, the liturgical or adulatory reproduction of the *récit* by which power legitimizes itself. A speech that is tied to the risk and event. *Parrhēsia* does not say what one ought to do; nor does it organize a "true" speech, which would be formal, abstract and would lie down on politics from the outside, in keeping with an unattainable localization with respect to the reality in which it is entirely situated. The parrhesiast exercises veridiction vis-à-vis those who govern, whether the "object" of this governing function is the subject himself who gets in touch with the parrhesiast or the others, those who are governed, inside a properly[16] political relationship.

To make these points – philosophy as a practice, veridiction as a risk, their constitutive relationship with the contingency of the situation – Foucault returns to two Platonic passages (Book VII in *The Republic* and Book IV in *Laws*) where the analysis of the relation between philosophy and medicine clarifies how the advisor's speech is produced. The philosopher is called upon to diagnose the diseases of the city; like the physician of free men – not that of slaves, who only need a straight prescription – he has to persuade, make the others listen to him; and like a good physician, the philosopher does not only deal with the symptom, but attends to the general, wide-ranging health of the city. This leads to a general fact that concerns Foucault's overall philosophical-political commitment.

If philosophy aims to get *accomplished*, that is, to not be mere discourse, but *exergazesthai*, to give effect to its own words, it cannot settle in the empty position of the negative critique: it cannot be only protest or contestation. Rather, philosophy has to tell the truth to those who listen and take up the gauntlet that listening entails, given that the latter can never be taken for granted and can become perilous. In this sense, the *kairos* is exactly the opportunity that arises as the conditions of listening obtain. And in the pact between the one who advises and the one who is advised the *ergon* of philosophy can be accomplished as the mobilization of truth and as a *transformative practice* both within the former and the latter.

In *Alcibiades* the *kairos* is marked by the love Socrates feels for the young boy who is destined to a remarkable political career. In the *Seventh Letter*, where Plato can take responsibility for his own philosophy, that is, *exergazesthai* his own speech, is occasioned by Dionysus' invitation because he needs help and is willing to listen. In either case, it is all about *parrhēsia*. Foucault (2008a: 259) comments: 'La *parrhēsia* est donc l'activité que Platon reconnaît et revendique au fond à la racine de son activité de conseiller'. It is worth repeating that the structure of the advice is the *couplage* that positions the governed in front of the governor, the model of a political practice that crosses Western constitutional history; a practice that marginalizes the state and that in the latter only finds a peripeteia of the fact of government (Foucault 2004a: 253); a partial and temporary formalization of the problem of the institutionalization of practices.[17] In the end, the advisor is the one who *is* his own speech, who is committed, who takes responsibility for his opinion, and who, although his opinion is based on the interplay of general principles and contextual analysis, and although he speaks to everybody, cannot but convince individually (Foucault 2008a: 259).

The last characteristic listed above by Foucault, the advisor's activity *as a* political speech that differs from the speech of those who hold *dunasteia*, the actual power, *omnes et singulatim* – the parrhesiast speaks to everybody, but also one by one – foregrounds, one might point out, the specular relation that weds *parrhēsia* to governmentality (Foucault 1981a/2001). And yet this is a further significant fact. Foucault (2008a: 259) seems to assert that a speech can be said to be true *if and only if it is put to the test of politics*: 'Tout cela donne un discours dont la vérité doit s'éprouver au fait qu'elle deviendra réalité'. And this is not in the sense that the truth of philosophy, in a manner that is modelled after the scheme theory/practice, can be derived from its own success, by its capacity to actualize its own project. Rather, in the sense of a truth that proves effective insofar as it supports the probes of subjectivation of a speech and a position-taking that shoulder the responsibility of what one says by facing the risk of saying so without any mediation or shyness.

As a consequence, it is important for philosophy to tell the truth with regard to politics and it is important for any political practice to nurture a continuous relation to philosophical veridiction. 'Mais bien entendu que le dire-vrai de la philosophie ne coïncide pas avec ce que peut et doit être une rationalité politique' (Foucault 2008a: 266). The practice of philosophy and the practices of politics cannot overlap, because the relation between those who hold the place of *dunasteia* and those who hold the place of critique is never a relation of correspondence. It does not presuppose any identity. The asymmetry of positions maintains the difference that is needed for the irruption of speech in the governed. A speech that challenges, that resists, a speech of truth insofar as it is subtracted from the bad image, from the mimicry, of legislative or administrative rationality.[18]

'Pour Platon, et d'une façon me semble-t-il pour la philosophie occidentale', Foucault (2008a: 267) writes, 'le véritable enjeu n'a jamais été de dire aux hommes politiques que faire. Leur enjeu a toujours été, en face des hommes politiques, en face de la pratique politique, d'exister comme discours philosophique et comme véridiction philosophique'. Philosophy *is actualized* as long as it requires courage; one's taking the risk of the situation. It does not replace the political, as it never tells or decides on what one should do. Like for Weber, after all, philosophy simply follows the daemon that holds the threads of life of those who prove to be philosophers; or, to put it otherwise, the life that materializes as a political form of life, as *subjectum*, not as *subjectus* (see Balibar 2011, esp.: 67 ff.).

3. Daemons, then. This takes us back to Socrates. For there is a third figure that Foucault recovers in Plato. It is the figure of Socrates in *Laches*, a dialogue that famously centres on courage. Three things are interesting to Foucault in *Laches*. First, what is it that authorizes Socrates to speak of courage? Why do his interlocutors, Laches and Nicias, involve him in the discussion on the education of the children of Lysimachus and Melesias? Foucault explains that it is not on account of Socrates' technical competence as a soldier in Delium that he is allowed to speak. Instead, what qualifies him is the fact that his actions are in tune with his words (*Laches* XIV, 188d: 'autós autóu toù bíou symphōnōn tois lógois pros ta érga'). It is in fact his *coherence in life* (Foucault 2009: 138).

Here comes the second thing that interests Foucault. There is a significant *décalage* between *Alcibiades* and *Laches* where the meaning of Socratic *parrhēsia* surfaces. It concerns the *didonai logon*, giving an account of oneself, that represents the objective of Socratic *parrhēsia*. In *Alcibiades* it concerns the *psychē*, that is, the pivot of the passage from the government of the self to the government of the others. *Laches* does not home in on the soul, but on *bios*, life as a work of art that has to do with a stylistics, a form, a *polishing* job (permit me to use the Stoic term: sculpting one's own statue by eliminating, carving out, particularizing to the essential – Epictetus, *Discourses*, II, 19: 23–24.) which goes from itself to itself and is a *tremendously serious* game.

According to Epictetus, one of the authors of the later Foucault, the philosopher is one who, by interrogating, plays. The arguments bounce off each other and accompany the becoming of philosophical *zētēsis*. Epictetus (*Discourses*, book II, ch. 5: 18–20) presents Socrates as a skilful ball player, who plays the serious game of philosophy even in court: 'And what was the ball he had to play with?'. Epictetus adds: 'Life, chains, exile, a draught of poison, separation from a wife, and leaving his children orphans. These were what he had to play with ('tauta en mesō ois epaîzein'); and yet he did play, and threw the ball with address'. I like this quotation very much, as it reminds me of another witness of truth in this Socratic sense. A comrade and master who, while waiting for a judgment that might have sentenced him to dozens of years in jail – and that eventually found him not guilty – after five and a half years of preventive detention, instead of turning up in court enchained, decided to remain in Rebibbia (a major Italian jail), with a feeling of philosophical serenity, to play a very earnest tennis match.

In *Laches*, then, it is all about *bios*, not *psychē*, of those who are brought up to hold the governing position to which they aspire. The third thing that Foucault underlines is the transmission of such a Socratism to other Hellenistic schools. This is an exceeding path that this philosophy, as a *testimony* and *activity* of truth, marks with respect to Platonism to redefine itself within Cynicism with a particularly radical twist. The Cynic, the dog-like philosopher, turns *bios* – one's own life, body, sharp tongue – into an immediate *alethurgia* of truth.

Who is the Cynic? First, as Hegel (1995: 479 ff.) remarks by drawing on Diogenes Laertius (VI, 103), Cynicism is a style, a way of life, more than a philosophy. A way of life that *embodies* a philosophy, we might definitely say. An integrally public life, entirely deployed as a dramatics of truth: without secret or dissimulation, generally unintentional. The Cynic lives a thoroughly natural life in which – as the kind of love Plato talks about in *Symposium* – there is no cause for shame.

The rescue of non-dissimulated naturalness gestures towards an aesthetics of pureness. It invites to a thorough animality as the paradigm of an *autarkeia* that squeezes the divine into the perfect immanence of a life with no needs or desires, high or low – a life that only comprises surfaces and bodies, shoves, tests and encounters (the Cynic commits himself to the startling and impersonal cult of *tuchē*, its *aloghistos* movement, in an utterly impersonal and anarchic form – see Goulet-Cazé 2001).

The Cynic's *adiaphoros bios* – indifferent life, without a doubt, but an indifference that gets defined through *talaiporia* and a myriad of efforts and *ponoi* to become a thickened, virile, *herculean* life – is the perfectly independent life where the sign (as well as the meaning of philosophy) is *altered*, *transvalued*. Diogenes the forger, as the doxography says (*paracharaxon to nomisma*, is the Cynic uniform). Moreover, a meagre life, where poverty is *activated*, not endured. It is the decision of self-dispossession and material insertion in the flow of events, without being afraid of losing anything, and as a strategy of thickening and withstanding empowerment: Cynics as the philosopher-athlete (see Deleuze 2003b). Life that calls for disgrace and challenges *adoxia* in order to be lived as a choice of radical deconstruction of the tyranny of desire. Diogenes Laertius (IV, 50) on Bion of Borysthenes: referring to a wealthy miser he said, 'He has not acquired a fortune; the fortune has acquired him'. Seneca speaks of Diogenes (*De Beneficiis*, IV 4, 3–4): there are those who are in the grip of desires, and can barely be touched by the needs of humanity; 'Of necessity I shall be outdone in benefits [. . .] by Diogenes who passed through the Macedonian treasures naked, trampling on the King's wealth [. . .]' – Seneca ruminates – 'far richer was he than Alexander, who then had all things in his power; for what Diogenes *would not accept was greater than what Alexander could give him*' (Seneca 2011: 115–116).

Here I cannot analyse in detail the doxography that deals with Cynicism.[19] It is sufficient to recall what I said above. Virile philosophy, philosophy of animality and the body, *philosophical theatre* (dramatization, performance, pithy and licentious word – see Kennedy 1999), where truth is the litmus test for the coherence between discourse and *bíos*. To return to my topic, the words by Dion of Prusa (IX, 18) will suffice:

> Therefore, it is not sufficient for anybody who wants to be a Cynic to adopt cloak, walking stick, haversack and long hair and walk, hairy and illiterate, like in a travel with no hairdresser and school, but has to take up as attributes of the Cynic School reason in lieu of the walking stick and the rule of life in lieu of the haversack. *Parrhēsia is fine when one has proven one's value.* This is, I believe, what Diogenes and Crates did.

What is of interest to Foucault is that Cynicism *transforms* – in the sense of a transvaluation, the passage from a form to *another* – the utterly relevant philosophical and political issue, within Greek thought, of the courage of truth. I think we know the various ways in which this occurs. The first is that of democracy or of the advisor: 'La hardiesse politique, celle du démocrate comme celle du courtisan', Foucault writes and by doing so recapitulates and clarifies his own path

> consiste donc à dire quelque chose d'autre, quelque chose de contraire à ce qui pense l'Assemblée ou le Prince. C'est contre l'opinion de ce Prince ou de cette Assemblée, et c'est pour la vérité que l'homme politique, s'il est courageux risque sa vie'.
>
> (Foucault 2009: 2015)

Foucault dubs this first formula 'bravoure politique du dire-vrai'. The second is that of Socratic irony, which bridges the philosophical establishment of *parrhēsia* and the Cynic courage of truth. In the Socratic irony, the risk – that of arousing the listener's irritation, rage, revenge, processes and condemnations – is assumed as evidence for coherence, while true speech as an instrument to glide ('glisser', says Foucault) inside a knowledge that they do not know to possess, one that gets men to take care of the self as a task. With Cynicism a third mode of *parrhēsia* or courage comes (this time *literally*) on *stage*. What Foucault identifies as the disgracefulness of Cynic life is the disgrace of truth itself: 'Le courage cynique de la vérité consiste en ceci que l'on arrive à faire condamner, rejeter, mépriser, insulter par les gens la manifestation même de ce qu'ils admettent ou prétendent admettre au niveau des principes' (on this topic, see Cesaroni 2013).

Cynic *parrhēsia* comes to the surface in the life itself of those who have to make truth visible as a form of existence: *alēthēs bios*. Banality of philosophy, maybe. But a banality that operates as the cracked mirror that reflects the disgrace that philosophy is when it truly gets embodied into a practice (see Foucault 2009: 214–215). The epitaph of Cercidas of Megalopolis in his *Meliambics*: generated by Zeus (*Diogenés*), dog of the heavens. Drawing on Demetrius' take on the philosopher and philosophizing, Seneca (*De Beneficiis*, VII, 13–7) avers:

> If he has dedicated his mind to virtue and thinks of any pathway to which virtue summons him as being smooth and level; if, being by nature a social animal and born for the common good, he looks upon the world as a common home for all and has opened up his private thoughts to the gods, living always as though under public scrutiny and more in fear of himself than of others – then this man has escaped the storms and taken a stand on firm ground under a clear sky; he has reached the summit of all useful and necessary knowledge. *Everything else* is but an amusement for his leisure.
>
> (Seneca 2011: 167; emphasis added)

Everything else. Which is to say, life as verbosity, discourse, doctrine: pure futility, for the sober dog-like philosopher. One only has to think of the dispute between Favorinus and Demonax handed over by Lucian: 'Who, pray, are you, that you should pour scorn upon me?', says Favorinus to the Cynic, evidently annoyed. 'I am the possessor of a critical pair of ears', Demonax replies. Favorinus continues: '*You* are no infant, but a philosopher, it seems; may one ask what marks the transformation?'. 'The marks of manhood (*orcheis*, literally)', the bearded Cynic replies to the beardless Favorinus. *Parrhēsia* as wit, scorn, mere gesture that moulds meaning.

4. While talking about his work in the famous interview conducted by Duccio Trombadori at the end of 1978 (published in *Il Contributo* in 1980), Michel Foucault uses a couple of expressions that in the past slipped my attention and I have now come to consider as extremely significant. It is as if, in this interview, Foucault inaugurated, with deep personal investment, the research line that he was developing in his lectures at Collège de France in the 1980s. I believe this takes us back to

the questions raised at the beginning of this chapter. While he was gathering the threads of his research activity for the umpteenth time, Foucault (1980d/2001: 863) replies to the interviewer's question as follows (emphasis added):

> Mon problème est de faire moi-même, et d'inviter les autres à faire avec moi, à travers un contenu historique déterminé, une expérience de ce que nous sommes, de ce qui est non seulement notre passé *mais aussi notre présent, une expérience de notre modernité telle que nous en sortions transformés.*

Foucault produces works of 'fiction historique' (see Chapter 5), that is, works that employ authentic documents, archive material, existing texts, not to portray the objectivity of a process, but

> de façon qu'à travers eux il soit possible d'effectuer non seulement une constatation de vérité, mais aussi une expérience qui autorise une altération, une transformation du rapport que nous avons à nous-même et au monde où, jusque-là, nous nous reconnaissions sans problèmes.

His goal is to engender experiences of transformation. Philosophy, critique, mobilization of 'philosophie en activité', not a sovereign claim to truth (Foucault 1980e/2001: 929).

This is what Foucault calls the 'game' between truth and 'fiction', between 'evidence and fabrication', between analytics and montage, around which his books are organized. It engenders an *effect of alteration* that redeems the possibles that have not been actualized in the time we live in. This game is mobilized, fluidified, to exalt the forces and the processes that crystallize the solid monolith that we take as reality and therefore to permit breaking free from its grasp. *Déprise* is one of the key terms of the later Foucault. It is exactly with this kind of awareness – on top of the problem of thinking of the *practice of philosophy* as an *experience* of de-subjection and subjectivation – I believe, that Foucault studies Ancient thought.

But there is more than that. While answering Trombadori, who presses him on this issue, and particularly on the type of teaching that should orient this transformation, Foucault (1980d/2001: 866) clarifies:

> Je refuse le mot "enseignement". Un livre systématique qui mettrait en œuvre une méthode généralisable ou qui donnerait la démonstration d'une théorie porterait des enseignements. Mes livres n'ont pas cette valeur-là. Ce sont plutôt des invitations, des gestes faites en public.

These are invitations, for sure. But above all they are public gestures, as well as non-dissimulated gestures, with no shed of rhetoric, integrally visible, as they are party to a knowledge that lies on the surface of things – Hellenistic philosophy, as Deleuze (1990) would have it, is a surface knowledge; different from the Pre-Socratic knowledge of depths and the Platonic philosophy of heights. These are the gestures of the parrhesiastic actualization of Cynic philosophy. Moreover, a few lines after reclaiming his 'Socratism', his claim to the *paralyzing* effect on prison guards and social workers after reading *Discipline and Punish*: 'Cette réaction prouve que le travail a reussi, qu'il a fonctionné comme je le voulais'.

Foucault's books are 'livres-expérience', consciously constructed as different from 'livres-vérité' or 'livres-démonstration' of the philosophical tradition within university or academia (Deleuze 1990). An altering philosophy, a philosophy in action, that does not have anything to teach but paralyses as it works on the 'problématisation' of Western rationality and its practices. It is highly unlikely that Foucault was not thinking of *Meno*.

In another interview, this time conducted by Alessandro Fontana, first published in May 1984 and then republished in *Le Monde* in July 1984 (*Une esthétique de l'existence*), Foucault is pressed to explain what lies behind his interest in Antiquity. One has to think of something like an interference between the Christian West and Greek thought motivated by the oscillation range of the history of morals. The passage from Antiquity to Christianity is marked by the subjection of what in Ancient Greece was an 'individual ethics' (whatever this might mean, as I find this observation quite problematic) to a dispositif of obedience to systems of rules. Elsewhere, Foucault confirms this: if there is anything literally unthinkable for Ancient Greeks, this is the idea of one's subjection to a power that lasts one's whole life. Therefore, his inquiry into these systems of discipline and obedience in Antiquity is motivated by the progressive evanescence of this obedience to rules and the need to rethink ethics in accordance with his Ancient existential formulas:

> Si je me suis intéressé à l'antiquité, c'est que, pour toute une série de raisons, l'idée d'une morale comme obéissance à un code de règles est en train, maintenant, de disparaître, a déjà disparu. Et à cette absence de morale répond, doit répondre, une recherche qui est celle d'une esthétique de l'existence.
>
> (Foucault 1984g/2001: 1551)

Still, it is necessary to clarify that his mention of an 'aesthetics of existence' does not signal an unpolitical *retrait*. On the contrary, he focuses his attention on the emergence of a politics of the subject[20] that marks an irretrievable surplus with respect to the boundaries of sovereignty and its normative dispositifs. I believe Foucault's problem is that the processes of subjectivation that characterize the present cannot be thought of with the codes and the dispositifs that in the modern era entrapped them by means of techniques of power such as political representation or sovereignty. The latter ones are categories that require one's absolute and irresistible compliance for one's whole life – an absolute and irresistible compliance that, in the end, Ancient Greeks only deemed to be suitable for slaves. Mine is not a childishly extreme assertion. One only has to call to mind again a great liberal thinker, Tocqueville (1848: 316), as he writes: 'Dans ce système' – the democratic system defined by representative decision-making procedures – 'les citoyens sortent un moment de la dépendance pour indiquer leur maître, et y rentrent'. So reads this Norman author's blunt prose.

And not only that. In the same interview, Foucault clarifies the irretrievability, for the purposes of critique, of the notion itself of the individual and individual rights, which liberalism traditionally opposes to the invasiveness of state apparatuses. At least for two reasons that deserve mention. There is no such thing as a sovereign subject, a founding and foundational subject, a universal form of subjectivity that we can find everywhere. This very (allegedly sovereign) subject is nothing but the outcome of practices of subjection that affect it. Foucault writes: 'Je pense au contraire que le sujet se constitue à travers des pratiques d'assujettissement, ou, d'une façon plus autonome, à travers des pratiques de libération, de liberté, comme dans l'antiquité'. In other words, not as practices that presuppose an absolutely free subject, but as practices able to bend and exploit the rules, conventions and stylistics that belong to the social environment – to the *Lebensform*, to use a term of the later Wittgenstein – in which the subject is situated by making them instrumental in the subject's creative and inventive use of freedom.

Here comes the last passage that interests me. Does this mean accepting reality as it appears in our eyes, with its dispositifs, its machines, its laws? Does this mean accepting reality as true? It is at this point that veridiction makes its appearance in the interview. And it does so in a form that refers it to the question of critique and governmentality. 'Je crois trop à la vérité pour ne pas supposer qu'il y a différentes vérités et différentes façons de la dire', says Foucault. 'Certes, on ne peut pas demander à un gouvernement de dire la vérité, toute la vérité, rien que la vérité' – truth is not, *à la* Hobbes, the monopoly of the sovereign, one might say – 'en revanche, il est possible de demander aux gouvernants une certaine vérité quant aux projets finaux, aux choix généraux de leur tactique, à un certain nombre de points particuliers de leurs programme: *c'est la parrhesie (la libre parole) du gouverné*' (Foucault 1984g/2001: 1552–1553; emphasis added).

Therefore, what is possible is a political *parrhēsia* that lives up to the present. A *parrhēsia* that is redeemed as it gets caught by philosophy and reinvested as a specific mode of critique and subjectivation at the centre of the governmentalization of power. This form of *parrhēsia* takes various shapes that however share one characteristic: they interpellate in a way that subjectivates the position of the governed and puts him in front of those who govern; the latter has to face him in order to govern effectively. Whether those who govern have to account for a choice, in the sense of an action, for why it happened, and regardless of the fact of being included in the fact of government as experts or intellectuals, subjects involved in what materially happens, or bare citizens.

Without exchanging seats, of course, if the function of the critique stabilizes a difference. What critique must avoid in order that it may be practised as such – to wit, as the fire of innovation, transformation and resistance in the governmental ellipse – is the enchantment with which power struggles to exorcise the *parrhēsia* of the governed as it tries to subsume its surplus in the dispositif of sovereignty. As it does with its 'mettez-vous à notre place et dites-nous ce que vous feriez'. Realism as the litmus test for the maturity of critique; the last bastion of the truth effect of power and its imagining the enunciation only as a programme, a design, a sovereign discourse that has a practice to organize.

Without exchanging seats, of course, if the function of the critique is to stabilize a difference. What critique must avoid in order that it may be practised as such – to wit, as the fire of innovation, transformation and resistance within the governmental ellipse – is the enchantment by which power struggles to exorcise the *parrhēsia* of the governed as it tries to recover its surplus in the dispositif of sovereignty. As it does with its 'mettez-vous à notre place et dites-nous ce que vous feriez'. Realism is the litmus test for the maturity of critique; the last bastion of the truth effect of power and its imagining the enunciation only as a programme, design, sovereign discourse that has a practice to organize.

Therefore, this is a question that has to be accurately put aside in that it is perfectly useless and dangerous for the purposes of veridiction. Regardless of what power requires, critique does not need a fictitious realism. As long as it is what it is (namely, courage of truth, *parrhēsia*, a risk taken in the first person), then it can never be internal to the discursive liturgy that sets realism and disenchantment as the hallmark of the reversibility of the positions of the governor and the governed, in which the latter is swallowed up and annihilated as such. The political subjectivation of the governed occurs in a speech that never says what to do but urges those who make decisions and govern *to account for their doings.*

'En tant que gouvernés' – not as subjects of law, not as represented, not as 'assujettis', therefore, but as governed, that is, as affected by a process where the gauge for assessing the legitimacy of the governmental action is an open confrontation with the governed – 'on a parfaitement le droit de poser le questions de vérité' (Foucault 1984f/2001: 1553).

The veridiction that is at stake here is the veridiction ensuing from a speech that subjectivates the position of the governed by assigning him the task of a permanent critique of the exercise of governmental functions. These can never evade the continuous interpellation that is addressed to those who govern to account for themselves. On the contrary, only the courage of such a constant demand for accountability is able to activate knowledge and de-passivate the subject. Once more, this revolves around the government of the self and the government of others. This is the pole star that guides the intellectual, political and personal path of the later Foucault.

Notes

1 For a preliminary account of the history of this term, see Peterson 1929; Jaeger 1959; Schlier 1964; Gigante 1969; Momigliano 1971. But above all see the book that Michel Foucault mostly draws on, along with Marcello Gigante's study: Scarpat 1964.

2 See Foucault's first course at the Collège de France in Foucault 2011. I would also like to recall the lecture on the Oedipus myth at Rio de Janeiro in 1973 (Foucault 2000). On these issues, see Brindisi 2010.

3 Foucault 1982a/2001: 1058.

4 Foucault 1984g/2001: 1553.

5 The text has not been included in *Dits et écrits*, as it appeared in 1990 in 'Bulletin de la société française de philosophie'.

6 This point, which is key to understanding Foucault's analytic of power, has been deftly clarified in Revel 2005; Artières and Potte-Bonneville 2007.

7 I should rather say 're-emersion', given that in the 1983 course *Le gouvernement de soi et des autres* he establishes a direct line of continuity and transmission between ancient parrhēsia and the modern attitude to critique in Kant (Foucault 2008a: 326).

8 Critique is the movement through which the subject gives itself the right to question truth concerning its power effects and to question power concerning its truth effects.

9 Foucault (1982d/2001: 1605) writes : 'Max Weber a posé cette question: si l'on veut adopter un comportement rationnel et régler son action en fonction de principes vrais, à quelle part de soi doit-on renoncer? De quel ascétisme se paie la raison? À quel type d'ascétisme doit-on se soumettre? J'ai, pour ma part, posé la question inverse: comment certains types de savoir sur soi sont-ils devenus le prix à payer pour certaines formes d'interdits? Que doit-on connaître de soi afin d'accepter le renoncement?'.

10 See Flynn 1985; more in general, Moss 1998; Gros and Lévy 2003; Detel 2005.

11 Foucault accurately distinguishes it from the performative utterance, as far as the latter is entirely ritualized, somehow liturgical: it requires the speaker to have a recognizable status and engenders effects that are predetermined by the intentionality which affects speech.

12 On this topic, see Sforzini 2013; Rametta 2013.

13 On this issue, a good analysis can be found in Büttgen 2007. But see also Karsenti 2005.

14 In Plato, as I will illustrate shortly, this occurs both in the education of the governor to come (Alcibiades) and in the test whereby philosophy encounters its own "real", to distinguish itself from mere chatter (*Seventh Letter*, *Fifth Letter*).

15 Not as a governed (that is, as one who occupies a position that is not the same as those who govern; a specific position, located within the partial circuits of power, intimately tied to needs and desires that urge subjectivation), but as a "governor" (modern democracy, as I pointed out above, is based on the indistinctness of the two figures, namely, the abstract, identity-making, double-edged figure of the sovereign people). In other words, by claiming to have a say and to have a universal competence that corresponds to the sovereign's gaze and comes down to the ability to speak, and that therefore works for the assembling of the doxai on which common sense, chatter, power discourse slide: discursive functions that do not require any form of courage – as Tocqueville first intuited: one only has to recall the conclusive chapters of the second volume of *Democracy in America* and the evocation of the new type of tyrant as the 'berger' of a flock of timid and hardworking animals (see Chignola 2011).

16 But this "properly" should be between quotes because in the 1980s Foucault is more and more interested in the politics of the subject.

17 Very close to this conclusion, see Bourdieu 2012.

18 Rosanvallon 2006 tackles these issues independently of *parrhēsia*.

19 Texts and doxography can be found in Paquet 1992.

20 A politics that touches on the body, sexuality, the relationships between the sexes, but also on irrepresentable needs and desires, exorbitant and decostitutive practices, social movements, environmental issues, feminism, same-sex sexuality, etc.

Bibliography

Abrams, J.J. (2002) 'Aesthetics of Self-Fashioning and Cosmopolitanism: Foucault and Rorty on the art of Living', *Philosophy Today* 46(2): 185–192.

Adorno, Th.W., and Horkheimer, M. (1972) *Dialectic of Enlightenment*, New York: Verso.

Agamben, G. (1998) *Homo Sacer: Sovereign Power and Bare Life*, Abingdon: Stanford University Press.

Agamben, G. (2007) *Il Regno e la Gloria: Per una genealogia teologica dell'economia e del governo. Homo sacer II*, Venezia: Neri Pozza.

Aladjem, T.K. (1995) 'Of Truth and Disagreement: Habermas, Foucault and Democratic Discourse', *History of European Ideas* 20(4–6): 909–914.

Allen, A. (2000) 'The Anti-Subjective Hypothesis: Michel Foucault and the Death of the Subject', *The Philosophical Forum* 31(2): 113–130.

Althusser, L., and Balibar, E. (1970) *Reading Capital*, Brewster, B. (ed.), London: New Left Books.

Amariglio, J.L. (1988) 'The Body, Economic Discourse and Power: An Economist's Introduction to Foucault', *History of Political Economy* 20(4): 583–613.

Arendt, H. (1958) 'The Modern Concept of History', *The Review of Politics* 20(4): 570–590.

Arienzo, A. (2004) 'Dalla Corporate Governance alla Categoria Politica di Governance', in Borrelli, G.F. (ed.), *Governance*, Napoli: Libreria Dante & Descartes.

Artières, Ph., and Potte-Bonneville, M. (2007) *D'après Foucault: Gestes, Luttes, Programmes*, Paris: Les Prairies Ordinaires.

Aron, R. (1938) *Essai sur la théorie de l'histoire dans l'Allemagne contemporaine: La philosophie critique de l'histoire*, Paris: Vrin.

Aron, R. (1996) *Les étapes de la pensée sociologique*, Paris: Gallimard.

Artières, Ph., and Potte-Bonneville, M. (2007) *D'après Foucault: Gestes, luttes, programmes*, Paris: Les prairies ordinaires.

Austin, J.L. (1975) *How to Do Things With Words*, 2nd ed., Oxford: Oxford University Press.

Baldry, H.C. (1959) 'Zeno's Ideal State', *Journal of Hellenistic Studies*, 75: 3–15.

Baldry, H.C. (1983) *L'unità del genere umano nel pensiero greco*, Bologna: Il Mulino, Bologna.

Balibar, É. (1989) 'Foucault et Marx: L'enjeu du nominalisme', in *Michel Foucault philosophe*, Paris: Seuil, pp. 54–75.

Balibar, É. (2011) *Citoyen Sujet et autres essais d'anthropologie politique*, Paris: PUF.

Basso, L. (2012) *Agire in comune: Antropologia e politica nel'ultimo Marx*, Verona: Ombre Corte.

Benveniste, É. (1969) *Le vocabulaire des institutions indo-européennes, I. Economie, parenté, société*, Paris: Les Editions de Minuit.

Berni, S., and Fadini, U. (2010) *Linee di fuga: Nietzsche, Foucault, Deleuze*, Firenze: Firenze University Press.

Bernini, L. (2006) 'Foucault: una libertà senza liberalismo: A proposito dei Corsi di Foucault al Collège de France (1977–79)', *Filosofia politica* 1: 129–141.

Bernini, L. (2008) *Le pecore e il pastore: Critica, politica, etica nel pensiero di Michel Foucault*, Napoli: Liguori.

Bert, J.F. (2006) *Proximité, Réserve et emprunt: la place de Michel Foucault dans la sociologie française*, Thèse pour obtenir le grade de Docteur de l'Université de Paris VIII.

Bonnafous-Boucher, M. (2004) *Un libéralisme sans liberté: Du terme "libéralisme" dans la pensée de Michel Foucault*, Paris: L'Harmattan.

Bourdieu, P. (2012) *Sur l'État: Cours au Collège de France 1989–1992*, Paris: Raisons d'agir/Seuil.

Brehier, É. (1962) *La théorie des incorporels dans l'ancien stoïcisme*, Paris: Vrin.

Brehier, É. (1971) *Chrysippe et l'ancien stoïcisme*, London-New York: Gordon & Breach.

Brown, P. (1978) *The Making of Late Antiquity*, Cambridge, MA: Harvard University Press.

Brown, P. (1982) *Society and the Holy in Late Antiquity*, Berkeley, Los Angeles and London: University of California Press.

Brindisi, G. (2010) *Potere e giudizio: Giurisdizione e veridizione nella genealogia di Michel Foucault*, Napoli: Editoriale scientifica.

Brunner, O. (1970) 'La "casa come complesso" e l'antica "economica" europea', in Schiera, P. (ed.), *Per una nuova storia costituzionale e sociale*, Milano: Vita e Pensiero, pp. 133–164.

Burchell, G. (1991) 'Peculiar Interests: Civil Society and Governing "The System of Natural Liberty"', in Burchell, G., Gordon, C., and Miller, P. (eds.), *The Foucault Effect: Studies in Governamentality*, Chicago: University of Chicago Press, pp. 119–150.

Burchell, G. (1996) 'Liberal Government and Techniques of the Self', in Barry, A., Osborne, Th., and Rose, N. (eds.), *Foucault and Political Reason: Liberalism, Neo-Liberalism and Rationalities of Government*, Chicago: University of Chicago Press, pp. 19–36.

Büttgen, Ph. (2007) 'Théologie politique et pouvoir pastoral', *Annales: Histoire, Sciences sociales* 5: 1129–1154.

Carnevale, F. (2005) 'La parrhesia, le courage de la révolte et de la vérité', in Michon, P., Hauser, Ph., Carnevale, F., Brossat, A. (eds.), *Foucault dans tous ses éclats*, Paris: L'Harmattan, pp. 141–210.

Cavalletti, A. (2005) *La città biopolitica: Mitologie della sicurezza*, Milano: Bruno Mondadori.

Cavarero, A. (1993) 'Il corpo politico come organismo', *Filosofia politica* 3: 391–414.

Cesaroni, P. (2010) *La distanza da sé: Politica e filosofia in Michel Foucault*, Padova: cleup.

Cesaroni, P. (2013) 'La filosofia in Il coraggio della verità', in Cesaroni, P., and Chignola, S. (eds.), *La forza del vero: Un seminario sui Corsi di Michel Foucault al Collège de France (1981–1984)*, Verona: Ombre Corte, pp. 132–160.

Cesaroni, P., and Chignola, S. (2013) *La forza del vero: Un seminario sui Corsi di Michel Foucault al Collège de France (1981–1984)*, Verona: Ombre Corte.

Chang-Uh, L. (2002) *Oikeiosis: Stoische Ethik in naturphilosophischer Perspektive*, München: Verlag Karl Alber.

Chantraine, P. (1968) *Dictionnaire étimologique de la langue grecque*, vol. I, Paris: Klincksieck.

Chevalier, L. (1958) *Classes laborieuses et classes dangereuses à Paris pendant la première moitié du XIXe siècle*, Paris: Plon.

Chevallier, Ph. (2014) *Michel Foucault and the Question of Right*, in Golder, B. (ed.), *Re-Reading Foucault: On Law, Power and Rights*, Abingdon: Routledge, pp. 171–187.

Chignola, S. (1993) '*Quidquid est in territorio est de territorio*: Nota sul rapporto fra comunità etnica e Stato nazione', *Filosofia politica* VII(1): 29–62.

Chignola, S. (2004a) *Fragile cristallo: Per la storia del concetto di società*, Napoli: Editoriale scentifica.

Chignola, S. (ed.) (2004b) *Governare la vita: Un seminario sui Corsi di Michel Foucault al Collège de France* (1977–1979), Verona: Ombre Corte.

Chignola, S. (2008) 'In the Shadow of the State: Governance, governamentalità, governo', in Fiaschi, G. (ed.), *Governance: oltre lo Stato?* Soveria Mannelli: Rubbettino.

Chignola, S. (2011) *Il tempo rovesciato: La Restaurazione e il governo della democrazia*, Bologna: il Mulino.

Colliot-Thélène, C. (2009) 'Les rationalités modernes du politiqu: de Foucault à Weber', in Bruhns, H., and Duran, P. (eds). *Les rationalités modernes du politique*, Paris: L.G.D.J., pp. 181–197.

Conze, W. (1954) 'Vom "Pöbel" zu "Proletariat": Sozialgeschichtliche Voraussetzungen für den Sozialismus in Deutschland', *Vierteljahrschrift für Sozial und Wirtschaftsgeschichte* 41(4): 333–364.

Cremonesi, L. (2008) *Michel Foucault e il mondo antico: Spunti per una critica dell'attualità*, Pisa: ETS.

Crouch, C. (2004) *Post-democracy*, London: Polity Press.

Crozier, M., Huntington, S.P., and Watanuki, J. (1975) *The Crisis of Democracy: Report on the Governability of Democracies to the Trilateral Commission*, New York: New York University Press.

Cuccorese, M. (2001) 'Marx tel que Foucault l'imagine', *Actuel Marx en ligne* 6, available on line at http://actuelmarx.u-paris10.fr/alr0006.htm, last accessed on 3 July 2017.

Cutro, A. (2004) *Michel Foucault: Tecnica e vita. Biopolitica e filosofia del bios*, Napoli: Bibliopolis.

Cutro, A. (2005) *Biopolitica: Storia e attualità di un concetto*, Verona: Ombre Corte.

Daraki, M. (1985) 'Le voyage en Grèce de Michel Foucault', *Esprit* 100: 55–83.

Dardot, P., and Laval, Ch. (2009) *La nouvelle raison du monde: Essai sur la société neolibérale*, Paris: La Découverte.

Dardot, P., and Laval, Ch. (2012) *Marx, prénom: Karl*, Paris: Gallimard.

Dean, M. (1994) *Critical and Effective Histories: Foucault's Method and Historical Sociology*, London-New York: Routledge.

Deleuze, G. (1986) *Foucault*, Paris: Minuit.

Deleuze, G. (1989) 'Qu'est-ce qu'un dispositif?', in AA.VV. (ed.), *Michel Foucault philosophe Rencontre internationale, Paris, 9, 10, 11 janvier 1988*, Seuil: Paris, pp. 185–195.

Deleuze, G. (1990) *The Logic of Sense*, London: The Athlone Press.

Deleuze, G. (2003a) 'Fendre les choses, fendre les mots', in *Pourparlers 1972–1990*, Paris: Minuit, pp. 115–128.

Deleuze, G. (2003b) 'La vie comme oeuvre d'art', in *Pourparlers 1972–1990*, Paris: Minuit, pp. 129–161.

De Maistre, J. (1821) *Les soirées de Saint-Pétersburg, ou Entretiens sur le gouvernement temporel de la Providence*, available on line at http://gallica.bnf.fr/ark:/12148/bpt6k41853t.r=.langFR, last accessed on 1 September 2017.

Detel, W. (2005) *Foucault and the Classical Antiquity: Power, Ethics and Knowledge*, Cambridge: Cambridge University Press.

de Tocqueville, A. (1848) *De la démocratie en Amérique (1840)*, Paris: Pagnerre.

Devine, F.E. (1970) 'Stoicism on the Best Regime', *Journal of the History of Ideas* 31(3): 323–336.

Devos, R. (2002) 'The Return of the Subject in Michel Foucault', *American Catholic Philosophical Quarterly* 76(2): 255–280.

Dews, P. (1989) 'The Return of the Subject in the Late Foucault', *Radical Philosophy* 51: 37–41.

Duso, G. (1999) *La logica del potere: Storia concettuale come filosofia politica*, Roma-Bari: Laterza.

Duso, G. (ed.) (2003a) *Il potere: Per la storia della filosofia politica moderna*, Roma: Carocci.

Duso, G. (ed.) (2003b): *Il contratto sociale nella filosofia politica moderna*, Milano: Franco Angeli.

Duso, G. (2003c) *La rappresentanza politica: Genesi e crisi del concetto*, Milano: Franco Angeli.

Duso, G. (ed.) (2004) *Oltre la democrazia: Un itinerario attraverso i classici*, Carocci: Roma

Eribon, D. (1989) *Michel Foucault*, Paris: Flammarion.

Ernout, A., and Meillet, A. (2001) *Dictionnaire étimologique de la langue latine*, Paris: Klincksieck.

Erskine, A. (1990) *The Hellenistic Stoa: Political Thought and Action*, London: Gerald Duckwoth & Co.

Esposito, R. (2008) *Bíos: Biopolitics and Philosophy*, Minneapolis: Minnesota University Press.

Essbach, W. (1997) 'Durkheim, Weber, Foucault: Religion, Ethos und Lebensführung', in *L'Éthique protestante de Max Weber et l'esprit de la modernité*, Paris: Éditions de la Maison des Sciences de l'Homme.

Evrard, F. (1998) *Michel Foucault et l'histoire du sujet en Occident*, Paris: Bertrand-Lacoste.

Ewald, F. (1986) *L'État providence*, Paris: Grasset.

Fabiani, J.-C. (2004) 'La sociologie historique face à l'archéologie du savoir', *Le Portique* 13–14: 1–17.

Ferrari, J. (1983) *Les philosophes salariès (1849)*, Paris: Payot.

Fimiani, M. (2007) *Erotica e retorica: Foucault e la lotta per il riconoscimento*, Verona: Ombre Corte.

Finley, M.I. (1970) 'Aristotle and Economic Analysis', *Past and Present* 47: 3–25.

Flynn, Th.R. (1985) 'Truth and Subjectivation in the Later Foucault', *The Journal of Philosophy* 82(10): 531–540.

Foucault, M. (1967a/2001) 'Nietzsche, Freud, Marx', in Defert, D., Ewald, F., and Lagrange, J. (eds.), *Dits et écrits I, 1954–1975*, Paris: Gallimard, pp. 592–607.

Foucault, M. (1967b/2001) 'Qui êtes-vous, professeur Foucault?', in Defert, D., Ewald, F., and Lagrange, J. (eds.), *Dits et écrits I, 1954–1975*, Paris: Gallimard, pp. 629–648.

Foucault, M. (1969/2001) 'Qu'est-ce qu'un auteur?', in *Dits et écrits I, 1976–1988*, Paris: Gallimard, pp. 817–849.

Foucault, M. (1970/2001) 'Folie, littérature, société', in *Dits et écrits I, 1976–1988*, Paris: Gallimard, pp. 972–996.

Foucault, M. (1971/2001) 'Nietzsche, la généalogie, in Defert, D., Ewald, F., and Lagrange, J. (eds.), *Dits et écrits I, 1954–1975*, Paris: Gallimard, pp. 1004–1024.

Foucault, M. (1975) *Surveiller et punir*, Paris: Gallimard.

Foucault, M. (1975/2001) 'La maison des fous', in *Dits et écrits II, 1976–1988*, Paris: Gallimard, pp. 1561–1566.

Foucault, M (1976a/2001) 'Questions à Michel Foucault sur la géographie', *Dits et écrits II, 1976–1988*, Paris: Gallimard, pp. 28–40.

Foucault, M. (1976b/2001) 'Le savoir comme crime', in *Dits et écrits II, 1976–1988*, Paris: Gallimard, pp. 79–86.

Foucault, M. (1976c/2001) 'La fonction politique de l'intellectuel', in *Dits et écrits II, 1976–1988*, Paris: Gallimard, pp. 109–114.

Foucault, M. (1977a/2001) 'Entretien avec Michel Foucault' réalisé par A. Fontana et P. Pasquino', in *Dits et écrits II, 1976–1988*, Paris: Gallimard, pp. 140–160.

Foucault, M. (1977b/2001) 'Non au sexe roi', in *Dits et écrits II, 1976–1988*, Paris: Gallimard, pp. 256–269.

Foucault, M. (1977c/2001) 'Le jeu de Michel Foucault. Entretien avec D. Colas, L. Grosrichard, G. Le Gaufey, J. Livi, G. Miller, J. Miller, J.-A. Miller, C. Millot, G. Wajeman', in *Dits et écrits II, 1976–1988*, Paris: Gallimard, pp. 298–329.

Foucault, M. (1977d/2001) 'Va-t-on extrader Klaus Croissant?', in *Dits et écrits II, 1976–1988*, Paris: Gallimard, pp. 361–365.

Foucault, M. (1977e/2001) ' "Le pouvoir, une bête magnifique", entretien avec M. Osorio, *Quadernos para el dialogo*, 1977', in *Dits et écrits II, 1976–1988*, Paris: Gallimard, pp. 368–382.

Foucault, M. (1978a/2001) 'Dialogue sur le pouvoir', in *Dits et écrits II, 1976–1988*, Paris: Gallimard, pp. 464–477.

Foucault, M. (1978b/2001) 'La philosophie analytique de la politique', in *Dits et écrits II, 1976–1988*, Paris: Gallimard, pp. 534–551.

Foucault, M. (1978c/2001) '"Précisions sur le pouvoir. Réponses à certaines critiques" entretien avec P. Pasquino in DEII', in *Dits et écrits II, 1976–1988*, Paris: Gallimard, pp. 625–635.

Foucault, M. (1978d/2001), 'La "gouvernementalité" ', in *Dits et écrits II, 1976–1988*, Paris: Gallimard, pp. 635–657.

Foucault, M. (1978e/2001) 'Sécurité, territoire et population', in *Dits et écrits II, 1976–1988*, Paris: Gallimard, pp. 719–723.

Foucault, M. (1979a/2001) 'Pour une morale de l'inconfort', in *Dits et écrits II, 1976–1988*, Paris: Gallimard, pp. 783–788.

Foucault, M. (1979b/2001) 'Inutile de se soulever?', in *Dits et écrits II, 1976–1988*, Paris: Gallimard, pp. 790–794.

Foucault, M. (1980a/2001) 'La poussière et le nuage', in *Dits et écrits II, 1976–1988*, Paris: Gallimard, pp. 829–838.

Foucault, M. (1980b/2001) 'Table ronde du 20 mai 1978', *Dits et écrits II, 1976–*1988, Paris: Gallimard, pp. 839–853.

Foucault, M. (1980c/2001) 'Foucault étudie la raison d'État', *Dits et écrits II, 1976–1988*, Paris : Gallimard, pp. 856-860.

Foucault, M. (1980d/2001) 'Entretien avec Michel Foucault', in *Dits et écrits II, 1976–1988*, Paris: Gallimard, pp. 860–914.

Foucault, M. (1980e/2001) 'Le philosophe masqué', in *Dits et écrits II, 1976-1988*, Paris: Gallimard, pp. 923-929.

Foucault, M. (1981a/2001) '"Omnes et singulatim": vers une critique de la raison politique', in *Dits et écrits II, 1976–1988*, Paris: Gallimard, pp. 953–980.

Foucault, M. (1981b/2001) 'Sexualité et solitude', in *Dits et écrits II, 1976–1988*, Paris: Gallimard, pp. 987–997.

Foucault, M. (1981c/2001) 'Les mailles du pouvoir', in *Dits et écrits II, 1976–1988*, Paris: Gallimard, pp. 1001–1020.

Foucault, M. (1982a/2001) 'Le sujet et le pouvoir', in *Dits et écrits II, 1976–1988*, Paris: Gallimard, pp. 1041–1062.

Foucault, M. (1982b/2001) '"Espace, savoir et pouvoir", Entretien avec P. Rabinow', in *Dits et écrits II, 1976–1988*, Paris: Gallimard, pp. 1089–1104.

Foucault, M. (1982c/2001) 'Sex, Power and the Politics of Identity: An Interview With B. Gallagher and A. Wilson, Toronto, juin 1982', in *Dits et écrits II, 1976–1988*, Paris: Gallimard, pp. 1554–1565.

Foucault, M. (1982d/2001) 'Technologies of the Self', in *Dits et écrits II, 1976–1988*, Paris: Gallimard, pp. 1602–1632.

Foucault, M. (1983a/2001) 'À propos de la généalogie de l'éthique: un aperçu du travail en cours', in *Dits et écrits II, 1976–1988*, Paris: Gallimard, pp. 1202–1230.

Foucault, M. (1983b/2001) 'Structuralisme et poststructuralisme', in *Dits et écrits II, 1976–1988*, Paris: Gallimard, pp. 1250–1276.

Foucault, M. (1984a/2001) *Histoire de la sexualité, II, L'usage des plaisirs*, Paris: Gallimard.

Foucault, M. (1984b/2001) 'Qu'est-ce que les Lumières?', in *Dits et écrits II, 1976–1988*, Paris: Gallimard, pp. 1381–1397.

Foucault, M. (1984c/2001) 'Le souci de la vérité', in *Dits et écrits II, 1976–1988*, Paris: Gallimard, pp. 1487–1497.

Foucault, M. (1984d/2001) 'Qu'est ce-que les Lumières?', in *Dits et écrits II, 1976–1988*, Paris: Gallimard, pp. 1498–1507.

Foucault, M. (1984e/2001) 'Le retour de la morale', in *Dits et écrits II, 1976–1988*, Paris: Gallimard, pp. 1515–1526.

Foucault, M. (1984f/2001) 'L'éthique du souci de soi comme pratique de liberté', in *Dits et écrits II, 1976–1988*, Paris: Gallimard, pp. 1527–1548.

Foucault, M. (1984g/2001) 'Une esthétique de l'existence', in *Dits et écrits II, 1976–1988*, Paris: Gallimard, pp. 1549–1554.

Foucault, M. (1985/2001) 'La vie: l'expérience et la science', in *Dits et écrits II, 1976–1988*, Paris: Gallimard, pp. 1582–1595.

Foucault, M. (1988/2001) 'Les techniques du soi', in *Dits et écrits II, 1976–1988*, Paris: Gallimard, pp. 1602–1632.

Foucault, M. (1990) 'Qu'est-ce-que la critique? Critique et Aufklärung', *Bulletin de la société française de philosophie* 84(2): 35–63.

Foucault, M. (1995) *Discipline and Punish: The Birth of the Prison*, New York: Vintage Books.

Foucault, M. (1997) *Il faut défendre la société, Cours au Collège de France 1976*, Paris: Gallimard/Seuil.

Foucault, M. (1998a) *The Will to Knowledge: The History of Sexuality*, vol. 1, Hurley R. (ed.), London: Penguin.

Foucault, M. (1998b) 'Nietzsche, Freud, Marx', in Faubion, J.D. (ed.), *Aesthetics, Method and Epistemology*, New York: The New Press, pp. 269–278.

Foucault, M. (2000) 'Truth and Juridical Forms', in *Power*, New York: New Press, pp. 31–45.

Foucault, M. (2001a) *L'Herméneutique du sujet, Cours au Collège de France, 1981–1982*, Paris: Gallimard/Seuil.
Foucault, M. (2001b) *Fearless Speech*, Los Angeles: Semiotext(e).
Foucault, M. (2002a) *The Order of Things: An Archaeology of the Human Sciences*, London and New York: Routledge.
Foucault, M. (2002b) *The Archeology of Knowledge*, London and New York: Routledge.
Foucault, M. (2003) *Le pouvoir psychiatrique: Cours au Collège de France, 1973–74*, Paris: Gallimard/Seuil.
Foucault, M. (2004a) *Sécurité, Territoire, Population: Cours au Collège de France 1977–78*, Ewald F., Fontana A., M. Senellart (eds.), Paris: Gallimard/Seuil.
Foucault, M. (2004b) *La Naissance de la biopolitique: Cours au Collège de France, 1978–1979*, Ewald, F., and Fontana, A. (eds.), Paris: Gallimard/Seuil.
Foucault, M. (2008a) *Le gouvernement de soi et des autres, Cours au Collège de France, 1982–1983*, Paris: Seuil/Gallimard.
Foucault, M. (2008b) 'Introduction à l'anthropologie', in Kant, I. (ed.), *Anthropologie du point de vue pragmatique*, Paris: Vrin, pp. 11–79.
Foucault, M. (2009) *Le Courage de la vérité. Le gouvernement de soi et des autres II, Cours au collège de France, 1984*, Paris: Gallimard/Seuil.
Foucault, M. (2011) *Leçons sur la volonté de savoir: Cours au Collège de France, 1970–71*, Ewald, F., Fontana, A., and Defert, D. (eds.), Paris: Gallimard/Seuil.
Foucault, M. (2012a) 'Du gouvernement des vivants', in *Cours au Collège de France, 1979–1980*, Paris: EHESS/Gallimard/Seuil.
Foucault, M. (2012b) *Sull'origine dell'ermeneutica del sé: Due conferenze al Dartmouth College*, Napoli: Cronopio.
Foucault, M. (2013) *La Société Punitive: Cours au Collège de France, 1972–73*, Ewald, F., Fontana, A. and Harcourt, B.E. (eds.), Paris: EHESS/Gallimard/Seuil.
Foucault, M. (2016) *About the Beginning of the Hermeneutics of the Self: Lectures at Dartmouth College, 1980*, Chicago: University of Chicago Press.
Foucault, M. et al. (1977) 'Entretien inédit entre Michel Foucault et quatre militants de la LCR, membres de la rubrique culturelle du quotidien culturel *Rouge*', *Question Marx*, available online at http://questionmarx.typepad.fr/files/entretien-avec-michel-foucault-1.pdf, last accessed 3 July 2017.
Fränkel, H. (1962) *Dichtung und Philosophie des frühen Griechentums*, München: Beck.
Fumagalli, A. (2007) *Bioeconomia e capitalismo cognitivo: Verso un nuovo paradigma di accumulazione*, Roma: Carocci.
Gane, N. (2002) *Max Weber and Postmodern Theory: Rationalization Versus Re-Enchantement*, New York: Palgrave Macmillan.
Gigante, M. (1969) 'Filodemo Sulla Libertà di Parola', in *Ricerche filodemee*, Napoli: Maccharoli, pp. 41–61.
Goldschmidt, V. (1977) *Le système stoïcien et l'idée du temps*, Paris: Vrin.
Gordon, C. (1997) 'The Soul of the Citizen: Max Weber and Michel Foucault on Rationality and Government', in Whimster, S., and Lash, S. (eds.), *Max Weber: Rationality and Modernity*, London: Allen & Unwin.
Goulet-Cazé, M.-O. (2001) *L'ascèse cynique: Un commentaire de Diogène Laërce VI, 70–71*, Paris: Vrin.
Graeser, A. (1975) *Zenon von Kition: Positionen und Probleme*, Berlin-New York: De Gruyter.
Gros, F. (2002a) 'Sujet moral et sujet éthique chez Foucault', *Archives de philosophie* 65(2): 229–237.

Gros, F. (2002b) 'La parrhêsia chez Foucault (1982–1984)', in Gros, F. (ed.), *Michel Foucault: Le courage de la vérité*, Paris: PUF.

Gros, F., and Davidson, A. (eds) (2011) *Foucault, Wittgenstein: de possibles rencontres*, Paris: Kimé.

Gros, F., and Lévy, C. (eds) (2003) *Foucault et la philosophie antique*, Paris: Kimé.

Gruppo di Ricerca sui Concetti Politici. (ed.) (2012) *Concordia Discors: Scritti in onore di Giuseppe Duso*, Padova: Padova University Press.

Guenancia, P. (2002) 'Foucault/Descartes: la question de la subjectivité', *Archives de philosophie* 65(2): 239–253.

Habermas, J. (1971) 'Dogmatismus, Vernunft und Entscheidung: Zur Theorie und Praxis in der verwissenschaftlichen Zivilisation', in *Theorie und Praxis: Sozialphilosophische Studien*, Frankfurt am Main: Suhrkamp, pp. 307–335.

Hadot, P. (2008) *N'oublie pas de vivre: Goethe et la tradition des exercises spirituels*, Paris: Albin Michel.

Hahn, B. (2002) 'The Analytic of Finitude and the History of Subjectivity', in Cutting G. (ed.), *The Cambridge Companion to Foucault*, Cambridge: Cambridge University Press, pp. 176–212.

Hannah, M.G. (2012) 'Foucault's "German Moment": Genealogy of a Disjunction', *Foucault Studies* 13: 116–137.

Hardt, M., and Negri, A. (2009) *Commonwealth*, Cambridge, MA: Belknap Press of Harvard University Press.

Hebel, K. (1990) 'Dezentrierung des Subjekts in der Selbstsorge: Zum ästhetischen Aspekt einer nicht-normativen Ethik bei Foucault', in Gamm, G., and Kimmerle, G. (eds.), *Ethik und Ästhetik: nachmetaphysische Perspektiven*, Tübingen: Diskord, pp. 226–241.

Hegel, G.W.F. (1995) *Lectures on the History of Philosophy: Greek Philosophy to Plato*, Lincoln, NE and London: University of Nebraska Press.

Hobbes, Th. (1998) *Leviathan, The Matter, Forme, & Power of a Common-Wealth Ecclesiasticall and Civill*, Oxford, NY: Oxford University Press.

Hofmann, H. (1974) *Repräsentation. Studien zur Wort – und Begriffsgeschichte von der Antike bis ins 19. Jahrhundert*, Berlin: Duncker & Humblot.

Huisman, D. (ed.) (1984) *Dictionnaire des philosophes*, Paris: PUF.

Isin, E.F. (2002) *Being Political: Genealogies of Citizenship*, Minneapolis: Minnesota University Press.

Jaeger, H. (1959) 'Parrhesia et fiducia', *Studia patristica I*: 221–239.

Kantorowicz, E. (1957) *The King's Two Bodies: A Study in Medieval Political Theology*, Princeton: Princeton University Press.

Karsenti, B. (2005) 'La politique du dehors: Une lecture des cours de Foucault au Collège de France (1977–1979)', *Multitudes* 22(3): 37–50.

Karsenti, B. (2006) 'La politica del "fuori": Una lettura dei Corsi di Foucault al Collège de France (1977–1979)', in Chignola, S. (ed.), *Governare la vita: Un seminario sui corsi di Michel Foucault al Collège de France (1977–1979)*, Verona: ombre corte, pp. 71–90.

Kelsen, H. (1937) 'The Philosophy of Aristotle and the Hellenistik-Macedonian Policy', *International Journal of Ethics* 28(1): 1–64.

Kennedy, K. (1999) 'Cynic Rhetoric: The Ethics and Tactics of Resistance', *Rhetoric Review* 18(1): 26–45.

Kluge, F. (1899) *Etymologisches Wörterbuch der deutschen Sprache, sechste verbesserte und vermehrte Auflage*, Straßburg: Trüber.

Lazzarato, M. (2005) 'Biopolitique/Bioéconomie', *Multitudes* 22: 51–62.

Leblanc, G. (2005) *L'esprit des sciences humaines*, Paris: Vrin.

Lemke, T. (2007) 'Oltre la biopolitica: Sulla ricezione di un concetto foucaultiano', in Cometa, M., and Vaccaro, S. (eds.), *Lo sguardo di Foucault*, Roma: Meltemi, pp. 85–107.

Lemke, T., Krasmann, S., and Bröckling, U. (2000) *Gouvernamentalität, Neoliberalismus und Selbsttechnologien*, in *Gouvernamentalität der Gegenwart. Studien zur Ökonomisierung des Sozialen*, Frankfurt a. Maine: Suhrkamp.

Leonelli, R.M. (1999) 'Fonti marxiane in Foucault', *Altreragioni* 9: 119–135.

Leonelli, R.M. (ed.) (2010) *Foucault – Marx: Paralleli e paradossi*, Roma: Bulzoni.

Legrand, S. (2004) 'Le marxisme oublié de Foucault', *Actuel Marx* 36: 27–43.

Long, A.A. (1968) 'The Stoic Concept of Evil', *The Philosophical Quarterly* 8(73): 329–343.

Long, A.A. (1982) 'Soul and Body in Stoicism', *Phronesis* 27: 34–57.

Long, A.A. (1986) *Hellenistic Philosophy: Stoics, Epicureans, Sceptics*, Berkeley-Los Angeles: University of California Press.

Lorenzini, D., Revel, A., and Sforzini, A. (eds.) (2013) *Michel Foucault: éthique et vérité 1980–1984*, Paris: Vrin.

Luce, S. (2009) *Fuori di sé: Poteri e soggettivazioni in Michel Foucault*, Milano: Mimesis.

Macherey, P. (2013a) *Il soggetto produttivo: Da Foucault a Marx*, Verona: Ombre Corte.

Macherey, P. (2013b) *Études de philosophie "française". De Sieyès à Barni*, Paris: Publications de la Sorbonne.

Maier, H. (1969) *Die altere deutsche Staats und Verwaltungslehre*, München: Beck.

Marx, K. (1962) *Das Kapital*, I, in Marx Engels Werke, hrsg. von Institut für Marxismus-Leninismus beim ZK der Sed, Berlin: Dietz Verlag, Bd. 40.

Marx, K. (1968) 'Ökonomisch-philosophisch Manuskripte aus dem Jahre 1844', in *Marx Engels Werke*, hrsg. von Institut für Marxismus-Leninismus beim ZK der Sed [= MEW], Berlin: Dietz Verlag, Bd. 40.

Marazzi, Ch. (1992) *Il posto dei calzini: La svolta linguistica dell'economia e i suoi effetti nella politica*, Torino: Bollati Boringhieri.

Mbembe, A. (2003) 'Necropolitics', *Public Culture* 15(1): 11–40.

Mcgushin, E. (2007) *Foucault's Askesis: An Introduction to Philosophical Life*, Evanston: Northwestern University Press.

Megill, A. (1979) 'Foucault's Structuralism and the end of History', *The Journal of Modern History* 51(3): 451–503.

Mezzadra, S. (2014) *Nei cantieri marxiani: Il soggetto e la sua produzione*, Roma: manifestolibri.

Mezzadra, S., and Neilson, B. (2013) 'Extraction, Logistics, Finance: Global Crisis and the Politics of Operations', *Radical Philosophy* 178(2): 8–18.

Meyer, A. (1969) 'Mechanische und organische Metaphorik politischer Philosophie', *Archiv für Begriffsgeschichte* 13: 128–199.

Michel, P. (1981) *Les barbares, 1789–1848: un mythe romantique*, Lyon: Presses Universitaires de Lyon.

Miller, J. (2000) *The Passion of Michel Foucault*, Cambridge, MA: Harvard University Press.

Moles, J. (1983) 'Le cosmopolitisme cynique', in Goulet-Cazé, M.O. and Goulet, R. (eds.), *Le cynisme ancien et ses prolongements*, Paris: PUF, pp. 259–280.

Momigliano, A. (1971) 'La libertà di parola nel mondo antico', *Rivista storica italiana* 83: 499–524.

Montiglio, S. (2000) 'Wandering Philosophers in Classical Greece', *Journal of Hellenistic Studies* 20: 86–105.

Moss, J. (ed.) (1998) *The Later Foucault: Politics and Philosophy*, London: Sage.

Näf, W. (1951) 'Die Frühformen des modernen Staates im Spätmittelalter', *Historische Zeitschrift* 171(2): 225–243.

Narducci, E. (1985) 'L'archeologia del desiderio: Michel Foucault sulla sessualità degli antichi', *Quaderni di storia* 11: 185–214.

Negri, A. (1979) *Marx oltre Marx: Quaderno di lavoro sui Grundrisse*, Milano: Feltrinelli.

Nehamas, A. (2000) *The Art of Living: Socratic Reflections from Plato to Foucault*, Berkeley-Los Angeles: University of California Press.

Niehues-Pröbsting, H. (1993) 'Die Kynismus-Rezeption der Moderne: Diogenes in der Aufklärung', in Goulet-Cazé, M.-O., Goulet, R. *Le cynisme ancien et ses prolongements*, Paris: PUF, pp. 519–555.

Nietzsche, F. (1954) 'Unzeitgemässe Betrachtungen, Nutzen und Nachteil der Historie für das Leben, Unzeitgemäße Betrachtungen', in *Werke in drei Bänden*, München: Hanser.

Nietzsche, F. (2006) *Menschliches Allzumenschliches: Ein Buch für freie Geister, I–II*, Kőln: Anaconda Verlag.

Oestreich, G. (1969) *Geist und Gestalt des frühmodernen Staates: Ausgewählte Aufsätze*, Berlin: Dunker & Humblot.

Oksala, J. (2012) *Foucault, Politics and Violence*, Evanston: Northwestern University Press Politics.

O'Neill, J. (1986) 'The Disciplinary Society: From Weber to Foucault', *British Journal of Sociology* 37(1): 42–60.

Owen, D. (1994) *Maturity and Modernity: Nietzsche, Weber, Foucault and the Ambivalence of Reason*, London-New York: Routledge.

Paltrinieri, L. (2012) *L'expérience du concept: Michel Foucault entre épistémologie et histoire*, Paris: Publications de la Sorbonne.

Pandolfi, A. (1998) 'L'etica come pratica riflessa della libertà. L'ultima filosofia di Foucault', in Foucault, M. (ed.), *Archivio III: Estetica dell'esistenza, etica, politica*, Milano: Feltrinelli, pp. 7–28.

Pankoke, E. (1990) *Die Arbeitsfrage: Arbeitsmoral, Beschäftigungskrisen und Wohlfahrtspolitik im Industriezeitalter*, Frankfurt an Maine: Suhrkamp.

Paquet, L. (ed.) (1992) *Les cyniques grecs: Fragments et témoignages*, Paris: Librairie Générale Française.

Pasquino, P. (1985) 'Moderne Subjekt und der Wille zum Wissen', in Essbach, W., Dane, G., Karpenstein-Eßbach, Chr., and Makropoulos, M. (eds.), *Anschlüße: Versuche nach Michel Foucault*, Tübingen: Edition Discord, pp. 39–54.

Peterson, E. (1929) 'Zur Bedeutungsgeschichte von Parrhesia', in Koepp, W. (ed.), *Festschrift für R. Seeberg I*, Berlin, pp. 283–297.

Piasenza, P. (1990) *Polizia e città: Strategie d'ordine, conflitti e rivolte a Parigi tra Sei e Settecento*, Bologna:Il Mulino.

Plowden, E. (1816) *Commentaries or Reports*, London: S. Brook.

Pohlenz, M. (1949) *Die Stoa: Geschichte einer geistigen Bewegung*, 2 vols., Göttingen: Vandenhoeck & Ruprecht.

Poster, M. (1982) 'Foucault and History', *Social Research* 49(1): 116–142.

Poster, M. (1984) *Foucault, Marxism and History: Mode of Production Versus Mode of Information*, Cambridge: Polity Press.

Procacci, G. (1993) *Gouverner la misère: La question sociale en France (1789–1848)*, Paris: Seuil.

Radice, R. (2000) '*Oikeiosis*': *Ricerche sul fondamento del pensiero stoico e sulla sua genesi*, Milano: Vita e Pensiero.

Radice, R. (ed.) (2002) *Stoici antichi: Tutti i frammenti raccolti da Hans von Arnim*, Milano: Bompiani.

Rametta, G. (2013) 'Autoctonia e parrhesia. Foucault lettore dello Ione', in Cesaroni, P., and Chignola, S. (eds.), *La forza del vero: Un seminario sui Corsi di Michel Foucault al Collège de France (1981–1984)*, Verona: Ombre Corte, pp. 102–131.

Rancière, J. (2014) *Les Mots de l'histoire: Essai de poétique du savoir*, Paris: Seuil.

Redfield, J. (1985) 'Le sentiment homérique du moi', *Le Genre humain* 12: 93–111.

Rediker, M. (1987) *Between the Devil and the Deep Blue Sea: Merchant Seamen, Pirates and the Anglo-American Maritime World 1700–1750*, Cambridge: Cambridge University Press.

Reesor, M.E. (1972) 'Poion and Poiotes in Stoic Philosophy', *Phronesis* 17(3): 279–285.

Reinfeldt, S., and Schwarz, R. (2004) 'Liberalismus und Biopolitik', in Reichert R. (ed.), *Governmentality Studies: Analysen liberalerdemokratischer Gesellschaften in Anschluß an Michel Foucault*, Münster: Lit Verlag.

Revel, J. (1975) 'Foucault et les historiens', *Magazine littéraire* 101: 10–12.

Revel, J. (2005) *Michel Foucault: Expériences de la pensée*, Paris: Bordas.

Revel, J. (2013) 'Promenades, petits excursus et régimes d'historicité', in Lorenzini, D., Revel, A., and Sforzini, A. (eds), *Michel Foucault: éthique et vérité 1980–1984*, Paris: Vrin, pp. 161–175.

Richter, G. (2005) *Oikonomia: Der Gebrauch des Wortes Oikonomia in Neuen Testament, bei den Kirchenvätern und in der Theologischen Literatur bis ins 20. Jahrhundert*, Berlin-New York: De Gruyter.

Riedel, M. (ed.) (1972–1974) *Rehabilitierung der praktischen Philosophie*, Freiburg I. B.: Rombach.

Riedel, M. (1975) 'Gesellschaft, Gemeinschaft', in Brunner, O., Conze, W., and Koselleck, R. (eds.), *Geschichtliche Grundbegriffe. Historisches Lexikon zur politisch-sozialen Sprache in Deutschland*, Stuttgart: Klett-Cotta, pp. 801–862.

Rigotti, F. (1989) *Metafore della politica*, Bologna: il Mulino.

Rist, J. (1977) 'Zeno and Stoic Consistency', *Phronesis* 22: 161–174.

Rorty, R. (1981) '*Volonté de savoir*, Beyond Nietzsche and Marx', *London Review of Books* 3(3): 5–6.

Rosanvallon, P. (1992) *Le sacré du citoyen: Du suffrage universel en France*, Paris: Gallimard.

Rosanvallon, P. (2006) *La contre-démocratie: La politique à l'âge de la défiance*, Paris: Seuil.

Rusche, G., and Kirchheimer, O. (1939) *Punishment and Social Structure*, New York: Columbia University Press.

Sassen, S. (2006) *Territory, Authority, Rights: From Medieval to Global Assemblages*, Princeton: Princeton University Press.

Scarpat, G. (1964) *Parrhesia: Storia del termine e delle sue traduzioni in latino*, Brescia: Paideia.
Scattola, M. (1994) *La nascita delle scienze dello Stato: August Ludwig Schlözer (1735–1809) e le discipline politiche del Settecento tedesco*, Milano: Franco Angeli.
Schiera, P. (1968) *Dall'arte di governo alle Scienze dello Stato: Il cameralismo e l'assolutismo tedesco*, Milano: Giuffrè.
Schiera, P. (1999) 'Il rapporto tra disciplina/disciplinamento fra sociologia del potere e storia llcostituzionale', in *Specchi della politica: Disciplina, melancolia, socialità nell'Occidente moderno*, Bologna: il Mulino.
Schlier, H. 'Parrhesia, parrhesiazomai', in Kittel, G., Bromiley, G.W., and Friedrich, G. (eds.), *Theological Dictionary of the New Testament*, vol. V, Grand Rapids: Eerdmans, pp. 871–886.
Schochet, G.J. (1975) *Patriarchalism in Political Thought: The Authoritarian Family and Political Speculation and Attitudes especially in Seventeenth-Century England*, Oxford: Basil Blackwell.
Schmitt, C. (1982) *Der Leviathan in der Staatslehre des Thomas Hobbes: Sinn und Fehlschlag eines politischen Symbols*, Hamburg: Hohenheim Verlag.
Scuccimarra, L. (2006) *I confini del mondo: Storia del cosmopolitismo dall'Antichità al Settecento*, Bologna: Il Mulino.
Sellars, J. (2007) 'Stoic Cosmopolitism and Zeno's Republic', *History of Political Thought* XXVIII(1): 1–29.
Seneca, L.A. (2011) *On Benefits*, Chicago and London: The University of Chicago Press.
Senellart, M. (1995) *Les arts de gouverner: Du regimen médiéval au concept de gouvernement*, Paris: Seuil.
Sforzini, A. (2013) 'Dramatiques de la vérité: la parrêsia à travers la tragédie attique', in Lorenzini, D., Revel, A., and Sforzini, A. (eds.), *Michel Foucault: éthique et vérité 1980–1984*, Paris: Vrin, pp. 139–160.
Skinner, Q. (1996) *Reason and Rhetoric in the Philosophy of Hobbes*, Cambridge: Cambridge University Press.
Skinner, Q. (2008) *Hobbes and Republican Liberty*, Cambridge: Cambridge University Press.
Skinner, Q. (2014) *Liberty Before Liberalism*, Cambridge: Cambridge University Press.
Sloterdijk, P. (1983) *Kritik der zynischen Vernunft*, II Bde, Frankfurt a. M.: Suhrkamp.
Snell, B. (1948) *Die Entdeckung des Geistes*, Hamburg: Claassen & Goverts.
Stimilli, E. (2011) *Il debito del vivente: Ascesi e capitalismo*, Macerata: Quodlibet.
Strauss, L. (1977) *Che cosa è la filosofia politica? Scritti su Hobbes e altri saggi*, Urbino: Argalia.
Striker, G. (1983) 'The Role of Oikeiosis in Stoic Ethics', *Oxford Studies in Ancient Philosophy* 1: 145–167.
Szakolczai, A. (1998) *Max Weber and Michel Foucault: Parallel Life-Works*, London-New York: Routledge.
Tarn, W.W. (1939) 'Alexander Cynics and Stoics', *The American Journal of Philology* 60(1): 41–79.
Taylor, C. (1985) 'Foucault on Freedom and Truth', in *Philosophical Papers*, vol. 2, Cambridge: Cambridge University Press, pp. 152–184.
Tellman, U. (2009) 'Foucault and the Invisible Economy', *Foucault Studies* 6: 5–24.
Thomas, Y. (2011) *Les opérations du droit*, Paris: EHESS/Gallimard/Seuil.

Thompson, T. (1966) *The Making of the English Working Class*, New York: Vintage.

Todescan, F. (1979) *Diritto e realtà: Storia e critica della* fictio iuris, Padova: Cedam.

Vadée, M. (1998) *Marx penseur du possible*, Paris: L'Harmattan.

Van Krieken, R. (1990) 'The Organization of the Soul: Elias and Foucault on Discipline and the Self', *Archives Européennes de Sociologie/European Journal of Sociology* 26: 353–371.

Vegetti, M. (1986) 'Foucault et les anciens', *Critique* 471–472: 925–932.

Ventura, D. (2009) *Giustizia e costituzione in Aristotele*, Milano: FrancoAngeli.

Vercellone, C. (ed.) (2007) *Capitalismo cognitivo: Conoscenza e finanza nell'epoca postfordista*, Roma: manifestolibri.

Vernant, J.-P. (1979) 'Catégories de l'action et de l'agent en Grèce ancienne', in Vernant, J.-P. (ed.), *Religions, histoires,raisons*, Paris: Maspero, pp. 85–95.

Vernant, J.-P. (1989) *L'individu, la mort, l'amour*, Paris: Gallimard.

Veyne, P. (1971) *Comment on écrit l'histoire*, Paris: Seuil.

Veyne, P. (1986) 'Le dernier Foucault et sa morale', *Critique* 471–472: 933–941.

Veyne, P. (2002) 'Foucault révolutionne l'histoire', in *Comment on écrit l'histoire*, Texte intégral, Paris: Seuil, pp. 383–429.

Veyne, P. (2008) *Foucault: Sa pensée, sa personne*, Paris: Albin Michel.

Virno, P. (2002) *Grammatica della moltitudine: Per un'analisi delle forme di vita contemporanee*, Roma: DeriveApprodi.

Volpi, F. (1986) 'La riabilitazione della filosofia pratica in Germania e il suo senso nella crisi della modernità', *Il Mulino* 35(308): 928–949.

Volpi, F. (1999) 'Rehabilitación de la filosofía práctica y neo-aristorelismo', *Anuario filosófico* 32(63): 315–344.

von Gierke, O. (1880) *Johannes Althusius und die Entwicklung der Naturrechtlichen Staatstheorie*, available on line at http://onlinebooks.library.upenn.edu/webbin/book/lookupid?key=ha001748272, last accessed on 3 July 2017.

von Treitschke, H. (1871) 'Frankreichs Staatsleben und der Bonapartismus: III Die goldenen Tage der Bourgeoisie', in *Historische und politische Aufsätze von Heinrich von Treitschke*, vol. 3, Leipzig: Vierte vermehrte Auflage, pp. 162–235.

Weber, M. (1904/1922) 'Die "Objektivität" sozialwissenschaftlicher und sozialpolitischer Erkenntnis', in *Gesammelte Aufsätze zur Wissenschaftslehre*, Tübingen: Mohr (Paul Siebeck), pp. 146–214.

Weber, M. (1905a/1922) 'Kritische Studien auf dem Gebiet der kulturwissenschaftlichen Logik. I. Zu Auseinandersetzung mit Eduard Meyer', in *Gesammelte Aufsätze zur Wissenschaftslehre*, Tübingen: Mohr (Paul Siebeck), pp. 215–265.

Weber, M. (1905b/1922) 'Kritische Studien auf dem Gebiet der kulturwissenschaftlichen Logik. II. Objektive Möglichkeit und adäquate Verursachung in der historischen Kausalbetrachtung', in *Gesammelte Aufsätze zur Wissenschaftslehre*, Tübingen: Mohr (Paul Siebeck), pp. 266–290.

Weber, M. (1985) *Wirtschaft und Gesellschaft: rundriss der verstehenden Soziologie*, Tübingen: Mohr.

Weber, M. (1986/1920) *Gesammelte Aufsätze zur Religionssoziologie, Zwischenbetrachtung: Theorie der Stufen und Richtungen religiöser Weltablehnung*, Tübingen: Mohr, Bd. II, pp. 536–576.

Weber, M. (1988) 'Schriften zur Religionssoziologie', in *Gesammelte Aufsätze zur Religionssoziologie*, Tübingen: Mohr, Bd. I.

Wittgenstein, L. (1977) *Vermischte Bemerkungen*, Frankfurt am Main: Suhrkamp.

Wolff, E. (1989) 'Éros et logos. À propos de Foucault et de Platon', *Revue de philosophie ancienne* 7(1): 47–78.

Weber, M. (1991/2002) 'Wissenschaft als Beruf', in *Schriften 1894–1922*, Stuttgart: Kröner, pp. 474–511.

Wolin, S. (1986) 'Foucault's Aesthetic Decisionism', *Telos* 67: 71–86.

Young, R. (2001) 'Foucault in Tunisia', in *Postcolonialism: An Historical Introduction*, Oxford: Blackwell.

Zanini, A. (2005) *Filosofia economica: Fondamenti economici e categorie politiche*, Torino:Bollati Boringhieri.

Zanini, A. (2010) *L'ordine del discorso economico: Linguaggio delle ricchezze e pratiche del governo in Michel Foucault*, Verona: Ombre Corte.

Index

Absolutism 14, 32
Agamben, Giorgio x
Alcibiades (Plato) 58, 116–118
Althusius, Johannes 70
Althusser, Louis 30, 32, 39
anarcho-capitalism, American 24
Anthropology from a Pragmatic Point of View (Foucault) 109
Antiquity 24, 44, 65, 67n38; of Christianity 53, 103, 108, 123; *histoire-fiction* of 105; individual ethics 62; Modernity and 45, 68–72; republican myth 84n3
Archaeology of Knowledge, The (Foucault), 92
Aristotle 17, 26, 36, 48, 51, 57, 69, 71, 72, 75–76, 78, 79, 84
asceticism 94, 102–105
attitude 53, 93; critique 111; hypermodern 54; limit 3; modern, of philosophy 5, 8, 49, 86, 99, 110, 126n7; modernity as 1–2; philosopher's 80; production of 30; psychological 23; systematic 30
Aufklärung 1–2, 86, 93
Aurelius, Marcus 73, 80, 107n39
Austrian ordoliberalism 20

Baader-Meinhof Gang 46
Bacchylides 108
Balibar, Étienne x
Benveniste, Émile 75–76
biopolitics: biopower to 20–21; concept of 10, 50; governmental scheme 15–18; sovereignty 13; technologies of 15–18; term 11, 43
biopower 106n21; concept of 10, 50; shift to biopolitics 20–21; term 11, 43
body natural 27
body politic 27
Brown, Wendy ix
Burchell, Graham viii

Calvinism 87
Cameralism 18, 20, 24, 115
Capital, The (Marx) 14, 29, 30, 31, 33
Catholicism 103
Cercidas of Megalopolis 121
Chatterjee, Partha x
choice 110, 120; accounting for 124; ethical, sexual and political 63; of liberation from subjection 81; options and 22; of philosophical life 54; of poverty and obedience 104
Christianity: Antiquity of 53, 103, 108, 123; morality 57, 62; pastoral power 110–111
Chrysippus of Soli 72, 74
Cicero 72, 78, 79, 81, 82, 85n20
Collège de France 10, 38, 42n15, 55, 90, 108, 109, 115, 121, 125n2
constitutional history 11, 19, 28, 99, 114, 117
constructivism 96
corporation, doctrine of 27
corpus, term 26
corpus mysticum 27
correction 14, 16, 74
Cousin, Victor 59
critique: *parrhēsia* and 109–111; term 2
Croce, Mariano ix
Croissant, Klaus 46–47, 49, 63
Crozier, Michel J. ix, 115
cynicism 112, 119–122; Stoicism and 78–80

Dartmouth College 102
dead labour 35

deconstitutionalization 99
Deleuze, Gilles 46, 53, 60
démas 26
Derrida, Jacques 58
Descartes, René 55, 56, 58
diagnosis 1, 5
Dielectic of Enlightenment (Adorno and Horkheimer) 86
discipline 14–16, 106n21
disobedience 110
dispersive rationality 88
dominion 16, 68, 70–71
Donzelot, Jacques viii
Dreyfus, Hubert 62
dunasteia 117–118

ellipse: of government x, 63, 109, 114, 124–125; of governmentality 49, 60, 63, 65, 100
Enlightenment 1, 2, 4, 6, 46, 61
Epictetus 72, 78, 80–81, 83, 112, 119
Epicureanism 112
Epicurus 73, 74
Esposito, Roberto x
ethopoiesis 61, 112
Euripides 112–114
evénementialisation 3, 87, 91, 95, 98, 101
Ewald, François viii, 53, 54

Faucher, Léon 42n12
Ferrari, Joseph 59
fiction: game of 122; *histoire-fiction* 95–98, 101, 105; *historique* 94, 112, 122; history and 94–98
Filmer, Robert 70
Fitzpatrick, Peter x
Florence, Maurice 109
Fontana, Alessandro 123
Fordist: compromise 22; social contract 32
Foucault, Michel 24, 29, 38, 40, 43, 54, 57, 64, 86, 101, 121
Frankfurt School 49, 56, 86–89, 93, 99, 100
freedom 22, 60, 61; power of 61–65; of speech 112–118
French Revolution 28, 100, 110
function-Psy 15

games: of fiction 122; of power 7–9, 90, 94; of truth 7–9, 59, 90, 94, 122; of veridiction 59, 63, 90, 92, 93, 96, 111

genealogy 3, 4; biopolitical technologies 16; of biopower 48; of Christian pastoral power 47; of governmentality 17, 19, 24, 43, 115; of knowledge 6; modern political form 70; of morality 53; of politics 12–13; of subject 90, 100, 104–105; valorization of 10
German ordoliberalism 21, 24
Goethe 68, 104, 107n38
Golder, Ben x
Gordon, Colin viii
governing: art of 16; concept of 23, 48, 115; developing technologies 36; governed and 51, 58, 109; object of 117; population 18; positions of 119, 125
government: production of truth and 11–13; reality of philosophy 59–61
governmentality 11, 19–24, 65, 99–100, 106n21; genealogy of 17; term 50–51
governmentalization 19, 50–51; biopolitics 100; of power 53, 88, 99, 109, 110, 124; procedures of 51
Guattari, Félix 46–47
Guizot, François Pierre Guillaume 36

Habermas, Jürgen 45, 63, 89–90, 99, 100
Hausväterliteratur 17
Hegel, Georg Wilhem Friedrich 30, 34, 44, 86, 88
Heidegger, Martin 62
Henry VIII 27
Heraclitus 77
histoire-fiction 95–98, 101, 105
history: fiction and 94–98; philosophy and 92–94; of rationality 94
Hobbes, Thomas 11–13, 27, 28, 39, 44, 50, 58, 69, 70–71, 84
Homer 26
Hunt, Alan ix
Huntington, Samuel P. ix, 115
human being: definition of 82–83; history and philosophy 92–94; nature of 78–80, 80–83; as political animal 69–73, 75–76; relationships 74–78; wisdom and wise life 82–83

ideology 7, 45, 60; critique of 5, 10; falsity of 8; legal 29; of the Political 115
individuation 9, 14, 44, 52, 54–57, 61, 68, 82, 90, 112
intensification 41, 105

interference 5, 23, 55, 95, 123
intern-exteriority 2
inversion of Clausewitz's principle 10, 31
irrationalism 91

Kant, Immanuel 1–7, 9, 20, 54, 61, 63, 86, 90, 93, 99, 107n40, 109–111, 126n7
Kantorowicz, Ernst 27
Kelsen, Hans 12
Keynesianism 24
Kirchheimer, Otto 105n2
Koyré, Alexandre 105n3
Kritik 1, 3, 4, 7, 20

labour, resistance 40–42
labour-force 35, 36
Laches (Plato) 105, 118–119
Lactantius, Lucius 73
language game 46
Laws (Plato) 117
lebendige Leiblichkeit 33–34
Legrand, Stephan 39
Le Monde (newspaper) 123
Leviathan 52
Leviathan (Hobbes) 27, 69
liberalism 20, 24, 51; era of 49
London Review of Books (journal) 89

Marx, Karl 28, 42n9, 44
Marxism 29, 30, 32
memory 1, 19, 48, 53–54, 56, 59, 66n32, 104
Mezzadra, Sandro x
mob 28, 36
modernity 57, 61; Antiquity and 68–72; as attitude 1–2
multiversum 55

naturalization 37
natural law theory 68–69, 71–72
Negri, Antonio ix, xi
Neilson, Brett x
neoliberal governmentality 23
neoliberalism 22
Nicomachean Ethics (Aristotle) 79
Nietzsche, Friedrich 1, 4, 7, 32, 44, 68, 69, 88, 93, 94, 95
normalization 8, 14, 15, 40, 52, 57

objectivation 40, 51–52
oikodespotêia 71
oikodespotēs 75
oikonomia 17, 24, 48, 78
oikos 71, 74–76
ordoliberalism: Austrian 20; German 21, 24
original accumulation 37–38, 40

parrhēsia: critique and 109–111; explosion of bad 115–116; freedom of speech and 112–118; notion of 108, 111; political speech and 117–118; rhetoric and 116–117; term 108–109
Pasquino, Pasquale viii
patriarchalism 70
people: opposition between bodies of 28–32; unity of the 28
phenomenology 7, 55, 87, 105n6
Philo 72
philosophical vocation 99
philosophy 44–46; history and 92–94; practice of 118; relation of politics and 59–61; sense as journalism 6; verification of 59
Physiocracy 24
Plato 6, 44, 53, 58–59, 69, 78, 109, 114–117
plebe 28
Plutarch 61, 73, 84n13
pneuma 76–78
Poetics (Aristotle) 36
police 15, 17–18, 20, 24, 46
polis 70–76, 81–83; Plato's *kallipolis* 59
political animal, human being as 69–73, 75–76
political philosophy, retrait of 45
political theology 28, 36, 50, 70, 109–111
politics: practice of 118; relation of philosophy and 59–61; of self 61–62
Politics (Aristotle) 26, 69
politics of truth 5–9
politikē koinōnia 72, 75
populace 28, 36, 39, 42n12
population 16–18; power as 20
positivity 90; critique and 109–111
power: of affirmation 63; of freedom 61–65; games 7–9, 46, 90, 94; governmentalization of 53; labour 40–42; law and political thinking 12–13; political theory 9–13; reformulation of Foucault's 43–44, 66n6; resistance and 110; resistance to 9; subjectivity 56; technologies of 57; tyrant and 80–81
Prince (Machiavelli) 16–18

problematization: Christian morality and 57; dispersion as 10; endlessness of 97; interplay of power 111–112; open 98; power of affirmation 63; of present 100; radical 90, 95; of the subject 53, 88; term 54–55
Procacci, Giovanna viii
production of truth, government and 11–13
programme, notion of 87–88
programmeless action 64
proletariat 28, 37
Protestantism 103, 109
Protestant Reformation 102
Puritan asceticism 104–105

Rabinow, Paul 62
rationalization 99, 104, 111
realism 65, 92, 124, 125
regulation 48
Republic (Zeno) 73
Republic, The (Plato) 117
republican myth 84n3
Restoration 31
Riedel, Manfred 76
Rorty, Richard 107n28
Rousseau, Jean-Jacques 12, 32, 39, 44
Rosanvallon, Pierre 27, 28, 59, 67n46
Rushe, George 105n2

Salvatore, Andrea ix
Sartre, Jean-Paul 45, 55, 62, 109
Sassen, Saskia x
Schmitt, Carl 50
self, politics of 61–62
Seventh Letter (Plato) 58, 116
sexuality, Ancient ethics of 101
social question viii, 18, 36
Socrates 60, 116, 117, 118, 119
Solon 44
sôma 26
sovereignty: concept of 43; core of political theory 12

statization 19
Stoicism 72–73, 112; cynicism and 78–80; view of nature 81–83
structuralism 105n6
subjectivation 112; function of 113; modern mode of 52
subjectivity, knowledge and powers 56
Surveiller et Punir (Foucault) 40, 43
Symposium (Plato), 119

thanatopolitics 13, 14, 43, 47
Thatcher, Margaret ix, 22
Thompson, Edward P. 37
Tocqueville, Alexis de viii, 36, 49, 123, 126n15
transformation, fiction denoting 94–95
Trilateral Commission 115
Trombadori, Duccio 121
truth games 7–9, 59, 90, 94
tyranny 84n3, 120

University of Vermont 100
Untimely Meditation (Nietzsche) 95

veridiction 5–6, 8, 58–60, 87, 124, 125; form of 103, 113; games of 59, 63, 90, 92, 93, 96, 111; practice of 104, 117, 118; site of 11, 20
Vernant, Jean-Pierre 58
Veyne, Paul 65, 91, 95
vocation 45, 75, 110; philosophical 99, 116; politics as 97, 109
Von Stein, Lorenz viii, 36

Watanuki, Joji ix, 115
Weber, Max 86, 93, 94, 96–98, 101, 102, 109
Wickham, Gary ix
Wieland Christoph Martin 116
Wittgenstein, Ludwig 44, 111

Zeno of Citium 73, 74, 80